AUTONOMOUS DISTRICT COUNCIL AND TRIBAL WELFARE

AUTONOMOUS DISTRICT COUNCIL AND TRIBAL WELFARE

Sukanta Sarkar
and
Suman Kalyan Chaudhury

KALPAZ

ISBN : 978-93-5128-043-9
Price : ₹ 975

First Published, 2014

Published by

Kalpaz Publications
C-30, Satyawati Nagar,
Delhi-110052
Ph. : 9212142040
E-mail: kalpaz@hotmail.com

Laser Typesetting : Gyan Prints (AB-II), Delhi
Printed at : G. Print Process, Delhi

Cataloging in Publication Data—DK
Courtesy: D.K. Agencies (P) Ltd. <docinfo@dkagencies.com>

Autonomous district council and tribal welfare / Sukanta Sarkar and Suman Kalyan Chaudhury.
p. cm.
Contributed articles.
Includes bibliographical references and index.
ISBN 9789351280439

1. India—Scheduled tribes—Social conditions. 2. India—Scheduled tribes—Government policy. 3. India—Scheduled tribes—Civil rights. 4. India—Scheduled tribes—Legal status, laws, etc. 5. North Cachar Hills Autonomous District Council. I. Sarkar, Sukanta. II. Chaudhury, Suman Kalyan, 1972-

DDC 305.800954 23

Contents

Foreword

I am glad to know that Dr. Sukanta Sarkar and Dr. S.K. Chaudhury have prepared manuscript of a book entitled *"Autonomous District Council and Tribal Welfare"* and the book is going to be published by the Kalpaz Publications, Delhi, India. Nineteen highly reputed scholars have contributed in this book. By reading the manuscript, I think most of the Autonomous District Councils of India and Government's tribal welfare strategies have been included in it. I am confident that this book will be very useful to the students and researchers of Tribal welfare, Sociology, Rural development, and Economics etc.

I wish academic endeavour of the editors and contributors of this book shall be fruitful and it will satisfy the academic queries of the readers.

With best wishes

Professor M.A. Rahman, Ph.D (USA)
Director, Centre for Global Environmental Culture (CGEC)
Coordinator, RCE Greater Dhaka and WWOOF Bangladesh
International University of Business Agriculture and Technology
Uttara Model Town, Dhaka, Bangladesh

Preface

Development of tribal is a basic agenda of government. Autonomous district council is a part of it. An autonomous area or autonomous entity is an area of a country that has a degree of autonomy, or freedom from an external authority. Typically it is either geographically distinct from the rest of the country or populated by a national minority. Autonomous district council is a real fact in North-East India. Autonomous district council and tribal are interconnected. It is a way for providing more autonomy power to tribal people is their own development. It is proving under the six schedule of Constitution of India. Government of India already set-up various district councils in North-East India. There are three district councils, (i.e., Bodoland Territorial Council, Karbi Anglong Autonomous Council and Dima Hasao Autonomous District Council) in Assam. There are three autonomous district councils in Mizoram, (i.e., Chakma Autonomous District Council, Lai Autonomous District Counci, and Mara Autonomous District Council) and Meghalaya, (i.e., Garo Hills Autonomous District Council, Jaintia Hills Autonomous District Council abd Khasi Hills Autonomous District Council). In Manipur there are six council and in Tripura one. The Arunachal Pradesh Assembly had passed a bill to create four Autonomous District Councils in the state in 2003 but the Parliament is yet to approve it. There are various village level institutions in ground level which have more autonomy power.

In this connection, we want to place on record our deep appreciation to Prof. Ajay Pathak, Vice-Chancellor, ICFAI University, Tripura, Agartala for providing valuable inputs.

We desire to express our heartiest thank to Prof. B.K. Panda, Department of Economics, Berhampur University, Odisha who despite his busy schedule and hectic academic engagements, all the time encouraged and supported us. We are also beholden to Dr. N.G. Pendse, Department of Economics, Rani Durgabati University, Jabalpur who's erudite and scholarly tidbits for preparing such a vast work are still fresh in our mind. We also thanks to Dr. Pradeep Kumar Pandey, Centre of Judicial Studies, Dibrugarh University, Assam; Dr. Suman Kalan Chaudhury, Department of Business Administration, Berhampur University, Odisha; Dr. Rakesh Joshi, Department of Economics, Saurashtra University, Gujarat; Dr. D. Pulla Rao, Department of Economics, Andhra University; Dr. Vibhuti Patel, Professor cum Director, Centre for Study of Social Exclusion and Inclusive Policy, SNDT Women's University, Mumbai; Dr. Wakar Amin, Department of Social Work, University of Kashmir, J & K.; Dr. Shazia Manzoor, Assistant professor Department of Social Work, University of Kashmir, J & K; Dr. Pallab Kanti Ghoshal, Department of Commerce, Nataji Subhas College, Udaipur, for their valuable suggestions and moral support.

We are heartily grateful to Prof. R. Prasad, Prof. Ashish Kumar Shivastava and Prof. L.S. Nigam, Pandit Ravishankar Shukla University, Raipur, Chhattisgarh who always encouraged us to carry on this constructive work. Further, we express our heartily thankfulness to each and every person who directly/indirectly helped us in preparing this work.

It is hoped that this book will be very useful for students of tribal study in particular. Comments and suggestions are most welcomed.

Sukanta Sarkar

Suman Kalyan Chaudhury

Abbreviations

AAGSU : All Assam Gorkha Students Union
ABAVP : Akhil Bharatiya Adivasi Vikas Parishad
ABSS : Ana-Bodo Surakhya Samity
ABSU : All Bodo Students Union
ADC : Autonomous District Council
AKS : Autonomous Karbi State
APHLC : All Party Hill Leader's Conference
ASHA : Accredited Social Health Activities
BABPA : Bodoland Autonomous Boundary Protection Association
BAC : Bodoland Autonomous Council
BLT : Bodo Liberation Tiger
BLT : Bodoland Liberation Tigers
BPAC : Bodo Peoples' Action Committee
BPCC : Bodoland Pradesh Congress Committee
BTAD : Bodoland Territorial Autonomous Districts
CADC : Chakma Autonomous District Council
CCD : Conservation-cum-Development
DGHC : Darjeeling Gorkha Hill Council
DHAC : Dima Hasao Autonomous Council
DHD : Dima Hasao district
EITU : Eastern India Tribal Union
GB : Goan Boora
GHADC : Garo Hills Autonomous District Council
GJM : Gorkha Janmukti Morcha
GNLF : Gorkha National Liberation Front
GoI : Government of India
GTA : Gorkhaland Territorial Administration
IAY : Indira Awaas Yojana

ILP	: Inner Line Permit
IPR	: Intellectual property Rights
ITDP	: Integrated Tribal Development Project
JHADC	: Jaintia Hills Autonomous District Council
KAAC	: Karbi Anglong Autonomous Council
KCP	: Kangleipak Communist Party
KHADC	: Khasi Hills Autonomous District Council
KLNLF	: Karbi Longri National Liberation Front
KPLT	: Karbi People's Liberation Tiger
KYKL	: Kanglei Yaol Kanba Lup
LADC	: Lai Autonomous District Council
LAHDC	: Ladakh Autonomous Hill Development Council
LAMPS	: (Large Agricultural Marketing Societies)
MADA	: Modified Area Development Approach
MADC	: Mara Autonomous District Council
MFPA	: Minor Forest Produce Act
MNF	: Mizo National Front
MPLF	: Manipur People's Liberation Front
NAREGA	: National Rural Employment Guarantee Act
NCMP	: National Common Minimum Programme
NDFB	: National Democratic Front of Bodoland
NEFA	: North-East Frontier Agency
NGOs	: Non-governmental organisations
NHTA	: Naga Hills Tuensang Area
NSCN-K	: Nationalist Socialist Council of Nagaland-Khaplang
OBC	: Other backward classes
PHE	: Public Health Engineering
PLA	: People's Liberation Army
PLRC	: Pawi-Lakher Regional Council
PREPAK	: People's Revolutionary Party of Kangleipak
PTG	: Particularly Vulnerable Tribal Groups
RPF	: Revolutionary People's Front
SFDA	: Small Farmers Development Agencies
SGRY	: Sampoorna Grameen Rozgar Yojana
SGSY	: Swarnjayanti Gram Swarozgar Yojana
SMED	: School and Mass Education Department
SP	: Samajwadi Party
SRC	: States Reorganisation Commission
SSA	: Sarva Shiksha Abhiyan
SSDD	: ST and SC development Department
ST	: Scheduled Tribe

TDB	: Tribal Development Blocks
TRI	: Tribal Research Institute
TRIFED	: Tribal Cooperative Marketing Development Federation of India Limited
TSP	: Tribal Sub Plan
TTAADC	: Tripura Tribal Areas Autonomous District Council
UGC	: University Grant Commission
UMFO	: United Mizo Freedom Organisation
UNLF	: United National Liberation Front
UPA	: United Progressive Alliance
UPDS	: United Peoples' Democratic Solidarity
VOs	: Voluntary Organisations
VTC	: Vocational Training Centre

List of Contributors

1. **Amitra Sudan Chakraborty,** Assistant Professor, Department of Law, Glocal University, Uttar Pradesh.
2. **D. Pulla Rao,** Professor, Department of Economics, Andhra University, Visakhapatnam, Andhra Pradesh.
3. **Dinesh Sarmah,** Assistant Professor, Department of Economics, S.D. Jain Girls College, Dimapur, Nagaland.
4. **Farzana Alim,** Professor, Department of Home Science, Aligarh Muslim University, Aligarh, Uttar Pradesh.
5. **Jangkhongam Doungel,** Associate Professor, Department of political science, Mizoram University, Aizawl, Mizoram.
6. **N.G. Pendse,** Professor, Department of Economics, Rani Durgabati University, Jabalpur, Madhya Pradesh.
7. **R. Prasad,** Professor, Department of Economics, Pandit Ravishankar Shukla University, Raipur, Chhattisgarh.
8. **Dr. Rakesh Joshi,** Associate Professor, Department of Economics, Saurashtra University, Rajkot, Gujarat.
9. **S.K. Chaudhury,** Associate Professor, Department of Management Studies, Berhampur University, Berhampur, Odisha.
10. **S. Haukhanlian Mate,** Associate Professor, Department of History, Govt. Saitual College, Saitual, Mizoram.
11. **P.K. Pandey,** Assistant Professor, Centre of Judicial Study, Dibrugarh University, Dibrugarh, Assam.

12. **Sukanta Sarkar,** Assistant Professor, Faculty of Management Studies, ICFAI University Tripura, Kamalghat, Agartala, Tripura.
13. **Tarun Kumar Bahadur,** Associate Professor, Department of Economics, Bongaigaon College, Bongaigaon, Assam.
14. **Falguni S. Vyas,** JJK College, Rajkot, Gujarat.
15. **Jamshed Ali,** Assistant Professor, Haflong Government College, Haflong, Dima Hasao District, Assam.
16. **Lalthlamuana Darlong**, Assistant Professor, Department of Economics, Ambedkar College, Fatikroy, Tripura.
17. **Prahelika Roy,** Student, Women's College, Agartala, Tripura.
18. **Subhash Chandra Panda,** Senior Consultant, National Institute of Open Schooling, Noida, Uttar Pradesh.
19. **Satyajit Das,** Ph.D. Scholar, Department of Political Science, Tripura University, Suryamaninagar, Agartala.

Introduction

British Indian administration had shrewdly governed the tribal areas by endorsing internal administrative freedom since the very inception of extending its (British) rule in the area. Tribals are very much deprived from the initial stages. They are sore simple and hard labourer people. Social security and special care is more important for their development. In Indian Constitution there are various provisions present which support needs of social security. Tribal development as a subject has been an important area of inquiry in the social sciences. In recent years, the subject has acquired immense importance both at the national and international level The active support and hectic campaign by a number of international Non-Governmental Organisations championing the cause of the *'indigenous people'* has made it a burning issue all over the world. Education greatly benefits personal health. Particularly powerful for girls, it profoundly affects reproductive health, and also improves child mortality and welfare through better nutrition and higher immunisation rates. In this book there are nineteen papers in two parts. In first part papers are link with tribal welfare and second part papers are of autonomous district council.

Dr. Jangkhongam Doungel in his paper "*Evolution and Functioning of the Sixth Schedule to the Constitution of India*" examined the provision of Autonomous District Council. It is incorporated in the Sixth Schedule to the constitution of India which is now popularly known as the *Sixth Schedule*. The provision of Sixth Schedule to the constitution of India is a unique feature because the process for materialisation of the Sixth Schedule had already begun since the very inception of British rule in the tribal area. *Dr. N.G. Pendse and Dr. Sukanta Sarkar* in their paper *"Situation of Tribal's in India: A Critical Analysis"* argued that tribal's constitute 8.14 per cent of the total population of the country, numbering 84.51 million (2001 Census) and cover about 15 per cent of the country's area. The fact that tribal people need special attention can be observed from their low social, economic and participatory indicators. *Dr. S. Haukhanlian Mate* in his paper *"Traditional Thangkhal Marriage System"* discusses the Thangkhals marriage system. The Thangkhals belongs to Tibeto-Burman family speaking the Tibeto-Burman language. Marriage is an important form of institution among the Thangkhals. *Dr. P.K. Pandey* in his paper *"The Socio Demography of the Tribal's in North-East India"* analyse the situation of tribal's in north-east India. North-East India is renowned for its tribal culture. North East India consists of a number of hills and few fertile plains. The undulating nature of the topography of the area has compelled the inhabitants to adopt mainly two methods of agriculture, permanent and shifting according to their suitability. The state of Assam comprises of relatively bigger plain areas, except, however, two districts, the North Cacher and the Karbi Anglong, which are hilly.

L. Darlong in his paper "Economic Problems and Prospects of Tribal Youth in Tripura: With Special Reference to Educated Unemployment" concluded that the economic problems of educated tribal youth is a serious problem, which needs timely attention and solution. As many educated tribal youth are not aware of the various facilities available for starting their own ventures leading to unemployment. *Prahelika Roy* in her paper *"Tribal life in India: Past vs. Present"* expressed that Hill and tribal are interconnected. Hilly areas are the base of tribal's. Previously they lived in isolated and simple life but their life is changing for education and social upliftment. *Dr. Turun Kumar Bahadur* in his paper *"Employment avenues in Government and Corporate Sectors for Tribal People"* observe the *goal of reservation in India. The government's job reservation policies placed little emphasis on improving the job-related attributes of persons from the ST. Prof. Fazana Alim* in her paper *"Social Security of Tribal's in India: Needs and Government Initiatives"* made an attempt to analyse the policy of government for protection of tribal's. The Ministry of Tribal Affairs was constituted in October 1999 with the objective of providing more focused attention on the integrated socio-economic development of the most under-privileged sections of the Indian society.

Prof. Subhash Chandra Panda in his paper *"Tribal Culture and Elementary Schooling of the Girls in the context of Odisha"* found that in most of the tribal sections the women hold a significant place in the society and home as well. Generally they are not addicted to liquor as their men folk. *Amitra Sudan Chakraborty* in his paper *"Tribal's in Andaman and Nicobar Islands: An overview"* argue that situation of tribal's in Andaman and Nicobar Islands are not good. The indigenous tribes are distinguished as two groups: the Onge, Sentinelese, Jarawa and Andamanese of Negroid descent living on the Andaman Islands and the Shompen and Nicobarese of Mongoloid descent living in the Nicobar Islands. *Dr. Rakesh A. Joshi and Falguni S. Vyas* in their paper *"Tribal and their labour problems"* found that many tribal areas in India are still identified as the areas of poverty, illiteracy, unemployment and exploitation. *Prof. D. Pulla. Rao* in his paper *"Status of Autonomous District Council's in India: An Overview"* analyse the situation of Autonomous District Council's in India. Autonomous district council is a real fact in North-East India. In North-East India more or less every state has autonomous district council. Autonomous district council and tribal are interconnected. Autonomous district council is a way for providing more autonomy power to tribal people is their own development. It is proving under the six schedule of Constitution of India.

Jamshad Ali in his paper *"Management of forest for sustainable development with reference to Dima Hasao Autonomous District Council, Halflong, Assam"* discuss about the Dima Hasao Autonomous District Council. Sustainable utilisation of forest resources need for the join participation of the local people in order to conserve, protect and utilised the natural resources, prevent further degradation of the declining forests resources of Dima Hasao district. *Dr. S.K. Chaudhury in his paper "Karbi Anglong Autonomous District Council in Assam: Historical Perspectives"* observed that the Karbis are one of the major ethnic groups in North-east India. The Karbis linguistically belong to the Tibeto-Burman group. Karbi Anglong district is the main district for them. Prahelika Roy in her paper *"Bodoland Territorial Council: Past vs. Present"* argue about the situation of Bodoland Autonomous Discrict Council. The Bodos are an ethnic and linguistic community, early settlers of Assam in the northeast part of India. According to the 2011 census, there are nearly two million Bodos in Assam which makes for 5.5 per cent of the total population in the state. Bodos belong to a larger ethnic group called the Bodo-Kachari. *Dr. Dinesh Sarmah* in his paper *"Situation of Tribal's and economic transition in Nagaland"* conclude that the Nagas, inhabitants of Nagaland, are said to belong to the indo-mongoloid stock, a race whose presence was first noted ten centuries before Christ, at the time of the compilation of the Vedas. The Nagas form many tribes, as well as numerous sub-tribes, each having a specific geographic distribution. Each tribe is distinct in character from the other in terms of customs, language and dress.

Prof. R. Prasad and Dr. Sukanta Sarkar in their paper *"Autonomous district council in Mizoram: Needs and Government Initiatives"* found that Autonomous district council is the real fact of Mizoram. Lai, Chakma ana Mara autonomous district councils are playing vital roles for the development of the southern part of the state. It also helps for solving the insurgency from of the state. Each district council is unique for its culture and religious believes. *Dr. P.K. Pandey* in his paper *"Gorkhaland Territorial Administration: Conflict and Progress"* argued that Gorkhaland movement grew from the demand of Nepalis living in Darjiling District of West Bengal for a separate state for themselves. The Gorkhaland National Liberation Front led the movement which disrupted the district with massive violence between 1986 and 1988. The issue was resolved, at least temporarily in 1988 with the establishment of the Darjiling Gorkha Hill Council within West Bengal. Satyajit Das in his paper *"TTAADC in Tripura and Tribal Welfare: An Overview"* found that Tripura tribal areas autonomous district council is a milestone in the path of development process of tribal people in Tripura. About 30 per cent of the total population of Tripura is scheduled tribe. They are still back ward in 21st century than that of other communities.

SECTION—A

TRIBAL SITUATION AND WELFARE

1

Evolution and Functioning of the Sixth Schedule to the Constitution of India

Jangkhongam Doungel

Introduction

Indian Constitution is the lengthiest and the bulkiest constitution of the world. The original constitution enforced on 26 January, 1950 comprised of 395 articles, eight schedules and 22 parts.[1] At present, the Indian constitution now contains 447 articles, 12 schedules and 22 parts (26 parts including four sub-parts) and it has been amended 95 times till 2010.[2] Many articles are deleted due to amendments of certain part of the constitution. Article numbers are incorporated in serial wise for easy identification of the contents of the constitution. Parts are further classified into chapters and sub-chapters, whereas guidelines which are required in different aspects of governance of the country are listed in schedule. The provision of Autonomous District Council is incorporated in the Sixth Schedule of the constitution of India which is now popularly known as the *Sixth Schedule.*

British Rule and its Impact in the Hill Areas of the North-east India

British Indian administration had shrewdly governed the tribal areas by endorsing internal administrative freedom since the very inception of extending its (British) rule in the area. With the acquirement of the Dewany (power to collect revenue) of Bengal by Robert Clive in 1765, British rule had extended as far as the border of Assam (North East India). Therefore problems broke out in Garo Hills, David Scot; Magistrate of Rangpur was deputed to undertake spot verification of the situation. David Scot submitted his report to the Governor-General-in-Council on August 1816, in which, he recommended the establishment of North East Rangpur Civil Commissioner by slicing some area of the Rangpur Magistrate jurisdiction and it was readily approved by the Governor General-in-Council. Consequently, Regulation X of 1822 was enforced and it happened to be the first regulation, enforced by the British Authority for administering the tribal areas of North East India. The Regulation X of 1822 laid down a special plan for administration of justice, adaptable to peculiar custom and prejudice of the region.[3] And thinking it as a necessary step for preservation of ethnic identity of the tribal's, Garo Hills was delinked from the jurisdiction of Civil, Criminal and Revenue Court of the government on first March, 1870 by the Garo Hills Act (Act XXII) of 1869. Further, the same Act was also enforced in the Naga Hills, Khasi Hills and Jantia Hills from first November 1871.[4] Thus, as a measure for preservation of custom, culture and ethnic identity of the tribal's as well as to avoid unproductive huge expenditure, shrewd arrangement was made in such a tactful way. Due to that Chin Hills Regulation of 1896 was also enforced in the Lushai Hills.[5]

The British Indian administration also took another step for safeguarding tribals of the eastern part of Bengal. So, Bengal Eastern Frontier Regulation, 1873, popularly known as Inner Line Regulation or Inner Line Permit (ILP) was enacted. Subsequently, *Inner Line Permit (ILP)* was enforced in Kamrup, Darang, Nowgong, Sibsagar, Lakhimpur, Garo Hills, Khasi and Jantia Hills, Naga Hills and Cachar from first January, 1873. The above mentioned districts and Goalpara were declared to be under the jurisdiction of the Governor General-in-Council by the Government of India Act of 1854. When the Chief Commissioner Province of Assam was created by reorganising the geographical area of Bengal in 1784, Inner Line Regulation or ILP continued to function in the above mentioned nine Hill districts. Over and above that, Scheduled Districts Act of 1874 was enforced in the hill districts where ILP was not yet extended and those areas were also subsequently brought under the Inner Line Regulation afterwards.[6] Scheduled Districts signify those backward districts where normal administration could not be carried out. Accordling all the tribal dominated backward districts were declared as Scheduled Districts by the Scheduled District Act of 1874.[7]

The Assam Frontier Tract Regulation had given wide powers to Chief Commissioner in order to enhance development of the backward districts of Assam. As per the notification issued by Section 52A(2)n of the Government of India Act of 1915-1919, the districts, declared as Backward Tracts by the Governor General-in-Council were listed as given below: [8]

1. Garo Hills District:
2. Khasi and Jantia Hills excluding Shillong Municipality;
3. Mikir Hills;
4. North Cachar Hills;
5. Naga Hills;
6. Lushai Hills;
7. Sadiya Frontier Tract;
8. Balipara Frontier Tract;
9. Lakhimpur Frontier Tract.

Simon Commission Report of 1930 highlighted that the geographical area of Backward Tribal Area in all over India was 1,20,000 sq. miles which comprised of tribal areas in Bihar, Orissa, Punjab, Burma, Bengal and Assam (North East India).[9] The terminology *"Backward Tract"* was changed into Excluded Area by the Government of India Act of 1935. Excluded Area means backward most tribal areas which were under the direct rule of the Governors and districts which were categorised as excluded area had no representation in the provincial legislature. Whereas, districts which were categorised as partially *'Excluded Area'* were under provincial government and they also had representatives in the provincial legislature. However, the law enacted by provincial legislature could not be enforced in the *'Partially Excluded Area'* without the approval of the Governor. Moreover, the Governor could also use his discretionary power without consulting the provincial government in the partially excluded area. As a result, the hill districts in Assam were classified as categorised below.[10]

Excluded Area

1. North East Frontier Tract (Sadiya, Balipara and Lakhimpur);
2. Naga Hills District;
3. Lushai Hills District;
4. North Cachar Hills.

Partially Excluded Area

1. Garo Hills;
2. Mikir Hills;
3. Khasi and Jantia Hills excluding Shillong Municipality.

As stated earlier, the Tribal Areas had drawn special attention of the administration since pre-independent era. The Cabinet Mission sent by the British Parliament under Sir Stafford Cripps had made a public statement on 16 March, 1946 which also had suggested for the formation of an Advisory Committee, to study upon the rights of minorities and tribal's of excluded area. Accordingly, an Advisory Committee on Fundamental Rights, minorities and Tribal and Excluded Area was set up with Vallabhai Patel as the Chairman on 24 January, 1947 by the Constituent Assembly. The main task of the committee was to work out a modus operandi in the constitutional arrangement for tribal's of excluded and partially excluded area and to enable them to safeguard their ethnic identity and culture in a democratic way. Subsequently, on 2nd February, 1947 the Advisory Committee set up three sub-committees which are given as given below:[11]

1. North East Frontier (Assam) Tribal and Excluded Area Committee;
2. North West Frontier Province and Baluchistan Tribal and Excluded Area Committee;
3. Excluded and Partially Excluded Areas in provinces other than Assam.

Bordoloi Committee and Acceptance of the Second Schedule by the Constituent Assembly

As a result of partition of the country into India and Pakistan on 14 August, 1947 and inclusion of North West Frontier Province (NWFP) and Baluchistan in Pakistan,[12] North West Frontier Province and Baluchistan Tribal and Excluded Area Committee became automatically defunct. As such, only two committees continued to function with respect to the rights and status of the tribal's. Gopinath Bordoloi was Chairman of the North East Frontier (Assam) Tribal and Excluded Area Committee and other members of the committee were Rev. JJM Nichols Roy, Rup Nath Brahma, A.V. Thakkar and Mayang Nokcha. Mayang Nokcha replaced Aliba Imti, the previous member who was from Naga Hills. The Committee was also popularly known as *Bordolai Committee* after the name of its chairman and the then Chief Minister of Assam, Gopinath Bordoloi. A.V. Thakkar was Chairman of the Excluded and partially Excluded Area (other than Assam) Sub-committee. Bordoloi committee extensively toured the Lushai Hills, North Cachar Hills, Mikir Hills and Naga Hills but could not visit Garo Hills and Jowai Sub-division of Khasi Hills due to bad weather and communication problem.[13]

The Bordoloi Committee tactfully analysed and compiled the facts which were collected and submitted its report to Vallabhai Patel, Chairman, Advisory Committee on Fundamental Rights etc., on 28 July, 1947. The report dealt with various aspects relating to administration of the tribal areas such as thoughts on development, special features of these areas, land, forest, jhumming, court, finance, control of immigration, service etc. The Advisory Committee discussed the report on 7 December, 1947 and 24 February, 1948. After that, Drafting Committee again studied the report on 13 February, 1948 and the report which B.N. Rau, Constitutional Adviser put in the Seventh Schedule was rearranged and put in the Sixth Scheduled by Dr. B.R. Ambedkar. The draft schedule was submitted to the President of the Constituent Assembly on 21th February, 1948 and the matter was discussed in the Constituent Assembly on 5, 6 and 7th September 1949. There was heated exchange of words between the supporters and opponents of the draft schedule. Rejeshwar Prasad from Bihar as well as Rohini Kumar Chaudhury and Kuladhar Chaliha from Assam were quite vocal in their arguments against the establishment of District

Council under the draft Sixth Schedule. They categorically stated that, instead of guaranting autonomy, the hill areas should be assimilated with the plains. Kuladhar Chaliha had even alleged that in the like manner in which Pakistan was created, the Sixth Schedule should create Tribalistan which would be a great threat to national integration. However, Dr. B.R. Ambedkar, Gopinath Bordoloi, A.V. Thakkar, Jaipal singh and Rev JJM Nichols Roy spoke strongly in favour of the sixth schedule provision. Dr. B.R. Ambedkar said *"The Tribal people in area other than Assam are more or less Hinduised more or less assimilated with the civilization and culture of the majority of the people in whose midst they live with regards to the tribals in Assam that is not the case. Their roots are still in their own civilization and culture."*[14]

Dr. Ambedkar further said that the position of the tribal's of Assam was somewhat analogues to the position of the Red Indians of the United States as against the white emigrants. The United States created boundaries or reservation in which the Red Indians live. They are no doubt, citizens of United States of America but they are actually independent people. The government of USA realised that their laws and mode of life, their habitat and manner of life were so distinct that it would be dangerous to bring them immediately at one time within the range of laws made by the white people for the whites and white civilisation. This was the main reason why we insisted upon the creation of District Councils and Regional Councils on the lines adopted by the USA for the Red Indians, he added.[15] In the course of the heated debate in the constituent Assembly, Rev. JJM Nichols Roy stated that there were different types of tribal's and tribals of Assam were lovers of democracy. So, the proposed democratic set-up would be convenient for them because they had already experienced such type of system from before. He further stated that ethnic Skirmish was frequent in Assam between Ahoms and Assamese, Bengalis and Muslims, tribals and non-tribal's. Therefore without taking political advantage out of such critical situation, experts of the specialised area, namely, doctors, social workers, academicians, philosophers, sociologists and Professors were engaged to find out an objective solution. Consequently, members of the Constituent Assembly were readily convinced by the influential argument of the tribal leader upon the ethnic identity, custom, culture and tradition of the tribal's.

In the meantime, Dr. B.R. Ambedkar and G.N. Bordoloi had been already convinced by Rev. JJM Nichols Roy on the perplexed issue. Over and above that, Rev. JJM Nichols Roy also had submitted a memorandum to the Cabinet Mission, demanding the creation of a political set-up where the tribal's would be able to govern themselves. Hence Rev. JJM Nichols Roy had enormously contributed in the genesis and emergence of sixth schedule of the constitution of India. As a matter of fact, Rev JJM Nichols Roy was regarded as an architect of the District Council autonomy.[16]

G.N. Bordoloi also played a vital role in the evolution of the Sixth Schedule. He wrote a letter to Sardar Vallabhai Patel, Chairman of the Advisory Committee and stated that, *social custom, tribal organisation, culture and language of tribal could be preserved only if an autonomous political set-up was established for them.* After along and heated debate in the Constituent Assembly and after certain amendments were made, the Sixth Schedule finally emerged and was incorporated in Articles 244 (2) and 275 (1) of the constitution of India. Along with that, preservation of custom, culture, language and ethnic identity of tribal's of Excluded and partially excluded areas other than Assam was incorporated in the Fifth Schedule in Article 244 (1) of the constitution of India. The constituent Assembly also accepted the suggestion of Bordoloi Committee and Excluded and partially Excluded Area (other than Assam) committee. As a result, tribal inhabited areas under Fifth Schedule are known as *"Scheduled Area"* and tribal inhabited areas under the Sixth Schedule are known as *"Tribal Area"*.[17] It is clearly incorporated in the constitution of India that even if an area is exclusively tribal dominated area, it can not be called a *Tribal Area* if Sixth Schedule provision to the constitution of India is not enforced in that area.

Eminent lawyer and former Vice President of India, M. Hidayatullah said *"Fifth and Sixth Schedules are constitution within a constitution"*.[18] He further highlighted that these two schedules incorporated the setting up of a peculiar political set-up in certain tribal areas. However, the difference with some other parts of the constitution is that some provisions of the constitution can be amended only by 2/3rd majority of members of the parliament and some provision with not just two third majority but approval by at least half of the state is required. But in case of the Fifth and Sixth Schedule, amendment can be done just by simple majority in Parliament.[19]

The Tribal Areas, as listed in the Sixth Schedule in the initial stage of the enforcement of the constitution of India are given below.[20]

Part A

1. United Khasi - Jantia Hills District;
2. Garo Hills;
3. Lushai Hills;
4. Naga Hills;
5. North Cachar Hills;
6. Mikir Hills.

Part B

1. North East Frontier Tract (Balipara Frontier Tract, Tirap Frontier Tract, Abor Hills District and Mishmi Hill District);
2. Naga Tribal Areas.

As shown above, Sixth Schedule Areas were cattegoriesed into two parts at the initial stage. Those areas where the people were a bit developed and where democratic political institution could be established were listed in Part A. Infact, the areas where District Council could be established were listed in Part A. On the other hard, the backward most areas where establishment of democratic system was not possible were categorised in Part B. As a matter of fact, some tribal's in Part B was still in primitive stage even at that time. Therefore, the Governor of Assam was given discretionary power for administering tribals in Part B of the Sixth Schedule.[21] Moreover, Part B is also identified as the Sixth Schedule where there are no District Council. However; even under Part A, District Council could not be established in Naga Hills due to rejection of District Council Status by the Nagas under the influence of insurgency movement spearheaded by A.Z. Phizo.[22]

Amendment of the Sixth Schedule and Emergence of States and Union Territories from the Sixth Schedule Area

As a necessary measure for betterment of the tribal's, the Sixth Schedule provision had been amended many a time. The North East Frontier Tract was placed under the administrative jurisdiction of the

External Affairs Ministry since 26 January, 1950 and Adviser to the Governor of Assam assumed direct charge of the Tract. The Naga Tribal Area was merged with the North East Frontier Tract in 1951 under the new designation as North East Frontier Agency (NEFA). The Nagas had not only rejected the sixth schedule but violently fought for independence. As a result, Sixth Schedule amendment bill was enacted by the Indian Parliament and Naga Hills Tuensang Area (NHTA) was created on 1st December, 1957 by amalgamation of the Tuensang Frontier Division of NEFA and Naga Hills District of Assam. Due to the intensified demand of Naga state by the Naga leaders, the Constitution Thirteenth Amendment act made provisions for creation of Naga state of Nagaland and was inaugurated by Dr. S. Radhakrishnan, the then President of India at Kohima on first December, 1963. As a result, Naga Hills and Naga Tribal Area no longer appeared in the Sixth Schedule. After that, NEFA also got Union Territory with a new name, Arunachal Pradesh in 1972 and it was no longer existed in the Sixth Schedule.[23]

The creation of Nagaland State had given an impetus to the tribal's of other hill areas of Assam to fight for statehood. As such, the demand for hill state was spearheaded by Eastern India Tribal Union (EITU) and All Party Hill Leader's Conference (APHLC). Indeed, the declaration of Assamese as a state language was a blessing in disguise for the Hill State movement. The United Mizo Freedom Organisation (UMFO) of Lushai Hills was merged with EITU in 1957 and the Mizo Union (M.U.) also supported APHLC in the initial stage. However, the M.U. parted ways with APHLC due to difference of opinion. Consequently, a bill for creation of Autonomous state of Meghalaya comprising Khasi and Garo Hills was passed by Indian Parliament on 24th December, 1969 and the Autonomous State of Meghalaya was created on second April, 1970. After that, Meghalaya was accorded the status of statehood on 21th January, 1972. On the very same day, Lushai Hills was also declarared as the Union Territory of Mizoram. The existing District Councils continued to function in Meghalaya but United Khasi-Jantia District Council was bifurcated into two, namely *Khasi District Council* and *Jantia District Council*. So far as the Union Territory of Mizoram is concerned, the Mizo District Council was abolished and the Pawi-Lakher Regional Council was trifurcated into three Regional Council and the three Regional

Councils were subsequently upgraded to the status of full-fledged Autonomous District Councils. As a result, Tribal areas in the Sixth Schedule were also then listed as Part–I, Part–II and Part-III. Part–I was list of District Councils in Assam, Part-II was that of Meghalaya and Part-III was the list of District Councils in Mizoram.[24]

Uniqueness of the Pawi-regional Council

The Pawi-Lakher Regional Council (PLRC) was established for the Pawi and Lakher tribes of the extreme south of the then Lushai Hills. The uniqueness of the PLRC was that, it was the only Regional Council, established under the provision of the Sixth Schedule of the constitution of India. After the formation of the Union territory of Mizoram, the PLRC was trifurcated into three Regional Councils, namely, Pawi Regional Council, Lakher Regional Council and Chakma Regional Councils on 2nd April, 1972 and the three Regional Councils were upgraded to the status of Autonomous District Councils on 29th April, 1972. Along with that, they are listed in part–III of the tribal areas in Paragraph 20 of the Sixth Schedule of the constitution of India.[25]

Amendment of The Sixth Schedule And Its Present Status

The Sixth schedule was amended again with the reorganization of Assam and creation of Nagaland, Meghalaya, Mizoram and Arunachal Pradesh from undivided Assam. Further, the category for listing Tribal Areas under the sixth schedule provision was also changed from Part-A and Part-B to Part–I, Part–II and Part-III. With the approval of the recommendation of the Tripura Legislative Assembly for creation of Autonomous District Council, the Parliament again amended the Sixth Schedule and Tripura tribal Area Autonomous District Council was included in Part-II A of the Sixth Schedule with effect from 1st April, 1985.[26]

As a result of the tripartite Bodoland Accord of Central Government, Government of Assam and All Bodo Students Union (ABSU) which was signed on 21st February, 1993, *Bodoland Autonomous Council (BAC)* was established. Yet, the Bodos were dissatisfied with the functioning of BAC and they claimed that enough power was not given to the BAC as it ought to be. So, a violent Bodoland movement was resumed under the banner of Bodo Liberation Tiger (BLT). Other than the BLT, there is also another Bodo insurgent group known as *National Democratic Front of Bodoland (NDFB)* which is fighting for sovereignty. Again, a tripartite agreement of the BLT, Central Government and Government of Assam was signed. Subsequently, Sixth Schedule was extended to the BAC with a new name Bodoland Territorial Council (BTC). Simultaneously, BTC is included in Part–I of the tribal Area in paragraph 20 of the sixth schedule of the constitution of India.[27]

After many deletions and additions in the Sixth Schedule due to frequent amendment of the constitution of India, the tribal areas of different councils under paragraph 20 of the Sixth Schedule should be listed as given below.[28]

Part –I

1. North Cachar Autonomous Council.
2. Karbi Anglong Autonomous Council.
3. Bodoland Territorial Council.

Part-II

1. Khasi Autonomous District Council
2. Jantia Autonomous District Council.
3. Garo Autonomous District Council.

Part-IIA

1. Tripura tribal areas District Council.

Part-III

1. Chakma Autonomous District Council.
2. Lai Autonomous District Council.
3. Mara Autonomous District Council.

Comparative Analysis of the Powers of Different Councils

Four different councils, namely, *Regional Council, District Council*, *Autonomous Council* and *Territorial Council* appear up till now in the provision of the Sixth Schedule of the constitution of India. Other than the Pawi Lakher Regional council, no other Regional council was established under the Sixth Schedule provision. So far as the District Council is concerned, it (District Council) is still functioning in Mizoram, Tripura and Meghalaya. Further, there are two Autonomous Councils and one Territorial Council in Assam.

The law making powers, incorporated in paragraph three of the Sixth Schedule of the constitution of India is the driving force of District Council autonomy. Certain subjects (departments) are handed over to District Councils for enabling them to effectively govern their respective autonomous area. District Councils in Mizoram are controlling about 18 subjects in average though some of the District Councils claimed that they control as many as 28 departments. Moreover, they control up to Middle School (Upper Primary School), i.e., up to class VIII in education and they have a parallel District Council Board of Education apart from the State Board. The syllabus, curriculum, academic calendar and examination etc., up to Middle school within the District Council area are under the control of District Council Board of School Education in each Autonomous District Council. The Power, responsibilities and subjects, administered by the District Councils of Mizoram, Meghalaya and Tripura are more or less the same. However, District Councils in Meghalaya seemed to constructively utilise their power to the maximum among the District Councils of the three states. The reason being, motor vehicle tax had been levied by District Councils in Meghalaya, many years before District Councils of the other two states are aware of it. With regard to enforcement of the legislation exacted by State Assembly and Parliament in the District Council area, it is included in Paragraph 12 A for Meghalaya, Paragraph 12 B for Mizoram and paragraph 12 BB for Tripura. Karbi Anglong Autonomous Council and North Cachar Autonomous Council look after more than 30 subjects in average and they are facilitated with administering 15 more departments which are not found in the District Councils. They also control up to Higher Secondary level in education. Lastly, the *Bodoland Territorial Council (BTC)* controls more than 40 subjects and looks after up to college level in education.[29]

Conclusion

The provision of Sixth Schedule of the constitution of India is a unique feature because the process for materialisation of the Sixth Schedule had already begun since the very inception of British rule in the tribal area. Moreover, the Sixth Schedule of the constitution of India important for different tribes of North East India. The reason being, those tribes who are not facilitated with the sixth schedule provision are clamouring for it because they are aware of the benefits of the Sixth schedule provision. As a matter of fact, tribals of the Hill areas of Manipur, some tribes from Assam, Gurkhas of Darjeeling Hills in West Bengal and Brus, Hmars, paites and minority tribes of Uiphum mountain range of Lawngtlai District of Mizoram are still demanding the inclusion of their respective area in the Sixth Schedule provision.

Exaggeration and misconception have often overshadowed rationalism of the Sixth Schedule. Opponents of the Sixth Schedule exaggerate it in such a manner that it amounts to breaking up of the state power whereas; supporters of the Sixth Schedule claim it again as a replica of Union Territory or statehood status. The above mentioned two extreme views should be carefully synthesized and objective approach should be adopted in this regard. Infact, terming the extension of Sixth Schedule as amounting to breaking away of the state boundary or diminishing power of the state in one hand and terming the Sixth Schedule as an analogue to Union Territory or state on the other are all Utopian misnomers. Mature and corrective approach should be adopted on the issue of the Sixth Schedule. The different councils, functioning now in Mizoram, Meghalaya, Tripura and Assam may not be free from certain loopholes, however, the little development works which they perform in their respective area may remain undone had sixth schedule provision been not extended there. It is an interesting feature that the tribal areas which are now facilitated with the Sixth Schedule are clamouring for more powers and those who are not in the sixth schedule list are intensifying their demands for extension of sixth schedule in their respective area. Further, there is no hard and fast rule in the Sixth Schedule about the set up of *District Council* by following a particular pattern. It is evident that there were three Autonomous District Councils in Undivided Chhimtuipui District of Mizoram from 1972–1998. And even after the bifurcation of Chhimtuipui District into Lawngtlai and Saiha Districts, there are still two Autonomous District Councils, namely, Lai Autonomous District Council (L.A.D.C.) and Chakma Autonomous District Council (C.A.D.C.) under Lawngtlai District. In Assam, one council is functioning within a district with respect to the case of Karbi-Anglong and North Cachar Hills. So far as Tripura is concerned, tribal areas are scattered and not geographically compact, as such, all the tribal areas are under one Autonomous District Council. Thus, rigid norms are not strictly followed in the establishment of District council but appropriate arrangement can only be made if the modus oparendi is judiciously adopted to suit the needs of the local people.

There are no hurdles in the geographical size of the area for establishment of Autonomous District Council. It is said the Government of Manipur emphasises upon the adoption of Tripura pattern where the whole tribal area would be under a unified District Council for implementation of the Sixth Schedule. However, it should be noted that there is no hard and fast rule in the Sixth Schedule to the constitution of India for adoption of only one Autonomous District Council for the whole tribal area.

References

1. Ojha, N. N., Indian Polity, Chronicle Books, New Delhi, 1993, p. 16.
2. (a) Pandey, Manoj, Our Constitution, JBA Publishers, New Delhi, 2005. (b) September 2012 Issue of the Competition Refresher, edited by Prof. Davinder Kaur, New Delhi, 2012.
3. Hansaria, B.L., Sixth Schedule to the Constitution of India—A Study, Jyoti Printers, Gauhati, 1983, pp. 1-2.
4. Chaube, S.K. Hill Politics in North East India, Orient Longman, Patna, 1999, p. 14
5. Chin Hills Regulation, 1896, Regulation No. V of 1896, printed by the Superintendent, Government Printing, Burma, 1897.
6. Chakraborty, P., The Inner-Line Regulation of the North East India, Linkman Publication, Titagarh, West Bengal, 1995, p. B
7. Hansaria, B.L., op. cit, pp. 3-4.
8. Hansaria, B.L., op. cit, pp. 3-4.
9. *Ibid.*
10. Singh, S.N., Mizoram, Mittal Publication, New Delhi, 1994, p. 113.
11. Chakraborty, P., Fifth and Sixth Schedules to the constitution of India, Capital Law House, Delhi, 2005, p. 5.
12. Chander, Parkash, Indian Political System, cosmos Bookhive (P.) Ltd, Third Edition, p. 134.
13. Hansaria, B.L., Op. Cit, pp. 9-10.
14. *Ibid.*, pp. 11-15.
15. *Ibid.*

16. Kyndiah, P.R. Rev. JJM Nichols Roy: Architect of District Council Autonomy, Sanchar Publishing House, New Delhi, 1993, pp. 103 and 120-122.
17. Government of India, The Constitution of India as on 1st June, 1996, Department of Publication, New Delhi, 1996, pp. 148 and 151 and 162.
18. Hidayatullah, M., The Fifth and Sixth Schedules to the constitution of India, Ashok Publishing House, Gauhati, 1979, pp. 1-2.
19. *Ibid.*
20. Hansaria, B.L. *op. cit,* pp. 28-30.
21. *Ibid.*, p. 50.
22. Singh, Chandrika, Political Evolution of Nagaland, Lancers Publishers, New Delhi, 1981, pp. 41-47.
23. Government of India, *op. cit,* p. 161.
24. Doungel, Jangkhongam, Evolution of District Council Autonomy in Mizoram, Spectrum Publications, Guwahati, 2010, pp. 62-65.
25. *Ibid.*
26. Chakraborty, P., Fifth and Sixth Schedules to the constitution of India, *op. cit.,* p. 82.
27. Deb., A.B., Nationality Question, Security and Development in North East, North East India Political science Association (NEIPSA), 2004, pp. 94-96.
28. Bakshi, B.M., (i) The Constitution of India, Universal Law Publishing Co. Pvt. Ltd., New Delhi, 2006, p. 358. (ii) Mizoram Gazette of 18.2.2003, Issue No. 386. (iii) Chakraborty, Fifth and Sixth Schedule to the constitution of India, *op. cit,* p. 293.
29. *Ibid.,* Bakshi, B.M., pp. 345-346.

2

Situation of Tribal's in India: An Overview

N.G. Pendse and *Sukanta Sarkar*

Introduction

Humans are the primates of the family Hominidae and the only extant species of the genus *Homo*. They are uniquely adept at utilising systems of symbolic communication such as language and art for self-expression, the exchange of ideas, and organisation. They create complex social structures composed of many cooperating and competing groups, from families and kinship networks to states. Humans began to practice sedentary agriculture about 12,000 years ago, domesticating plants and animals which allowed for the growth of civilisation. Humans subsequently established various forms of government, religion, and culture around the world, unifying people within a region and leading to the development of states and empires. The rapid advancement of scientific and medical understanding in the 19th and 20th centuries led to the development of fuel-driven technologies and improved health, causing the human population to rise exponentially. In 1974-1975, about 22 per cent of India's total geographical area was covered by forests. This forest region, interspersed all over the country, consists of evergreen forests, deciduous forests, dry forests, alpine forests, riparian forests and tidal forests. According to the 1971 Census Report, a majority of the tribals lived in the countryside and relied mainly on agriculture. From an economic point of view, the tribes could be classified as semi-nomadic, the Jhum cultivators and the settled cultivators, living completely on forest produce. Forests are the main source of subsistence for them. They collect their food from them; use the timber or bamboo to construct their houses; collect firewood for cooking and in winter to keep warm; use grass for fodder, brooms and mats; collect leaves for leaf plates; and use harre behra for dyeing and tanning. The forest regions are also inhabited by non-tribals, who depend on forests for fuel, fodder and so on.

Tribal's constitute 8.14 per cent of the total population of the country, numbering 84.51 million (2001 Census) and cover about 15 per cent of the country's area. The fact that tribal people need special attention can be observed from their low social, economic and participatory indicators. Whether it is maternal and child mortality, size of agricultural holdings or access to drinking water and electricity, tribal communities lag far behind the general population. Nearly 52 per cent of Tribal population is Below Poverty Line and nearly 54 per cent tribal's having no access to economic assets such as communication and transport. These indicators underline the importance of the need of livelihood generating activities based on locally available resources so that gainful employment opportunities could be created at the doorstep of tribal people.

Constitutional Provisions

The Constitution of India does not define Scheduled Tribes. However Article 366(25) refers to scheduled tribes as those communities who are scheduled in accordance with Article 342 of the Constitution. According to Article 342 of the Constitution, *the Scheduled Tribes are the tribes or tribal communities or part of or groups within these tribes and tribal communities which have been declared as such by the President through a public notification*. The Constitution of India incorporates several special provisions for the promotion of educational and economic interest of Scheduled Tribes and their protection from social injustice and all forms of exploitation. These objectives are sought to be achieved through a strategy known as the *Tribal Sub-Plan strategy*, which was adopted at the beginning of the Fifth Five Year Plan. The strategy seeks to ensure adequate flow of funds for tribal development form the State Plan allocations, schemes/ programmes of Central Ministries/Departments, financial and Developmental Institutions. The cornerstone of this strategy has been to ensure earmarking of funds for TSP by States/UTs in proportion to the ST population in those State/UTs.

However, the Constitution of India refers tribal areas within the States of Assam, Meghalaya, Tripura and Mizoram, as those areas specified in Parts I, II, IIA and III of the table appended to paragraph 20 of the Sixth Schedule. In other words, areas where provisions of Sixth Schedule are applicable are known as *Tribal Areas*. In relation to these areas Autonomous District Councils, each having not more than thirty members has been set up. These councils serve as an instrument of self-management and have powers of legislation and administration of justice apart from executive, developmental and financial responsibilities.

Tribals in North India

The Government of India defines the North India Cultural Zone as including the states of Jammu and Kashmir, Punjab, Himachal Pradesh, Haryana and Rajasthan, as well as the Union Territory of Chandigarh. Indo-Gangetic Plain and the Himalayas are demarcating the region from Tibet and Central Asia. Tribes of Punjab are scattered throughout the state. Amongst them the prominent ones are *Jats, Khatris, Aroras, Sainis, Kambohs and Sansis*. The Sikh Jats form a bulk of the total population of the state. They mainly belong to the agricultural class. Sikh Jats are considered as highly industrious by nature. Next to them are the Khatris and Aroras. The several nomadic tribes of Punjab, like *Sainis, Bawris, Bazigars* etc., are considered as aboriginal in their derivation. Tribes of Haryana mostly belong to Indo Aryan and Indo-Dravidian families. In the state of Haryana, Jats occupy a major place, being one of the largest groups in the region. In Haryana, Ahir community is mainly concentrated in Mahendragarh district. They are considered quite similar to the Jats having a number of clans.

Tribes of Himachal Pradesh are scattered in different parts of this state and have occupied a considerable percentage of India. The tribes of Himachal Pradesh belong to the famous Indo-Aryan family group. The major tribes of this region include *Kinnaura tribe, Lahaule tribe, Gaddi tribe and Gujjar tribe*. As far as the occupations are concerned, these tribes of Himachal Pradesh have taken up the occupations including rearing of cattle and also raising of wool. The five major tribes found in Uttar Pradesh are Tharu, Jaunsari, Raji, Bhotia and

Bhoksa. They are mainly found in the present state of Uttarakhand comprising areas like Uttarkashi, Pauri Garhwal, Tehri Garhwal, Haridwar, Nainital, Chamoli, Bageswar, Udham Singh Nagar, Pithoragarh, Champawat, Almora, Dehradun and Rudraprayag. Tribes of Uttarakhand mainly comprise five major groups namely *Jaunsari tribe, Tharu tribe, Raji tribe, Buksa tribe* and *Bhotiyas*. In terms of population Jaunsari tribe is the largest tribal group of the state. Every district of Uttarakhand has more or less a moderate percentage of tribal population. In the state of Uttarakhand, the main concentration of tribal population is in the rural areas.

Jammu and Kashmir is an abode to quite a number of tribal communities, who have settled down in every nook and corner of this hilly countryside. Just like many other Indian tribesmen, most of the tribes of Jammu and Kashmir have accepted rice, wheat, pulses as their staple food. Tribes of Rajasthan constitute 12 per cent of the total population. At the core of the state of Rajasthan, the Garasia tribes live with its treasure of cultural tradition as depicted in its superb language, food habits and gorgeous clothes. Some other tribal communities or *'adivasis'* that are found in different parts of Rajasthan are *Bishnoi Tribe, Meena tribes, Meghval* and *Rabari Tribe*.

Tribals in East India

East India comprises the states of West Bengal, Orissa, Bihar and Jharkhand. The diversity of East India is evident from its population, individual count and of course the intellectual stamina of the people residing in this region. East Indian tribes are absolutely engrossed in religious revelry and ceremonies associated with primeval faiths. The bulk of the region lies on the east coast of India by the Bay of Bengal and on the Indo-Gangetic plain. Jharkhand, on the Chhota Nagpur plateau is a hilly and a heavily forested state rich in mineral wealth.

Tribes of West Bengal have occupied a large section of the total population of West Bengal. Among the various tribal groups of West Bengal, most significant tribes are the *Garo Tribe, Lohara Tribe, Mahli Tribe, Mru Tribe, Munda Tribe, Oraon Tribe, Paharia Tribe, Kora Tribe* etc. These tribes comprises of less than one-tenth of the total population of the state. The Bhutia tribes are mostly farmers, producing several vegetables and fruits. Garo tribes are located mainly in Burdwan district, Meghalaya, Cooch Bihar, Jalpaiguri and Dinajpur of West Bengal. Oraon tribes of West Bengal are one of the biggest tribes in the whole of south Asia. These Oraon tribes converse with each other in Kurukh, a popular language belonging to the Dravidian family. Most of the Oraon tribal communities have taken up the profession of cultivation. Munda tribes are one of the largest tribes of India. Main languages spoken by these tribes include *'Munda'* or *'Killi'*, Santali and Mundari. These Munda tribes are pious and religious minded, and mainly practice Hinduism.

Most of the tribes of Bihar reside in mud houses with thatched roofs. There are baked tiles for roofs. The most important festival for the tribes of Bihar is Sarhul which commemorates the blossoming of Sal trees. Tribes of Jharkhand include near about 32 tribal groups that inhabit the state. As per 2001 Census, total population of Jharkhand is around 26.90 million. The total tribal population of this state is nearly 28 percent of the total population of the state. Tribes of Jharkhand are scattered in all parts of the state. The ancient tribes of Jharkhand consist of *Birhor tribe, Asur tribe, Birajia tribe, Hill Kharia tribe, Parahiya tribe, Mal Paharia tribe, Sauriya Paharia tribe,* and *Korba tribe*. Of all the states of India, Orissa has the largest number of tribes, as many as 62. Each of these tribal groups has its own indigenous customs and continues to practice them even today. In terms of percentage they constitute an impressive 24 percent of the total population of the state. These tribes mainly inhabit the Eastern Ghats hill range, which runs in the north-south direction. More than half of their population is concerned in three districts of Koraput (undivided), Sundergarh and Mayurbhanj.

Although the tribal population in Odisha has around 25 per cent; their contribution in the development process of the state is outstanding. Their tradition and culture is broad and uncommon. And the cultural history of tribal's of this undivided Koraput has special importance all over India. The tribal population consists of 53.74 per cent in the undivided Koraput (now divided into 4 districts Koraput, Rayagada, Nawarangpur and Malkangiri) as per 2001 census operation. They all live in the above district although their number is so small. As far as the population of a tribe is concerned the Bhumia, Bhatra, Gond, Koya, Paraja, Kondh constitute above one lakh each, while other 26 tribes population is around 1000.

Tribals in West India

West India consists of the states of Goa, Gujarat and Maharashtra, along with the Union Territories of Daman and Diu and Dadra and Nagar Haveli. The states are roughly bounded by the Thar Desert in the northwest, the Vindhya Range in the north and the Arabian Sea in the west. A major portion of Western India shares the Deccan Plateau with South India. Before the partition of India, Sindh and Balochistan were also included in this region.

Tribes of Goa are few in number but they truly represent the unique culture of the state. The recent economical, technological and scientific changes have not affected their ways of living and traditional customs. The major tribal communities of Goa live in isolated villages. Their indigenous lifestyles, traditions, ceremonies, customs, religious beliefs, practices and superstitions form a significant part of the culture of the state. Tribes of Gujarat are primarily resided in the rugged regions of Aravallis, Vindhya, Satpura and Sahiyadri ranges. The tribal belt in Gujarat consists of the districts of Danga, Surat, Broach, Baroda, Panchmahals, Sabarkantha and Banaskantha. Various sects of adivasis, mainly of Bhil Tribe and Konkan origin reside in this region. Tribes such as the *Siddhis, Rabari tribe, Padhar tribe, Mers and Bharwads* live in the coastal Saurashtra districts of Junagadh, Jamnagar and Kutch. There are over 5 million adivasis or tribal communities in Gujarat. Tribes with Bhil features account for more than 50 per cent of the Gujrat's adivasi population. The tribal people of Gujarat are religious and are animistic in religion.

Tribes of Maharashtra are the primitive people of this region and are scattered in different parts of the state. Mostly they are the inhabitants of the hilly areas. Some of the tribes are of primitive and nomadic character. Tribes like *Warli Tribe, Bhil Tribe, Koli Tribe* and *Halba Tribe* are some of the tribes that inhabit in the land of Maharashtra. Tribes of Daman and Diu make a statement of their own in whatever field they have specialised. Tribes have always been impressed and affected upon by Portuguese and British domination, which still bears ample proofs.

Central India is known as heart of India. Madhya Pradesh and Chhattisgarh are the important states in this region. Tribes of Chhattisgarh account for around one third of the total population of the state. Some of the major tribes of Chhattisgarh include *Gond tribe, Baiga Tribe, Korba, Abhuj Maria, Bison Horn Maria tribe, Muria tribe, Halba tribe, Bhatra* and *Dhurvaa tribes*. In Chhattisgarh, Bastar District is considered as the largest tribal district. Bastar District has over 70 percent tribal population. Tribes of Madhya Pradesh represent the culture of their state. In the state of Madhya Pradesh the Jhabua district has the highest density of tribal population.

Tribals in South India

South India is the area encompassing India's states of Andhra Pradesh, Karnataka, Kerala and Tamil Nadu as well as the union territories of Lakshadweep and Pondicherry, occupying 19.31 per cent of India's area (635780 km^2 or 245476.030 mi^2). The region is also known as *Dravida* as is used in the National anthem. South India lies in the peninsular Deccan Plateau and is bounded by the Arabian Sea in the west, the Indian Ocean in the south and the Bay of Bengal in the east. Tribes of Pondicherry in fact, divide amongst themselves under various categories, like the *Irulars, the Kattunaickens, the Malaikuravars, the Yerkulas or the Kurumans. Karaikal and Yanam* are the major locations under Puducherry where such tribal populations swarm to perform daily activities. The tribal life in Puducherry is governed under their own sweet way, like hunting or working in farms.

Tribes of Kerala belong to the famous family group of Dravidians. The mountainous regions of Kerala are inhibited by the tribal communities. The major tribes of Kerala are namely *Urali tribe, Paniyan tribe, Kapu tribe, Kanikkar tribe, Kadar tribe* etc. The Panyan tribal people of Kerala reside in some parts of Wayanad district, Malappuram district and Kannur district. Tribes of Karnataka flaunt ample exquisite clothes festivities, dance and theatres in their lives. The long list of the tribes of Karnataka state includes *Bedar tribe, Toda tribe, Hakkipikki tribe, Jenu Kuruba tribe, Kadu Kuruba tribe, Kattunayakan tribe, Konda Kapus tribe, Sholaga tribe* etc. Another important tribal group, *Sholaga tribe*, has a belonging to the Kannada group.

Tribes of Andhra Pradesh have added grandeur to the region with their rich heritage of culture, innocent lifestyle and age-old ethnicity. The tribes of Andhra Pradesh are classified into two groups.

One of the groups is present across the hilly tracts of the Deccan Plateau and by the Godavari River and Krishna River. There are around 38 tribes and sub-tribes in Tamil Nadu, and Literacy rate is 27.9 per cent of the population. The tribal people are predominantly farmers and cultivators and they are much dependant on the forest lands. Tribes of Tamil Nadu are concentrated mainly in the district of Nilgiris. Of all the distinct tribes, the Kotas, the Todas, the Irulas, the kurumbas and the Badagas form the larger groups, who mainly had a pastoral existence. Other tribes include, Kattunayakan and Paniyan amongst others.

Tribals in North-east India

Northeast India is a slightly sliced region between eastern region in India and Purvanchal Range—it is an eastward extension of the Himalayas in the northern belt of India that primarily consists of all the regions that have been carved out of the original *Province of Assam* of British India that consists the present day Assam or Assam Valley and rest of the contiguous—Arunachal Pradesh, Meghalaya, Mizoram, Nagaland and former Princely States of Manipur and Tripura.

Tribes of Nagaland include a major part of the Nagaland community. The fourtheen types of Nagaland are *Angami, Ao, Chakhesang, Chan, Khemungan, Konyak, Lotha, Phom, Pochury, Rengma, Sangtam, Sema, Yimchunger* and *Zeliang*. While almost 80 percent of population is engaged in agriculture which are located at the hill slopes and receives sufficient amount of rainfall. The tribes keep parity in selecting the crop which depends on the setting of the crops. Tribes of Mizoram largely include four types of tribal communities. The tribal people of Mizoram largely include the Chakma tribes, Pawi tribes, Ralte tribes and the Kuki tribes who travelled from upper regions of the continent.

Tribes of Manipur which represent a unique feature of the land include at least 29 communities that originated from Tibetan Burmese tribal group of Mongoloids. The state of Manipur is largely inhabited by four types of tribes along with other tribes. This includes the Meities and Pangals who inhabit the lower regions of the valley; while the hilly regions of Manipur are mainly populated by the Naga tribes and Kuki tribes. Along with these tribal community of Manipur include 29 more tribal communities which are *Aimal, Anal, Angami,*

Chiru, Chote, Gangte, Hmar, Kabui, Kachanaga, Kairao, Koirang, Kom, Lamgang, Mao, Maram, Maring, Mizo, Monsang, Moyon, Paite, Purum, Ralte, Sema, Simte, Sabte, Tangkul, Thadou, Vaipha and *Zou*. Tribes of Manipur also include a huge group of Kuki tribes who migrated to these regions from upper lands.

Tribes of Tripura, who inhabit a major part of Tripura, largely resemble the Tibeto-Burman origin. The territory is inhabited by 19 tribes who are enlisted as scheduled tribes under the Constitution of India. These tribes include *Bhil, Bhutia, Chaimal, Chakma, Garo, Halam, Jamatia and Khasia. The Kuki* includes seventeen sub-tribes - *Lepcha, Lushai, Magh, Munda, Noatia, Orang, Riang, Santhal, Tripuri* and *Uchai*. A mong these the dominant tribes ar*e Tripuri, Riang, Jamatia, Chakma, Halam, Noatia* and *Magh* and so on. Tribes of Arunachal Pradesh which include at least 25 types of tribes highlight their own cultural and ethnic traditions. Tribes of Arunachal Pradesh largely includes the tribes like *Adi, Apatanis, Buguns, Hrusso, Singphos, Khambas and Membas, Mishmish, Monpas, Nyishi, Sherdukpens, Tagins, Kamtis, Wanchos, Notchets* and *Ypobins*. Along with this there are tribes like Adi is one of the important tribes of the Siang Frontier Division. They are believed to have migrated from Burma.

Tribes of Assam found in both the valley and plain areas of Assam. The land of Assam is decorated with a number of Hills which include Karbi Anglong and North Cachar hills and expansive rivers like Brahmaputra and Barak which create the valley of Assam. The tribes of Assam include a number of tribes *Chakma, Dimasa, Garo, Hajong, Hmar, Khasi, Jaintia, Khamti tribes, some Kuki tribes, Lakher, Barmans in Cachar, Boro, Borokachari, Deori, Hojai, Kachari, Sonwal, Lalung, Mech, Miri* and *Rabha* who form the core of Tribal community of Assam. Tribes of Assam also include Karbi tribes who are found in the hilly areas of Assam. Their domain is Karbi Anglong district. Tribes of Assam further include the Mishing tribes who are also called as Miri by the local people. They are mainly concentrated Tinsukia, Dibrugarh, Sibsagar, Jorhat, Golaghat, Darang, Sonipur, North-Lakhimpur and Dhemagi. Linguistically they belong to Tibeto-Burman sub-family. They also speak Assamese language.

Tribals in Andaman and Nicobar Islands

Tribes of Andaman and Nicobar Islands are known for their unique and indigenous traditions and ways of living. Basically there are five primitive tribes residing in Andaman and Nicobar Islands. The *Great Andamanese, Jarawa tribe, Sentinelese tribe, Onges tribe and Shompens tribe* are the five native tribes that mainly inhabit the islands of Andaman and Nicobar Islands. Great Andamanese tribal group resides in the Strait Island. Onges are related to the Negrito racial stock and they have been relegated to the reserved pockets both at Dugong Creek and South Bay of Little Andaman Island. The people of Shompens tribe belong to the Mongoloid Group. They inhabit the Nicobar Island. This tribe has two divisions. The smaller division is Mawa Shompens that live very close to the coastal region along the river valleys and are very shy. However, they are friendly with the Nicobarese. The main group of Shompens is hostile and resides in Alexendra and Galathia river areas and also on the east coast of the area in the interiors.

Tribals in Lakshadweep Islands

Lakshadweep Islands lies pretty close to Kerala, bearing major semblances to the marine state. Tribes of Lakshadweep amount to huge in number, with the Indian government administering the union territory as a tribal dominating area, with hundreds of sects surviving. The major tribal communities that dwell in Lakshadweep comprise *Aminidivi, Koyas, Malmis and Malacheris*. Aminidivis are considered to be the first group of people to have initiated inhabiting these islands. They started living in an island called Amini and in present times it teems with Aminidivi people. They are most recognised for their hand-made crafts. On the other hand Koyas are the land-owners of Lakshadweep and the Malmis are the ones who work for them. Malayalam is the most commonly spoken language in Lakshadweep.

Finally we can say that tribals are scattered more or less in all states of India. They are the ancient people in the sub-continent. Forest and hills are the integral part of their life. Tribals in Jharkhand and Nortn Eastern states are renowned for movement against the British. In North-Eastern states their proportion is higher than other states. They are facing various challenges. They have their own culture and traditions. They lives in backward areas and are more innocents. Migration and outsider touch effects their culture and livelihoods. Government of India already implemented various policies for the welfare of the tribal's. Given autonomous status to tribal areas is an initiative for protecting their life from outsiders.

References

1. Dr. Debashis Patra (2011).*The cultural history of the tribal's of the Koraput Region*, Retrieved from http://orissa.gov.in/e-magazine/Orissareview/2011/Dec/engpdf/47-50.pdf.
2. *East India* (2012). Retrieved from http://en.wikipedia.org/wiki/East_India
3. *Jarawa People (Andaman Islands),* Retrieved from http://en.wikipedia.org/wiki/Jarawa_people_%28Andaman_ Islands%29.
4. *Ministry of Tribal Affairs (2012).* Retrieved from http://tribal.nic.in/index.asp
5. *North-East India* (2012). Retrieved from http://en.wikipedia. org/wiki/Northeast_India
6. *North India* (2012). Retrieved from http://en.wikipedia.org/wiki/North_India
7. *Tribles in India (2012)*. Retrieved from http://tribesindia.com/
8. *The Times of India* (Nov 16, 2012). Tribal's have not been given their rights, Retrieved from http://articles.times ofindia.indiatimes.com/2012-11-16/ranchi/35155635 _1_tana-bhagats-tribal-land-panchayat-extension.
9. *The Times of India (Nov 12, 2012)*. Red ants spice up tribal diet, Retrieved from http://articles.timesofindia. indiatimes. com/2012-11-12/bhubaneswar/35068537_1_red-ants-forest-dwellers-tribals.
10. *Tribals of Orissa* (2012). Retrieved from http://orissadiary. com/orissa_profile/tribal/index.asp.
11. *Tribals of Orissa* (2012). Retrieved from http://www.orissa tourism.gov.in/new/tribes.html
12. Information about *Tribes of Himachal Pradesh, Tribal people of Orissa, Tribals in Lakshadweep, Tribes of Jharkhand, Tribes of Chhattisgarh, Tribes of West Bengal, Tribes of Bihar, Tribes of Goa, Tribes of Maharashtra, Tribes of Gujarat, Tribes of Daman and Diu, Tribes of Madhya Pradesh, Tribes of Punjab, Tribes of Haryana, Tribes of Uttar Pradesh, Tribes of Uttarakhand, Tribes of Jammu and Kashmir, Tribes of Rajasthan, Tribes of Pondicherry, Tribes of Kerala, Tribes of Karnataka, Tribes of Andhra Pradesh, Tribes of Nagaland, Tribes of Mizoram, Tribes of Manipur, Tribes of Tripura, Tribes of Arunachal Pradesh, Tribes of Assam, Tribes of Andaman* and *Nicobar Islands* Retrieved from http://www.indianetzone.com.
13. JoshiGopa (2010). Forest polity and tribal development, Retrieved from http://www.culturalsurvival.org/our publications/csq/article/forest-policy-and-tribal-development.

3

Traditional Thangkhal Marriage System

S. Haukhanlian Mate

Introduction

The Thangkhals are one of the many tribes found mostly in Manipur state. However, till today, the Government of Manipur did not recognise them a separate tribe. As such, many of them uncomfortably remain attached to any one of their cognate tribe of Chin-Kuki-Mizo ethnic groups. The purpose of writing this paper is to throw some light on the Thangkhal tribe of Manipur with special reference to their marriage system. Before making an attempt on their marriage system, let me highlight a brief historical background of the people. The Thangkhals belongs to the Mongolian stock[1] of the Chin-Kuki-Mizo group of tribes presently spreading across the Indo-Burma border and as far as the Chittagong Hill Track in Bangladesh. They claimed their origin from *'Khul'*[2] which means cave, a place which has not been ascertained to any degree of certainty as their traditional home.

The Thangkhals belongs to Tibeto-Burman family speaking the Tibeto-Burman language.[3] The original home of these people is not definitely known but must be somewhere between Kansu in South China and Burma is believed to be their earliest known home.[4] According to Hall[5] the earliest known home of the Tibeto-Burmese speaking people was somewhere between Gobi desert and Northeast of Tibet also possible Kansu. This region forms parts of Southern China where the tribal people are found and distributed widely over the mountainous area of Kweichow, Szechwan and Yunnan. The Thangkhals, who were also a tribal people, is believed to have lived with other tribes in these areas. The southern China between Kansu and Burma may be considered as the original homes of the tribal peoples including the Thangkhals.[6] From southern China, the people with other tribal groups started their sojourn and some had gone to Tibet, some to Nepal and some moved towards Burma and lived there. As there was peace in Burma, they started moving in different directions and the Thangkhal group moved towards the south and lived mostly with what we called now as the Sukte tribes. Till now, no tribal group has their own identity.

According to Thang Tuan, the Yos, Zos (Thangkhals) were originally from Ciimnuai.[7] From this place, they spread to other places in the Chin Hills[8] and founded a new village called *Taitaam*. After living for several years in this village, they moved to a village called *Mualbem*. It was believed that till now the Thangkhals lived together with their cognate tribes of Kuki-Chin-Mizo groups. From Mualbem village, a group of people moved out and founded a new village known as the *Thangkhal village*. In course of time, the people who lived in this village developed a distinct culture, tradition and dialect which are quite distinct from other tribes of the Kuki-Chin-Mizo groups. As such, taking the name of the village, the people called themselves *'Thangkhal'*.[9] Thus, the Thangkhal tribe came into existence who have distinct custom, tradition and dialect and customary laws which are quite different from that of their cognate tribes.

From the Thangkhal village which is in the Chin Hills of Burma, the people moved to Manipur. The first known permanent place where they settled in Manipur was at Mulam. From this place, they spread to different places in Manipur especially in Churachandpur district and few of them scattered outside Manipur. Unfortunately, though the Thangkhals have their own customs and traditions which are quite different from their cognate tribe, they were not recognised as a Scheduled tribe in Manipur by the government. To develop and safeguard the interest of the people specially the tribal, it is necessary for the government to recognise those tribes who have their own customs and traditions. Sometimes, the Thangkhals are treated like a lost tribe who are not recognised by others even though they exist as a tribe. They should be recognised as a Scheduled tribe or else the tribe will be endangered.

Marriage System

Kiteng' is a Thangkhal word for marry. The institution of marriage occupies an important place in the Thangkhal society. It is the backbone of their society which knits the family relationship close. Basically, marriage among the Thangkhal was a civil contract made at the consent of both the parties concerned. Normally, it was arranged by the parents. The parents exercise utmost care and solemnity in the selection of a life partner of their children. They did not look only at the outward character and accomplishments for the partner of their children. They carefully enquire into his or her lineage. Many characteristics such as insanity, epilepsy, talkativeness, thieving, laziness, etc., are considered hereditable and the children of such persons are not liked by the parents for their children.[10]

Traditionally, monogamy was the common form of marriage among the Thangkhals. Polygamy was not common. However, as time passed on, some of the chief and few others have a secondary wife called *'Mei'*[11] and practiced polygamy in spite of its condemnation by the society. There is no civil law against its practices.[12] The legitimate wife or the first wife is called Zipi and the concubine or secondary wife is called Mei. The *'Mei'* did not, however, occupy the same status with the first wife[13] and the status of the Mei is much lower than the Zipi. According to the Customary Law of the Thangkhal, the eldest son of the Zipi will inherit his father's property and the Mei's son had no share in it.

Marriage is an important form of institution among the Thangkhals. Free mixing of boys and girls are allowed but pre-marital sex relationships are not common[14] For selecting their life partners; great importance was attached to the relationship of the mother's brother's daughter and sister's son which is called *'Neita'* in the Thangkhal society. This system gives the sister's son certain special rights over mother's brother's daughter who is his *'Neita'*. The relationship between mother's brother and sister's son may be described as follows:

(a) Sister's son (uterine nephew) is the object of special attention on the part of his mother's brother. (Maternal uncle)

(b) As a prospective son-in-law, the sister's son is at liberty to do or take anything he likes, including taking food as he pleases in the house of his mother's brother who gives unlimited indulgence to him.

(c) Sister's son has a rightful claim on the daughter of mother's brother, his Neita.

(d) Mother's brother has an obligation on his sister's son about giving marriage of his daughter to him.

(e) Sister's son is bound by custom to marry mother's brother's daughter.

(f) Mother's brother is bound to give his daughter to his sister's son in marriage.[15]

Traditionally, there are two types of marriage among the Thangkhals- arranged marriage and elopement.

Arranged Marriage

This type of marriage is socially and customarily a recognised marriage among the Thangkhals. As marriage among the Thangkhals was a civil contract made at the consent of both parties concerned, the parents will arranged the marriage.[16] They were not restricted to any particular clan or family. Theoretically, a man can marry almost any women except his mother, sister, daughter and aunt.[17] However; they were restricted not to marry the sisters of his sister's husband.[18] If they marry the sister of his sister's husband, it is called *'Luang ki khek'* and it is not permitted by the Thangkhal custom. However, preference was given to cross cousin marriage that is marrying mother's brother's daughter called Neita. This kind of arranged marriage often takes place during the childhood of the boy and the girl. When the parents of a boy are determined that their son should marry no other than his mother's brother's daughter called *Neita*, the marriage negotiations is initiated by the parents of the boy during the childhood of the boy and the girl. In some extreme cases, when a daughter is born in a family, her father's sister and her husband initiated on her birth the claim that the baby girl being the *'Neita'* of their son, should not be given in marriage to anybody else. She should go to them as their son's wife. Such earmarking is called '*Ki khau khih*' meaning that the girl has been reserved for a particular boy and that no one should set his eye on her, either for marriage or for love.[19] The girl is the most eligible and suitable for the boy to marry. The boy is expected to marry his Neita to bring the family relationship more closely. It also signifies the respect and deep rooted love for their uncles.[20] As marrying the Neita was the expected law of marriage among the Thangkhals, if anyone involved in the marriage process and married the Neita, he will be accused of *'Sial Khau Sattan'* (cutting of the mithun's rope) which literally means separating one's affinity and will be legally sued with a fine of *"Sialpi leh Salam"* (a fine of mithun and pig).[21] Thus, no one was allow to interfere in the marriage proposal of the Neita.

Elopement

Another type of marriage which prevailed among the Thangkhals was elopement. This type of marriage was socially and customarily unrecognised. It takes place when both the boy and girl fall in love but their parents did not consent to the marriage. When there appears a third person in between the boy and the girl who is likely to stand in their way, because of being a serious contender to win the hand of the girl in marriage or when the economic consideration that involves in the event of all formalities of marriage are to be fulfilled in the case of either the boy or the girl being in abject poverty, or even when the girl is impregnated by either of the lovers. In all these cases, marriage by elopement are resorted.[22] For this type of marriage, courting was done and in the process, both the boy and girl fall in love with each other without the consent of their parents. As the parents did not consent to their marriage, the boy elopes with the girl. The young man and the girl who were in love would secretly go to some other village and get married without the consent of their parents and hide themselves from the girl's parents. This was regarded as disgraceful for the girl.[23] The first duty of the boy's family is to send their mediator to the girl's parents to apologies and report the elopement of the girl and request to consent the marriage. If the girl's parents are not willing, they can take back the girl even though she has lost her virginity.[24] After negotiations were made, the couple will come back to the boy's house. This type of marriage may be called *love marriage*.

Marriage Proposal

The method of finding a partner for a boy was traditionally regulated by the boy's parents. The boy's parents usually sent their mediators called *'Bangkual'* and *'Tanu'*[25] to the girl's parents with a jar of zu for initial negotiation when their son was of marriageable age. If the girl's parents drank the zu, it was taken as they accepted the proposal and further negotiations follows. Usually the boy's family will send their mediators for three times. In the process, the girls were hardly asked anything about their opinion. If the parents were convinced about the suitor, she was bound to accept the proposal. However, in certain cases, the girls were asked about their opinion and if she accepts it, she will just say as you wish but if not, she can also reject the proposal. In many cases, both the couples never knew or meet each other before they married.[26]

Bride Price

Bride price exists among the Thangkhals. Customarily, the bride price was fixed as *'Sial Nga'* (five mithun).[27] Though it was fixed as five mithun, it did not necessarily stick to mithun alone. It can also be paid in money. If it is to be paid in money, it depends on the mutual understanding of both the parties. They can even pay Rs 10/- or Rs 100/- as equal to a mithun if there is mutual understanding or else it may be very high.[28] The marriage prices are never paid down at once; in fact, they are allowed to remain unpaid for many years.[29] Usually an instalment is paid on the wedding day and the balance of the price is paid up in easy instalments.[30]

Marriage Ceremony

After all the arrangements were ready for the marriage, the girl's parents will arrange a feast called *'Inlam Zonsa'*[31] as a token for a bride looking for a new house and all the villagers will take part in it. Then, the bride will be conveyed to the groom's house by her relatives. The official wedding ceremony usually takes place when the bride was brought to the groom's house. For this, the priest would administer the wedding ceremony by tying a bundle of white feathers of a cock around the neck of the bride with words of blessings. This was done to introduce the bride to the *'Pusa'* (house hold god) of the groom and to accept her as their own family member from that day onward.[32] Thus, in this way, the wedding ceremony was celebrated among the early Thangkhals.

Mouvan Ken (Dowry)

When a Thangkhal girl married, she takes some materials to her husband's houses as dowry. Some materials are compulsory while some depends upon the capability of the bride's family. Some of the compulsory materials are:

1. *Seu 1 (a basket made of bamboo);*
2. *Nam 1 (a strap made of cane meant for carrying seu)*
3. *Puandum 1 (a traditional shawl);*
4. *Tutang 1 (a hoe);*
5. *Heitang 1(an axe);*
6. *Zanpuan 1 (a woven rough blanket made of* cotton).[33]

Besides the above mentioned materials, a bride can also take any materials in kind or in cash to her husband's house. Some of the materials specially clothes and utensils are distributed among the near relatives of the groom. However, all these materials depend on the capability of the bride's family and are not compulsory.

Tunsa

According to the customary law of the Thangkhal, a feast prepared in honour of the bride by her family was called *Tunsaa*.[34] This is the first marriage feast[35] when a Thangkhal girl married. Generally, the bride family kills three animals compulsorily for Tunsaa[35] but not necessarily at a time. It depends on the affluence of the party concerned. Pigs are normally used for Tunsa that is killing of animals on the occasion of marriage.[36] On such occasion; they will give away the head, both fore and hind legs, hip and the chest portion of the slaughtered animal or animals to the family of the son-in-law. With the remaining portion, they will throw a feast. When the feast is ready, the Indongta from both the parties including Upa, Zawl, parents and others will seat together and take the meat and swear that they were witness to the marriage.[37] This Tunsa was one of the most important and compulsory thing to be done when a Thangkhal girl marries.

Sasengsin

When animal or animals are killed on the occasion of Tunsaa, the meat which are given to the family of the son-in-law are kept in a basket known as *Seu* and was usually covered with a shawl or any kind of cloth. Such shawl or cloth is called *Sasengsin*.[38] This Sasengsin will be owned by the one who carried the Seu.

Pusum

According to the customary law of the Thangkhals, it is compulsory for the groom to pay a sum of Rs 3/- to the maternal grandfather or if he is not there to the maternal uncle of the bride which is called *Pusum*.[39] Perhaps, Pu, the bride's maternal uncle is the most important person to get a share of the marriage price.[40] If this is not given, a boy cannot marry a Thangkhal girl.

Tha-man

According to the Thangkhal custom, when a woman married, the groom had to give a sum of Rs 3/- to the mother of the bride which was known as *Tha-man*.[41] This was given to the mother as a reward for looking after her daughter.[42]This Tha-man was compulsorily given to the mother of the bride.

Sial Ak Mat

According to the Thangkhal custom, when the groom's party paid a mithun or money as marriage price of the bride to the girl's family then they will in return give a cock or a sum of Rs 10/- with a shawl to the groom's party. This is called *Sial Ak Mat*.[43]

Sialkhumsa

Sialkhunsa is the second feast in honour of the newly wed bride. It strictly depends on the good condition of the girl's parents. It is meant for paying the marriage price due of the girl, if any, or even if nothing is due, the feast is a must and is customary for the girl's parents to give Sialkhumsa to the groom. In the early period, this feast was rarely rare feast which was highly honoured by all, and on this occasion, one and all dear relatives from different places were invited, take zu (rice beer) till one got drunk and fighting was a necessary evil.[44]

Divorce

Kikhen is a Thangkhal word for Divorce. Among the Thangkhal, divorce occasionally occurred though it was strongly condemned by the society. There are two types of divorce among the Thangkhals:

1. A Husband Divorcing his wife

If a husband wants to divorce his wife according to the Thangkhal Customary law, it is done as: (a) He must give a mithun as a fine to the family of his wife, (b) He must return back all the things brought by his wife as dowry at the time of marriage, and (c) He cannot make claim of whatever he had paid for the marriage price instead he should paid up all the balance of the marriage price if he did not clear up.[45]

2. A woman leaving her husband

According to the customary law of the Thangkhals, if a woman wants to leave her husband, it is done in the following manner: (a) she has to return back the whole of the marriage price that her husband had paid to her relatives. (b) All the things brought by her as dowry at the time of marriage must remain with her husband and she cannot make claim on it. (c) She also cannot made claim at anything she had acquired while staying with her husband. and (d) Nothing will be said and discuss about all the animals slaughtered and all the zu drank in her favour in the process of her marriage.[46]

Besides the above mentioned types of divorces, if a husband divorces his wife having a child, according to the customary law of the Thangkhals, it should be done as follow: (a) The mother should take care of the child for a period of three years or till the child reach the age of three. During that period, if the child is sick or ill, all the expenditure on medicine and any other things will be borne by the father. (b) After the expiry of three years, the father can claim the child by paying a mithun to the mother, and (c) If the father refuses to take the child after the expiry of three years, the child is to remain with the mother and uncle and automatically became a part and parcel of the family. However, in many cases, when the child got maturity, he himself took his father's title and not his mother and become part of his father's family.[47]

Thus, the Thangkhal marriage system was different from many of their cognate tribe though it looks like very similar. Their preference to cross cousin marriage known as marrying their Neita was a peculiar one which was to bring the family relationship more closely with their maternal uncles. It also signifies their respects and deep rooted love for their uncles. Taking of the bride price, Thaman, Pusum and others in the process of the marriage are not meant to sell the girl or to give burden to the groom but to make good relationship between the couple and their families. This Thangkhal marriage system may have many similarities with many of the tribal groups especially with those of Manipur but a critical study will reveal many of its difference.

References

1. Thangkhal Bible Church, Silver Jubilee (1981-2006), Souvenir, p. 1.
2. Gougin,T., *The Discovery of Zoland*, Zomi Press, Churachandpur, Manipur, 1980, p. 3.
3. Grierson, G.A., *Linguistic survey of India, Part 3, Vol. III,* Delhi, Motilal Banarsidas, 1967, p. 16.
4. Mizoram College Teachers' Association Silver Jubilee (1978-2003) Souvenir, p. 11.
5. Hall. D.G.E; *A History of South East Asia*, Macmillan Co. Ltd. London, 1995, p.123.
6. Mate, S. Haukhanlian; *Social and Religious Transformation among the Mizos, (1891-1972)*, Ph.D. Thesis (Unpublished), Department of History, Manipur University, 2005, p. 14.
7. SingKhawkhai; *Zo People and their Culture*; Published by Khampu Hatzaw, Churachandpur, Manipur, 1995, p. 23.
8. Vumkohau; *History of the Zoumi (Chin) Race;* Zougam Research Publications, Lamka, Manipur, 1990, p. 1.
9. History of the Thangkhal People's Organisation, Published by Thangkhal People's Organisation, Churachandpur, Manipur, 2003, p. 3. (Hereafter cited as Thangkhal People).
10. Mate, S. Haukhanlian; op. cit. p. 31.
11. *Paite in Mizoram*; Tribal Reaearch Institute, Mizoram, 2011, p. 69. (Hereafter cited as Paite).
12. Pudaite, Rochunga; *The Education of the Hmar People*, Indo-Burma Pioneer Mission, Sielmat, Manipur, 1963, p. 69.
13. Paite; op. cit. p. 69.
14. Lamkang, Sankhil Shethon; *The Social and Cultural Life of the Lamkang Tribe*; M. Phil. Dissertation (Unpublished), Department of Political Science, Manipur University, Canchipur,1994, p. 22.
15. Gangte, T.S.; *The Kukis of Manipur, A Historical Analysis;* Gyan Publishing House, New Delhi, India, 2003, p. 59.
16. Haukhanlian Mate, S., op. cit., p. 31.
17. Sangkima, Dr., *Mizos: Society and Social Change*, Spectrum Publications, Guwahati, 1992, p. 27.
18. Kamkhenthang, H., *The Paite: A Transborder Tribes of India and Burma*; Mittal Publications, Delhi, India, 1988, p. 97.

19. Gangte, T.S., op. cit. p. 79.
20. Kampau Mate Interviewed on 4.5.2011.
21. Niangdeihnuam; op. cit. p. 77.
22. Gangte,T.S., op. cit. p. 79.
23. Ray, Animesh; *Mizoram*, National Book Trust, India, Second Edition, 2002, p. 88.
24. Ruwndar, Kanthung ; *The Social and Political Life of the Anal Tribe of Manipur*, M. Phil. Dissertation (Unpublished), Department of Political Science, Manipur University, Canchipur, 1995, p. 39.
25. Rev. Khamchinhang interviewed on 8.5.2011.
26. Niangdeihnuam; op. cit. p. 77.
27. Kampau Mate interviewed on 4.5.2011.
28. Thangkhal Sinlai Pawlpi Souvenir, Sinlai Suangphum (1987-2008), 2008. p. 58. (Here after cited as Thangkhal Sinlai Pawl)
29. Shakespear, J; *The Kushei Kuki Clans*, Tribal Research Institute, Aizawl, Mizoram, 1988, p. 51.
30. Parry, N.E.; *A Monographon Lushai Customs and Ceremonies*, Tribal Research Institute, Aizawl, Mizoram, Reprint: 1988, p. 24.
31. Khamsuanpau interview on 8.5.2011.
32. Niangdeihnuam, op. cit. p. 78.
33. Thangkhal People, op. cit. p. 35.
34. Niangdeihnuam; op. cit. p. 79.
35. Thangkhal Sinlai Pawl; op. cit. p. 59.
36. Gougin, T. : op. cit. p. 16.
37. Kampau Mate interviewed on 4.5.2011.
38. Thangkhal People; op. cit. p. 35.
39. Thangkhal Sinlai Pawlpi; op. cit. p. 59.
40. Kipgen, Mangkhosat; *Christianity and Mizo Culture,* Published by The Mizo theological Conference, Mizoram, 1996. p. 80.
41. Thangkhal Sinlai Pawlpi, op. cit. p. 59.
42. Thangkhal People; op. cit. p. 36.
43. Thangkhal Sinlai Pawl; op. cit. p. 59.
44. Gougin, T.; op. cit. p.17.
45. Thangkhal People, op. cit. p. 36.
46. *Ibid*. p. 37.
47. *Ibid*.

4

The Socio Demography of the Tribals in North-east India

P.K. Pandey

"Our duty is to encourage everyone in their struggles to live up to their own higher ideals and strive at the same time to make the ideal as near as possible to the truth."

—Swami Vivekananda

Introduction

From the ancient time people are living together but some lives in plain areas and others in hilly areas. Lives in hilly areas are hard than the plain. A tribe is viewed, historically or developmentally as a social group existing before the development of states. Many anthropologists used the term *tribal society* to refer to societies organised largely on the basis of kinship, especially corporate descent groups. *Adivasi* is an umbrella term for a heterogeneous set of ethnic and tribal groups claimed to be the aboriginal population of India. Many smaller tribal groups are quite sensitive to ecological degradation caused by modernisation. The Constitution of India, Article 366(25) defines Scheduled Tribes as "*such tribes or tribal communities or part of or groups within such tribes or tribal communities as are deemed under Article 342 to the scheduled Tribes (STs) for the purposes of this Constitution*". The Scheduled Tribe groups who were identified as more isolated from the wider community and who maintain a distinctive cultural identity have been categorised as *'Particularly Vulnerable Tribal Groups'* (PTGs) (previously known as Primitive Tribal Groups) by the Government at the centre. So far seventy-five tribal communities have been identified as *'particularly vulnerable tribal groups'* in different States of India. These hunting, food-gathering, and some agricultural communities, have been identified as less acculturated tribes among the tribal population groups and in need of special programmes for their sustainable development.

There is a substantial list of Scheduled Tribes in India recognised as tribal under the Constitution of India. Tribal people constitute 8.2 per cent of the nation's total population, over 84 million people according to the 2001 census. One concentration lives in a belt along the Himalayas stretching through Jammu and Kashmir, Himachal Pradesh, and Uttarakhand in the west, to Assam, Meghalaya, Tripura, Arunachal Pradesh, Mizoram, Manipur, and Nagaland in the northeast. In the northeastern states of Arunachal Pradesh, Meghalaya, Mizoram, and Nagaland, more than 90 per cent of the population is tribal. However, in the remaining northeast states of Assam, Manipur, Sikkim, and Tripura, tribal peoples form between 20 and 30 per cent of the population. The tribal people were the earliest inhabitants of India with four major tribes which together constitute the Indian people. They are:

(a) *The Austro-Asiatic Tribes:* In a very primitive form, they comprise the Mundas, the Khasis and the Nicobarees.

(b) *The Mongoloids*: These belong to the Sino-Tibetian race inhabiting the Sub-Himalayan regions such as the Nagas, Bodos and Kuki tribes.

(c) *The Dravidians:* These are tribes which speak Dravidian tongues like the Gonds, Sauras, Oraons etc.

(d) *The Aryans:* These are represented by the Caucasian Tribes which came from the Caspian Seas and includes the Shakas, Kushanas, Huns and other tribes which invaded India at various were assimilated into Indian society.

Since time immemorial forest has been the habitat of the tribal people in all the countries with tribal population. In India almost all

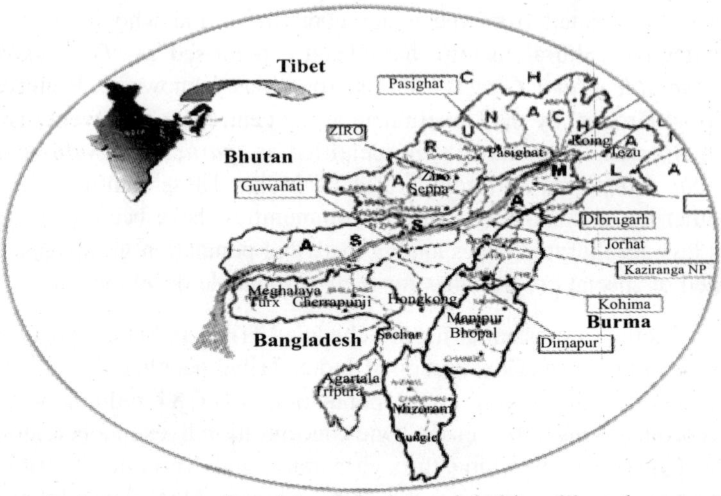

the tribal groups are found in their forest inhabit, although some of the tribal population may also be found in non-tribal villages, towns and cities. Most of the tribal communities inhabit the placid forest as a perennial source of natural resources. Till 1952 tribal people enjoyed freedom to use the forest and this has given them a feeling that the forest belongs to them. The constituent Assembly of India and its sub-committee on tribal affairs had devised a structure of constitutional provisions for providing legal safeguards to millions of tribes living in different parts of the country. Tribes are usually composed of a member of local communities and are often aggregated in clusters of a higher order call nation. The United Nation had proclaimed 1993 the *"International year for the world's indigenous people"*, with a view to give *"an opportunity to call attention to their ways of life and to the discrimination and disadvantages they face."* Maintaining and enhancing tribal sovereignty and self-determination is a key goal in Indian country. One way to strengthen self-determination is to control assets and that affect tribal members and tribal lands. The most common features of all these tribes are:

1. They live away from the civilised world in the inaccessible parts lying in the forests and hill;
2. They belong either to one of the three stocks: Negritos, Australoids or Mongoloids;
3. Speak their own tribal dialects;
4. Follow primitive occupation;
5. They are largely carnivorous;

6. They live either naked or semi-naked;
7. They have nomadic habits love for drink and dance;
8. Profess primitive religion known as 'Animism' in which the worship of ghosts and Spirits is the most important elements.

Tribal's in Assam

North East India consists of a number of hills and few fertile plains. The undulating nature of the topography of the area has compelled the inhabitants to adopt mainly two methods of agriculture, permanent and shifting according to their suitability. The state of Assam comprises of relatively bigger plain areas, except, however, two districts, the North Cacher and the Karbi Anglong, which are hilly. The total population of Assam in 2001 Census has been 26,655,528. Of them, 3,308,570 persons are Scheduled Tribes (STs), constituting 12.4 per cent of the total population of the state. The state has registered 15.1 per cent decadal growth of ST population in 1991-2001. There are total twenty three notified STs in the state. Of these, no population of Pawi has been returned in 2001 Census. Pawi is a small community of Mizoram.

Table 1 Population of Major STs, 2001 Census

Sl. No.	*Name of the Schedule Tribe*	*Total Population*	*Proportion to the Total ST Population*
1.	All Scheduled Tribe	3,308,570	100%
2.	Bodo	1,352,771	40.9
3.	Miri	587,310	17.9
4.	Mikir	353,513	10.7
5.	Rabha	277,517	8.4
6.	Kachari	235,881	7.1
7.	Lalung	170,622	5.2
8.	Dimasa	110,976	3.4
9.	Deori	41,161	1.2

Source: Ministry of Tribal Welfare.

The ST population in Assam is predominantly rural with 95.3 per cent rural and only 4.7 per cent urban population. Of the eight major STs, Dimasa have recorded the highest 10.4 per cent urban population, followed by Mikir (8.3 per cent). On the other hand Miri have recorded the lowest 1.8 per cent urban population. North Cachar Hills and Karbi Anglong the two autonomous hill districts of Assam are predominantly tribal housing two important STs of Assam — the Dimasa and Mikir (now recognised as Karbi).

Tribes of Assam are the aborigines of the land who have inhabited the area for ages. The land of Assam is decorated with a number of Hills which include Karbi Anglong and North Cachar hills and expansive rivers like Brahmaputra and Barak which create the valley of Assam. Tribes of Assam are often recognised as the first inhabitants of the land who belong to various tribal groups. The origin of the tribal groups which exist in Assam can be traced within the *Negritos, Dravidian, Alpines, Tibeto-Burmese and Aryan race* which travelled from far off areas and settled in the centrally located regions of Assam. These tribes unite to form the colourful tribes of Assam. The tribes of Assam include a number of tribes *Chakma, Dimasa, Garo, Hajong, Hmar, Khasi, Jaintia, Khamti tribes, some Kuki tribes, Lakher, Barmans in Cachar, Boro, Borokachari, Deori, Hojai, Kachari, Sonwal, Lalung, Mech, Miri* and *Rabha* who form the core of Tribal community of Assam. Tribes of Assam also include Karbi tribes who are found in the hilly areas of Assam. Their domain is Karbi Anglong district. Some are also found in North Cachar Hills District, Nagaon, Golaghat, Kamrup, Jorhat, Sonipur and Lakhimpur districts of Assam. The karbis originally belonged to the western China and entered Assam from central Asia through migration. This community initially settled in the Khasi and Jaintiya hills from where they slowly migrated to other areas.

Tribes of Assam further include the Mishing tribes who are also called as Miri by the local people. They are supposed to be a branch of Adi tribes of Arunachal Pradesh, who came down to Assam as a result of inter-tribal feuds. They are mainly concentrated Tinsukia, Dibrugarh, Sibsagar, Jorhat, Golaghat, Darang, Sonipur, North-Lakhimpur and Dhemagi. Linguistically they belong to Tibeto-Burman sub-family. They also speak Assamese language. Dimasa tribes are the other tribes found in Assam. They are mostly found in the North Cachar district and the Karbi along districts of Assam. Dimasa is their mother tongue which belongs to the Bodo group of the Tibeto-Burman family of languages and there are the Bodo tribes who are supposed to be the earliest tribes of the land. They are no more restricted to some particular area but are scattered in all parts of Assam and are largely found as the workers in the tea plantation. Along with this there are the Phake tribes who reside in Dibrugarh and Tinsukia district of Assam, along Dihing River. Phake tribe are said to have come here from Thailand in the late 18th century and speak Assamese language as well as Phake language.

The Bodos are an ethnic and linguistic community, early settlers of Assam in the northeast part of India. According to the 2011 census, there are nearly 2 million Bodos in Assam which makes for 5.5 per cent of the total population in the state. Bodos belong to a larger ethnic group called the *Bodo-Kachari*. The Bodos are recognised as a plains tribe in the Sixth Schedule of the Indian Constitution. Udalguri and Kokrajhar are considered the centre of the Bodo area. The Bodo people constitute a diverse range of the Indigenous people of North-east India. The Bodo language is a member of the Tibeto-Burmese family. Weaving is integral part of Bodo culture. Many families rear their own silkworms, the cocoons of which are then spun into silk. Bodo girls learn to weave from a young age, and no Bodo courtyard is complete without a loom. They are practicing Hinduism, Christianity and Bathouism. As of 2001, more than 90 per cent of the Bodos living in Assam were Hindus. However, the percentage of Christians is growing. In 1991, only 8.58 per cent of the Bodo were Christian, but that amount had increased to 9.40 per cent by 2001. In 2012, violence broke in Assam out between Bodos and Muslims causing the displacement of over 400,000 people. Over 5,000 houses have been razed.

The Karbis are the principal tribal community in the Karbi Anglong district of Assam, a district administered as per the provisions of the Sixth Schedule of the Constitution of India, having an autonomous district of their own since 17 November 1951. In 2006 the Indian government named Karbi Anglong one of the country's 250 most backward districts (out of a total of 640). The district has three sub-divisions: *Diphu, Hamren and Bokajan*. Besides Karbi Anglong district, the Karbi-inhabited areas include Dima Hasao, Kamrup, Marigaon district, Nagaon, Golaghat, Karimganj and Sonitpur districts of Assam; Balijan circle of Papumpare district in Arunachal Pradesh, Jaintia Hills, Ri Bhoi and East Khasi Hills districts in Meghalaya, and Dimapur District in Nagaland. Apart from Assam, the Karbis are also recognised as Scheduled Tribes in Meghalaya, Mizoram and Nagaland. The Karbis linguistically belong to the Tibeto-Burman group. The Karbis traditionally practice jhum cultivation (slash and burn cultivation) in the hills. They grow variety of crops which include foodgrains, vegetables and fruits like rice, maize, potato, tapioca, beans, ginger and turmeric. They are quiet self-sufficient and have homestead gardens with betel nut, jackfruit, oranges, pineapple, etc. The Karbi women are expert weavers and they wear home-made clothes. Their main attire consist the pekok, a piece of cloth with designs wrapped around the upper part of the body and tied into a knot on the right shoulder, the pini, similar to a sarong and a vamkok, a decorative piece of cloth tied around the waist over the pini.

The Dimasa people are a group of people in Assam, in northeastern India. Dimasa mythology says they are the children of Bangla Raja and the great divine bird Arikhidima. Dimasa Kachari is mainly found in the present day Dima Hasao District of Assam. They also have a sizable population in *Cachar, Karbi Anglong and Nowgong Districts* of the State and also Dimapur region of Nagaland state. According to the 2001 Census of India, more than 98 per cent of all Dimasa living in Assam are Hindu. Agricultural is the principal occupation and main source of livelihood of the Diamsa Kacharis. Dimasa were compelled to adopt shifting cultivation, commonly known as jhum, in hilly areas. Bishu is an important festival celebrated by Dimasa with the celebration of great pomp and splenduor among the Dimasa. Bishu is celebrated after completion of harvest.

Thus the land of Assam has been rightly called the unexplored paradise which has provided livelihood to a number of tribal communities. These tribes are no more restricted to any particular area or the hilly regions but are scattered over the entire state with distinct cultural trends.

Tribal's of Meghalaya

Tribes of Meghalaya represent the inhabitants of Meghalaya who reside in the foothills as well as within the mountain ranges of Garo, Khasi and Jaintias. The origin of these tribes can be traced from the Tibeto- Burman race and Proto Austroloid Monkhmer race. While the Garos can be traced as the descendents of Tibeto-Burman race, the Khasis and the Jaintiyas are claimed to have belonged to the Proto

Austroloid Monkhmer race. Along with this there are a number of tribes like the Bhois, Khynriams and the Wars who reside in the northern, southern and central parts of Meghalaya.

Garos are the tribes which are mainly found in the southern part of Garo hills which gives it the name. They originally belong to the Bodo family from the Tibetan- Burmese race; also reside in the plains of Assam and Bangladesh. The most popular food of the Garo tribes is rice with capsicum, onion and salt. The second type of tribe which is largely seen is *Khasis*. They are the largest tribal group of North eastern region. Khasis are known with a number of names in different parts of Meghalaya. Those living in the foothills of Jaintiya hills are known as *Jaintiyas* while those living in northern plains and foot hills are known as *Bhois,* those living in southern hills are known as *Wars*. All these tribes are coupled together under Hynniewtrep which is regarded as the descendents of Proto Austroloid Monkhmer race.

The total Khasi population may be estimated at 1.2 million people. According to the 2001 Census of India over 1.1 million Khasi lived in Meghalaya, in the districts of East Khasi Hills, West Khasi Hills, Ri-Bhoi and Jaintia Hills. In Assam their population reached 13,000. The Census of Bangladesh ennumerated 12,280 Khasi are for the whole country in 1991. It is generally considered that the Khasis consist of four sub-tribes: Khynriam, Pnar, Bhoi and War. The Khynriam inhabit the uplands of the Khasi Hills District, the Pnar or Syntengs live in the Jaintia Hills. The Bhoi live in the lower hills to the north and north-east of the Khasi Hills and Jaintia Hills towards the Brahmaputra valley. The War, usually divided into War-Jaintia, in the south of the Jaintia Hills and War-Khasi in the south of the Khasi Hills, live on the steep southern slopes leading to Bangladesh.

The people living in Jaintia Hills District of Meghalaya are ethno linguistic group of people and are believed to be of Indo-Mongoloid race although speaking a distinct Austric language belonging to the Mon-Khmer group. With regard to the social origin of the Jaintia people there is an indigenous theory according to which they belonged to a common race which occupied a large area of Northern India, Burma, Indo-China and parts of South China in the Neolithic period. The people residing in the central region of Jaintia Hills are called "*Pnars*" by those living in the southern and northern regions and who are in turn called as *"Wars"* and *"Bhois"* respectively by the Pnar. All three are collectively known by the generic name: *"Jaintias"* or *"Synteng"*. Women are entrusted to take care of property as the legal custodian, the family purse, valuable, movable and immovable properties. In Jaintia Hills traditionally, inheritance of real property passes from mother to the youngest daughter called as *'khadduh'*. Other sisters also share the property but the youngest one shares more because of her responsibility to the family. Tribes of Meghalaya which include a number of large as well as small tribal groups represent the colours of Meghalaya. The traditional dress of Meghalaya is known as *'Jymphong'* which is often worn during the festivals and ceremonies. Regarding food the tribes of Meghalaya are fond of fish while they also take mutton and rice which are their hot favourites accompanied with rice beer.

Thus the tribal groups in Meghalaya are scattered all over the region and known by separate names. Overall they belong to the same anthropological entities which demarcate them as one soul group. These groups may have some minute differences but overall they belong to one group of tribe.

Tribal's of Manipur

Tribes of Manipur which represent a unique feature of the land include at least 29 communities that originated from Tibetan-Burmese tribal group of Mongoloids. The state of Manipur is largely inhabited by four types of tribes along with other tribes. This includes the Meities and Pangals who inhabit the lower regions of the valley; while the hilly regions of Manipur are mainly populated by the Naga tribes and Kuki tribes. Along with these tribal community of Manipur include 29 more tribal communities which are *Aimal, Anal, Angami, Chiru, Chote, Gangte, Hmar, Kabui, Kachanaga, Kairao, Koirang, Kom, Lamgang, Mao, Maram, Maring, Mizo, Monsang, Moyon, Paite, Purum, Ralte, Sema, Simte, Sabte, Tangkul, Thadou, Vaipha* and *Zou*. Tribes of Manipur also include a huge group of Kuki tribes who migrated to these regions from upper lands. The migratory habit of the people encourages the cultural practice of handing down leadership from the father to the son, who inherits the wealth of the deceased father. The Naga group tribes have great ethnic and cultural affinities with the people of Nagaland, whereas the Kuki group has the affinity with the Chin and Mizos of the south.

Tribes of Manipur along with the major Naga group and non Naga group include many core tribal groups, among which Hmar is one of the prominent sub-tribes of Mizo. They are settled in Manipur since the year 1872. The Hmars are a distinct community with respect of their traditions, culture and social customs. Kabui tribes are the second popular tribe which is one of the sub-tribes of the Naga tribe. They call themselves as *Rongmei*. They are divided into four clans-*Kamai, Golmai, Gangmai,* and *Langmai*. Manipuri and Hindi languages are spoken by them fluently. They are mainly found in Tabudi sub-division of Senapati district of Manipur. Angami tribe is another tribal group often found in Manipur who follow a simple lifestyle, quite similar to all the other tribes of Manipur. Thus, the colourful state of Manipur is largely inhabited by the tribal communities which define the cultural traditions of Manipur and its strength of assimilation.

Tribal's of Nagaland

Tribes of Nagaland include a major part of the Nagaland community. They include fourteen types which are largely known as *Angami, Ao, Chakhesang, Chan, Khemungan, Konyak, Lotha, Phom, Pochury, Rengma, Sangtam, Sema, Yimchunger* and *Zeliang*. The people of Nagaland are distinctly marked by their looks which are usually marked by medium height, with low facial features, straight hair and brownishn skin. The tribes of Nagaland have their own distinctive language. In Nagaland, the tribes speak around sixty different dialects, which belong to the Sino-Tibetan language family. The colourful festivals usually centre on agriculture which is the main occupation of the land. All the tribes celebrate different seasonal festivals with a pageantry of colour and local music. Tribes of Nagaland are primarily engaged in agriculture. While almost 80 per cent of population is engaged in agriculture which are located at the hill slopes and receives sufficient amount of rainfall. The tribes keep parity in selecting the crop which depends on the setting of the crops. The tribes of Nagaland largely include the hilly tribes who are responsible for farming.

The people are simple, straightforward, hard-working and honest people with a high standard of integrity. They possess a strong sense of self-respect and rarely submitted to anyone who ran roughshod over them. The Naga traditionally live in villages. The family is the basic unit of the Naga society. In the classless, casteless Naga society, women have traditionally enjoyed a high social position, with a pivotal role in both family and community affairs. However, being a patriarchal society with strong warrior tradition, it is considered an honour to be born as a man. The Naga tribes are expert craftsmen. Their dwellings are made of wood and straw and these are ornately carved and arranged. Folk songs and dances are essential ingredients of the traditional Naga culture. The oral tradition is kept alive through the media of folk tales and songs.

The Naga tribes can be found in the contiguous adjoining states of Manipur, Assam, Arunachal Pradesh and across the border in Burma. The Naga tribes practiced headhunting and preserved the heads of enemies as trophies before the 19th century. The Naga people traditionally are tribally organised, with a strong warrior tradition. Their villages are sited on hilltops and until the later part of the 19th century, they made frequent armed raids on the plains below. Apart from cultural contacts with the neighboring Ahoms, the rulers of Assam from 1228, the Nagas had little or no contact with the outside world. Real exposure to the outside world came with the British annexation of Assam in 1828 following the Treaty of Yandabo in 1826. The most important landmark in the history of the Naga people with considerable social, cultural and political ramifications is the arrival of missionaries and the spread of Christianity among the Naga tribes. The acceptance of Christianity marked a departure from their many tribal customs and traditions, and along with the spread of English education, heralded the arrival of modernity in the Naga Hills. Today, more than 95 per cent of Naga people claim to be Christians. Christianity has changed the Naga society entirely and it bears little resemblance to the tribal society that it was a century ago. The Christian missionaries interfered in the social and cultural practices to a far greater extent than the government.

Tribal's of Mizoram

Tribes of Mizoram have inhabited the region since its origin. This small state of India has great scenic beauty with rolling hills, valleys, lakes and rivers. Like other states of seven sisters Mizoram too is largely populated with the tribal population of India. Tribes of Mizoram largely include four types of tribal communities. The tribal people of Mizoram largely include the *Chakma tribes, Pawi tribes, Ralte tribes* and *the Kuki tribes* who travelled from upper regions of the continent. Chakma tribes are the most important tribal group of Mizoram who practice a combined religion of Hinduism, Buddhism and animism. The history of Mizoram can be largely marked by three phenomenons; while the initial phase of Mizoram is largely captured by the tribal raids of various tribal communities, the second phase witnessed some level of literary awareness which gave primary political awareness to the people of Mizoram which helped the people of Mizoram to fight their independence movement. Within the third phase of Mizoram's history the political requirement and security of the area paved the way for the creation of the new state of Mizoram under Union of India as a Union territory in 20th February 1985. As such the history of Mizoram includes its independence move and its association with India along with the tribal culture of the land. Tribes of Mizoram primarily reside within the small clans which have turned out to be small villages that have a separate house for its village head.

The Mizo people are an ethnic group native to north-eastern India, western Burma (Myanmar) and eastern Bangladesh who speak any of various Kukish languages. A great majority of ethnic Mizo people are Christians. The multi-ethnic and pluralistic state of Mizoram exhibits a co-existence of different communities, such as the Mizo *(majority)*, the Riang, and the Chakma. With 91.58 per cent literacy, the second highest in Indian states, Mizoram is now leading towards the spread of education in a substantial manner, the recognition of Mizo ṭawng awng in the 8th Schedule of the Indian constitution is an undercurrent demand that is evident in various aspects of social and political life. The dominance of the English language is evident especially in the fields of education, official matters and other formal domains as in other parts of India. English had already penetrated the life and blood of the Mizo people for a long time along with the spread of education. Christian missionaries in the 19th century developed the current alphabetic system adopted for the Mizo language. Thus Tribes of Mizoram represent another string of Indian culture which has developed within the surrounding of hills and developed as a distinctive culture by itself. This reflects a distinct type of society that exists within the mountainous regions of India.

Tribal's of Sikkim

The majority of Sikkim's residents are of Nepali ethnic origin. The native Sikkimese consists of the *Bhutias*, who migrated from the Kham district of Tibet in the 14th century, and the *Lepchas*, who are believed to have migrated from the Far East. Sikkim was inhabited in pre-historic times by three tribes namely *Naong, Chang and the Mon*. The Lepcha who entered Sikkim sometimes later absorbed them completely. The origin of Lepchas is shrouded in mistery but it seems that they belonged to the clan of the Nagas of the *Mikir, Garo and Khasia hills* which lie to the south of the Bramaputra valley. Some believe they came from somewhere on the borders of Tibet and Burma. Lepchas themselves were reportedly originally Nagas of the Mikir, Garo and Khasi hills who came to Sikkim and absorbed into their fold the pre-historic tribes of *Naong, Chang and the Mon* of Sikkim. It is also inferred that their cultural traits of dress and family values is akin to the Khasis of Meghalaya and their language has close affinity to that of Tangkul Nagas of Northern Manipur.

The Bhutia shares 63.1 per cent of the total ST population of the state. The highest concentration of Bhutia has been reported from East. The population of Sikkim in 2001 Census has been 540,851. Of these 111,405 are Scheduled Tribes (STs), which constitute 20.6 per cent of the total state's population. The state has registered 22.6 per cent decadal growth of ST population in 1991-2001. The Bhutia and Lepcha are the two notified STs in the state. The Bhutia has recorded 10.9 per cent urban population and Lepcha 4.5 per cent. Thus, the tribal population is typically concentrated in the rural areas.

West Sikkim has equally mixed communities living in different villages. The Bhutias on of the indigenous tribe of Sikkim are found

Table 2 Populations of STs, 2001 Census

Name of the Scheduled Tribe	*Total Population*	*Proportion to the total ST Population*
All Scheduled Tribes	111,405	100%
Bhutia	70,308	63.1
Lepcha	40,568	36.4

Source: Government of India.

in the villages of Naku Chumbong, Singyang Sindrang, Yuksam, Tashiding, Melli, Nambu, Gayzing, Yangthang, kyongsa Tigjya and Lingchom. The Bhutias houses are comparatively bigger traditionally made of timber and stones with most having big prayers flags in front. They are farmers and cattle herders by professions. Their unique food is Tosha Gyari a set non veg rice meal served in brassware rice plate and their traditional drink is solchhyang Brewed millet beer served in bamboo decorated with silver strips. Their main celebrations are Lossong Naysol, Bumkor and marriages.

Lepchas the indigenous tribe of Sikkim is found in the villages of Sindrang, Singlitam, Khecheopalri, Lethang and Gangyap. These villages are in the distances of 5 kms to 30 kms from Pelling. They speak their own dialect and they too follow the same Tibetan form of Buddhism besides their local faith. Their Religious priests are called *Bong things*. Their main festival is Tendong Lhorum faat. Gurung an indigenous tribe of Sikkim from Nepali stock is found in the villages of Khorong, Sardon, Singyang and Beghaa, about 5 kms to 20 kms from Pelling. They are shepherds and their woman weave a kind of traditional carpet called *Rari* and coat called *Lukuni*. They call themselves Tamu and their main celebration is their Tamu Lochar. They are Buddhist. Tamangs are one of indigenous Nepali origin tribe of Sikkim having their own language, costume, culture and way of life. They follow Tibetan form of Buddhism having monasteries in their area. In Sikkim they are found quite scattered and available every where. Newaris are one of the indigenous Nepali origin tribes of Sikkim. They are historically recorded as the money minters of Sikkim the noted families of which are called Taxari and Vansari. They have their own language, script, costume, culture, traditions and way of life. They are either Hindu or Buddhist.

Tribal's of Arunachal Pradesh

The Indian state of Arunachal Pradesh has a total population of roughly 1.4 million (as of 2011) an area of 84,000 km^2, amounting to a population density of about 17 km^2 (far below the Indian average of 370 km^2). Much of Arunachal Pradesh is forested, and home to many of India's Scheduled Tribes. It is also known as *'Land of the Dawn-lit-Mountains'* this is the first Indian soil to greet the morning sun. In addition to the forests, the rich handicrafts add to the ethereal beauty of majestic Arunachal Pradesh. Weaving is a very common craft in the region. Highly artistic carpets, shawls, gales and jackets are the high-quality fruit of its looms. Art and craft has been playing a vital role in the life of most of the tribesmen group of Arunachal Pradesh since time immemorial. Tribes of Arunachal Pradesh which include at least 25 types of tribes highlight their own cultural and ethnic traditions. Tribes of Arunachal Pradesh form the major part of demography of Arunachal Pradesh. Along with this there are tribes like Adi which is one of the important tribes of the Siang Frontier Division. the Adis are divided into different groups, such as *Padam, Minyong, Shimong, Pangis, Pasi, Asing, Bori, Bokar, Karko, Ramo, Milan, Tagin, Gallong, Tangam* and *Pailiba*; the main concentrated areas of the Khamti are sixteen villages of Lohit district of Arunachal Pradesh. They are believed to have migrated from Burma.

The Adi is a major collective tribe living in the Himalayan hills of Arunachal Pradesh, and they are found in the temperate and sub-tropical regions within the districts of East Siang, Upper Siang, West Siang and Lower Dibang Valley and Lohit. The Adi celebrate a number of festivals, in particular Solung, in first week of September for five days or more. It is a harvest festival performed after the sowing of seeds and transplantation, to seek for future bumper crops. The Adi practice wet rice cultivation and have a considerable agricultural economy. Rice serves as the staple foods for the Adi. The majority of Adi traditionally followed the animist Donyi-Polo religion, which involves the worship of the sun, the moon, and the ancestral god, the shaman, called *Miri*, can be a female. They are basically agriculturist and their entire economic life centres around land.

The Nyishi people, principaly found in the Indian state of Arunachal Pradesh. They are also called *"Nyashang"*, meaning 'people of the land or the human being', by people belonging to Kurung Kumey district. They inhabit the Papum Pare, East Kameng Lower Subansiri, Kurung Kumey, parts of Upper Subansiri districts of Arunachal Pradesh, as well as the Sonitpur District and North Lakhimpur district of Assam. Polygyny is prevalent among the Nyishi. The Nyishi, who traditionally wear cane helmets surmounted by the crest of a hornbill beak, have considerably affected the population of this bird.

The Monpa are a major people of Arunachal Pradesh in northeastern India. Most Monpas live in the Indian state of Arunachal

Pradesh, with a population of 50,000, centered in the districts of Tawang and West Kameng. They also share very close affinity with the Sharchops of Bhutan. The Monpa are sub-divided into six sub-groups because of their variations in their language. The Monpa are known for wood carving, Thangka painting, carpet making and weaving. The traditional dress of the Monpa is based on the Tibetan Chugba, although woolen coats and trousers may be worn as well. The Monpa practice shifting and permanent types of cultivation. The Monpas of Kalaktang area developed trade in Udalguri area of Assam and Bhutan and with their counterparts, the Monpas of Tawang and Dirang areas. The people in group with their pony and trade items proceed to the camps at the advent of the winter season.

The Galos constitute a tribe inhabiting the West Siang, southwestern side of East Siang, southeastern side of Upper Subansiri, as well as in some small pockets in Itanagar and Lower Dibang Valley, Changlang districts of Arunachal Pradesh, Northeast India. Galo is a Tibeto-Burman language of the Western Tani branch. The Wancho are one of the major tribes of the Tirap District of Arunachal Pradesh. They are basically agriculturists and practice shifting cultivation to a great extent. They inhabit the western part of the district on the border of Nagaland. The Akas inhabit most of the eastern valley of the Bomdila range in West-Kameng district of Arunachal Pradesh. The Akas are also found in the East Kameng. The Lisus from a small ethnic group inhabit the remote easternmost corner of Tirap District. They having their own culture with Indonesian love to live in the isolated areas. On the eastern extremity of the state is the district of Lohit. The major tribes inhabiting this district are the Mishmis, Padams, Khamtis and the Singphos. Habitats of the Singphos are the lower regions, drained by the rivers Tengapani and Noa-Dihing. The area lies to the north of the Lohit River and is contiguous to the Tirap district of Arunachal Pradesh and Tinsukia District of Assam. The Singphos are Buddhists by religion. They like the Khamtis are well advanced in agriculture. They cultivate on permanent plots ploughed by either the buffaloes or oxes.

Tribal's of Tripura

Tribes of Tripura largely constitute thirty one percent of its total population who represent themselves through their culture and traditions. While largely located in the mountainous areas of Tripura, these tribes vary from region to region. The territory is inhabited by 19 tribes who are enlisted as scheduled tribes under the Constitution of India. These tribes include *Bhil, Bhutia, Chaimal, Chakma, Garo, Halam, Jamatia and Khasia*. The Kuki including seventeen sub-tribes —*Lepcha, Lushai, Magh, Munda, Noatia, Orang, Riang, Santhal, Tripuri and Uchai*. A mong these the dominant tribes are *Tripuri, Riang, Jamatia, Chakma, Halam, Noatia and Magh and so on. Largely Tripura is inhabited by Tripuri, Reang, Chakma, Mog, Halam* and *Murasin.*

The Chakma tribes are found in Tripura's south-eastern hills bordering Chittagong Hill tract. Traditionally they are good cultivators. Animal husbandry, basketry, horticulture, foraging, fishing and weaving are the subsidiary occupation of this tribe. The Chakma tribal group usually possesses faith in the Buddhist tradition which is scattered in various parts of Tripura. The Riang tribes are found in Mizoram, Assam and the Chittagong Hill Tract. In Tripura, their main concentration areas are in the eastern hills. Cultivation is major occupation of this tribe. This community hardly possesses any access to education which keeps it restricted towards traditions. The festivals of this tribe are largely marked by the faith, age old customs and traditions of the land. Tripuri has two synonyms—*Puran Tripuri* and *Dev Varma*. The dynasty has ancestral relation with the Lunar dynasty of the Mahabharata. They are found all over Tripura though the western and northern parts of the Tripura are the main concentrated areas. Mog tribes are claimed to have originated from Arakan, Burmese and Chinese clan who have migrated to Tripura during 957 AD. This clan largely believes in Buddhism and largely depends on agriculture for their subsistence. Halam tribes are supposed to be the offshoots of Kuki tribes who have settled in Tripura and accepted their raja's rule. Primarily this tribe practices Vaishnava faith and Saka cult. Originally there are twelve groups found in Halam tribes which are divided into 16 subsections. Murasin Tribes who inhabit the area are distinctively marked by the tradition of hanging the horns of dead animals. This clan which inhabits the regions of Tripura had been a part of the royal army of Tripura. Since the 1960s, the federal government has been gradually encouraging tribes to take a larger and larger part in self-administering programmes for their members.

Conclusion

North-East India is renowned for its tribal culture. The tribes of Assam include a number of tribes Chakma, Dimasa, Garo, Hajong, Hmar, Khasi, Jaintia, Khamti tribes, some Kuki tribes, Lakher, Barmans in Cachar, Boro, Borokachari, Deori, Hojai, Kachari, Sonwal, Lalung, Mech, Miri, Rabha who form the core of Tribal community of Assam. Manipur include 29 more tribal communities which are Aimal, Anal, Angami, Chiru, Chote, Gangte, Hmar, Kabui, Kachanaga, Kairao, Koirang, Kom, Lamgang, Mao, Maram, Maring, Mizo, Monsang, Moyon, Paite, Purum, Ralte, Sema, Simte, Sabte, Tangkul, Thadou, Vaipha and Zou. Tribes of Nagaland include fourteen types which are largely known as Angami, Ao, Chakhesang, Chan, Khemungan, Konyak, Lotha, Phom, Pochury, Rengma, Sangtam, Sema, Yimchunger and Zeliang. The tribal people of Mizoram largely include the Chakma tribes, Pawi tribes, Ralte tribes and the Kuki tribes who travelled from upper regions of the continent. Tribes of Arunachal Pradesh which include at least 25 types of tribes highlight their own cultural and ethnic traditions. There are 19 tribes who are enlisted as scheduled tribes under the Constitution of India in Tripura.

References

1. *Assam data highlights: The scheduled tribes census of India 2001,* Retrieved from http://censusindia.gov.in/Tables_ Published/SCST/ dh_st_assam.pdf.
2. Banerjee, B. (2004). The Wancho wood carving: An anthropological study about its traditionality, charges and destiny, Bibhas Dhar and Palash Chandra Coomar (Eds), *Tribes of Arunachal Pradesh*, First edition, Abhijeet Publications, New Delhi, p. 48.
3. Barik, R. (2006). Faulty planning in a tribal region: The Dandakaranya Development Authority, *Tribal development in India: Contemporary debate*, Govindra Chandra Rath (Ed), First dition, Sage Publication, New Delhi, p. 92.
4. Behura, N. (1996). Planned development and quality of life among Indian tribes, *Tribes of India: Ongoing challenges,* Mann, R. (Ed). First edition, M.D. Publication Private Limited, New Delhi, p. 5.
5. *Bodo people* (2012). Retrieved from http://en.wikipedia.org/wiki/Bodo people.
6. Borgohain, H. (2004). Customary, land law of the Adia, Bibhas Dhar and Palash Chandra Coomar (Eds), *Tribes of Arunachal Pradesh*, First edition, Abhijeet Publications, New Delhi, p. 92.

7. Chowdhury, S. (2004). An ethnographic note on the Singphos of Lohit, Bibhas Dhar and Palash Chandra Coomar (Eds.), *Tribes of Arunachal Pradesh*, First edition, Abhijeet Publications, New Delhi, p. 48.
8. Das, S. (1993). *Life style: Indian Tribes*, First edition, Gyan Publishing House, pp. 2-3.
9. Dutta. D. (2004). The Lisus of Arunachal Pradesh: An ethnographic account, Bibhas Dhar and Palash Chandra Coomar (Eds), *Tribes of Arunachal Pradesh*, First edition, Abhijeet Publications, New Delhi, p.119.
10. Datta, P. (2004). The Wanchos of Arunachal Pradesh: Their cultural and Historical background, Bibhas Dhar and Palash Chandra Coomar (Eds), *Tribes of Arunachal Pradesh*, First edition, Abhijeet Publications, New Delhi, pp. 27-28.
11. Duarah, D. (2004). Fairs and festivals of Arunachal Pradesh with special reference to festivals of the Nishis, Bibhas Dhar and Palash Chandra Coomar (Eds), *Tribes of Arunachal Pradesh*, First edition, Abhijeet Publications, New Delhi, pp. 37-38.
12. Dutta, P. (2004). The problems of agricultural transforma-tion in the highlands: A study on the Noctes and Wanchos of Arunachal Pradesh, Bibhas Dhar and Palash Chandra Coomar (Eds), *Tribes of Arunachal Pradesh*, First edition, Abhijeet Publications, New Delhi, p. 61.
13. Karmakar, K. (2002), *The silenced drums: A review of tribal economy development*, First edition, Northern Book Centre, New Delhi, pp. 4-5.
14. Koley, R. (2004). The Akas- A cognate tribe of Arunachal Pradesh and their customary laws, Bibhas Dhar and Palash Chandra Coomar (Eds), *Tribes of Arunachal Pradesh*, First edition, Abhijeet Publications, New Delhi, p. 106.
15. Mahapatra, L. (1997). Parameters of forest policy for tribal development, *Forest management in tribal areas: Forest policy and people participation*, Mahapatra, P., and Mahapatra, P (Eds), First edition, Concept publishing house, New Delhi, p. 26.
16. Pati, R., and Dash, J. (2002). *Tribal and Indigenous people in India: Problems and Prospects*, First edition, A.P.H. Publishing Corporation, New Delhi, p. 4.
17. *People their culture traditions and way of life* (2012). Retrieved from http://www.gopelling.net/people_culture_traditions.html
18. *Sikkim date highlights: The scheduled tribes census of India*, Retrieved from http://censusindia.gov.in/Tables_Published/SCST/dh_st_sikkim.pdf
19. *The People of Jaintia Hills (2012)*. Retrieved from http://jaintia.nic.in/People.htm.

20. Various informations are collected from Wikipedia, *like as Dimasa People, History of Sikkim, Kabi Lungchok, Karbi People, Khasi People, Mizo People, Monpa People, Naga People,* Nishi People, *Adi People, Adivasi, Tribe.*
21. Various information are collected from indianetzone, like as, *Tribes of Nagaland, Tribes of Meghalaya, Tribes of Manipur, Indian Tribals, Tribes of Tripura, Tribes of Mizoram, Tribes of Assam, Tribes of Arunachal Pradesh, Arunachal Pradesh Tribal Tour.*
22. Verma, M, (1996). *Tribal Development in India*, First edition, Mittal Publication, New Delhi, p. 3.
23. Walter Hillabrant and Nancy Pindus (2003). *Operating TANF: Opportunities and Challenges for Tribes and Tribal Consortia*, Retrieved from http://aspe.hhs.gov/hsp/tanf-tribes03/report.pdf

5

Economic Problems and Prospects of Tribal Youth in Tripura: With Reference to Educated Unemployment

Lalthlamuana Darlong

Introduction

Young women and men are the greatest asset of the state for the present and future, yet they represent a group that is seriously vulnerable when it comes to employment. Of all the severe problems the state encounters. Unemployment is the most critical. Though Tripura has achieved some in progressing in education, health services, social welfare measures and infrastructural development, the state has not been able to solve the problem of unemployment particularly educated unemployment. It is a large problem that makes the youth idle, worried and inactive. Here, educated unemployed means above matriculation.

According to Employment Exchange and Manpower Department, the number of registered job aspirants were 5, 71, 217 as quoted in the daily newspaper. Out of total unemployed youth, the numbers of graduate job aspirant's stands at 42,442. Unemployed B.A., B. Com. B.Sc., graduates are 32,874, 2,937 and 6,631 respectively while Madhyamik and XII pass are 1,62,275 and 49,196 respectively. According to Puttaswamaiah (1977), the educated unemployed are dangerous threat to the state. They can become dangerously vocal and influential to give constant threat to the security and stability of the state. He nurses a sense of personal injury and if the grievance is long continued and the numbers involved are large, the situation can become decidedly explosive. The unemployed persons belonging to this category are *'not dumb, driven cattle'*, but intelligent people, and will not accept an unenviable position lying down. It is the wastege of the best of our human resources as they remain ideals. This important section of the population can respond to the needs of society, country and state only if they are offered fruitful opportunities for growing up as useful citizens.

It has been said that among human resources of any nation, the vital chunk happens to be in youth. Since the beginning of planning in India, the youth have been recognized as *"the most vital section of the community"*. The importance of manpower planning can be observed by the following statement given in the Third Five Year Plan: *"As this process develops, there is a certain rhythm of expansion in the development of the people, and a sense of enterprise and achievement comes to them. They are conscious of a purpose in life and have a feeling of being participants in the making of history. Ultimately, it is the development of the human being and the human personality that counts. Although planning involves material investment, even more important is the investment in man"*.[1]

The recently released report on unemployment by the Union Labour ministry has some starling data. Tripura is the worst performer. The state has the highest percentage of unemployed in the whole country among all states. The state has 141 unemployed youths per thousand. The report prepared by the labour bureau, based on studies for the fiscal 2011-12, states that the unemployment of women in rural areas at the national level was 280 persons per 1,000 populations, compared to 179 in urban areas. Tripura is one of the states in India that has always suffered higher incidence of unemployment than that of the national average. This is particularly true of the educated unemployment. The whole country's unemployment rate is put at 3.8 per cent. In the urban sector, the highest unemployment rate is estimated in Tripura—236 persons per 1,000 population, followed by 229 in Sikkim, 145 in Kerala, 142 in Arunachal Pradesh and 139 in West Bengal. In the case of unemployment among females, it was high at 69 persons per 1,000 populations, when it is 29 in the case of males. Female unemployment rate was highest in Goa at 462, followed by 344 in Tripura, 262 in Kerala and 212 in West Bengal. The highest female unemployment rate in urban areas is in Sikkim at 511 persons per 1,000 populations, followed by 446 in Tripura, 402 in West Bengal and 375 in Kerala.[2]

The unemployment of the educated youth is not only a problem of theirs, but has become the problem of the family, the society and the nation at large. After spending the hard-earned money of one's parents and about two decades of precious time, the educated youth finds himself at the crossroads. He is desperate for any kind of job but finds no one to buy him. Thus, every educated youth is humiliated in two ways: (i) He cannot contribute anything to the familial economy because he could not work during the course of his study, and (ii) His two decades devotion to education is a waste without any fruits. Not only this, he finds himself answerable to the aspirations and expectations of the family. He is answerable to the family, who has spared everything on him, who has invested on him; its sweat earned income/money with a hope that he would emancipate the family from all socio-economic curses after his education. As Atchly (1977) believes that the greatest tragedy for a woman is widowhood and for a man unemployment (joblessness). Due to weak in industrial and underdeveloped agriculture sectors in Tripura, bulk of the educated population being dependent on the service sector. But employment opportunities in this sector are limited in relation to its supply, thereby, leading to unemployment.

The educated unemployment is a part and parcel of the overall unemployment, it has its own peculiarities, the educated unemployment differs from the general unemployment that job continuity and security is more important to them than their uneducated counterpart. They have their own expectations, aspirations and inclinations about the jobs in which they have to work. They generally, dislike manual work, whereas for the uneducated it is a common practice. The *'recognition'* and *'willingness'* aspects of employment are more sensitive in case of the educated.

Situation of Tribal's in Tripura

According to Census of 2001, the total population of Tripura is 31,99,203. Out of the total population 9,93,426 persons belong to

Table-5.1: Growth of Tribal Population in Tripura

Year	*Tribal Population*	*Total Population*	*Percentage of Tribal Population*	*Percentage Decadal Variation of*	
				Tribal Population	*Total Population*
1901	91,679	1,73,325	52.89	—	—
1911	1,11,303	2,29,613	48.47	21.40	32.47
1921	1,71,610	3,04,437	56.37	54.13	32.59
1931	2,03,327	3,82,450	53.16	18.48	25.62
1941	2,56,991	5,13,010	50.09	26.39	34.14
1951	2,37,953	6,45,707	36.85	-7.40	25.87
1961	3,60,070	11,42,005	31.53	51.31	76.86
1971	4,50,544	15,56,342	28.95	25.12	36.28
1981	5,83,920	20,53,058	28.44	29.60	31.91
1991	8,53,345	27,57,205	30.95	46.14	34.30
2001	9,93,426	31,99,203	31.05	16.41	16.03

Source: Various Census Reports.

Table 5.2: Growth of Literacy among the Tribes of Tripura

Year	*Scheduled Tribes*	*Overall Literacy Rate*
1961	10.1	20.24
1971	15.03	30.98
1981	23.07	42.12
1991	32.25	60.39
2001	56.5	73.2
2011 (P)	NA	87.8

Source: Census Reports 1961, 1971, 1981, 1991, 2001, 2011
*P: Provisional, NA: Not Available

Scheduled Tribe (ST) which constitutes 31.05 per cent. The proportion of Scheduled Tribes in the total population of the state was reported to be 64 per cent in 1874-75 and 52.89 per cent in 1901 and 36.85 per cent in 1951. In almost all socio-economic studies of Tripura, it is emphasised that owing to continuous immigration of non-tribal population (speeded up spectacularly after the partition of India) the proportion of tribal population has fallen drastically since 1931 reducing them to the minority position. Table 5.1 shows that the proportion of tribal population to total population in Tripura was as high as 56.37 percent in 1921 and it came down to 28.44 percent in 1981. Curiously the Census of 1991 shows an increase in the proportion of tribal population to 30.55 percent. The State has registered 16.41 per cent decadal growth of ST population during the period 1991-2001.

It is evident from Table 5.2 that the scheduled tribes literacy is 56.5 per cent in the state (2001 census), which also has been recorded as higher than the national average for scheduled tribes in India (47.1 per cent). It is also shown that the scheduled tribe's literacy increases from different census period i.e. from 10.1 per cent to 56.5 per cent in 1961 and 2001 census respectively. It shows that they give due importance on education in modern days. However, there is high gender disparity in literacy between the male (68 per cent) and female (44.6 per cent) and also disparity with the overall literacy of the state (73.2 per cent) in the same period. Thus, even after more than 65 years of independence, the tribal's are confronted with diverse problems and this problems need to be addressed for taking a concrete step towards the path of economic development.

Economic Problems Faced by Educated Tribal Youth

The problems faced by tribal youth differ on the basis of sex (male-female), economic (rich-poor), residence (rural-urban), education (educated-uneducated), physically and mentally challenged youth. Saxena (1979) conducted a study on the problem of educated unemployment in India. He opines that the growing imbalance between the development of general and vocational or professional type of education manifested in huge output of matriculates and graduates in Arts, Science and Commerce, far in excess of demand, has created the explanation for the growing number of educated unemployed in the country lies partly in the erroneous system of education which is book centred, neither providing *'academic excellence'* nor professional skills or capabilities. An attempt was made by T.N. Dhar (1979) to study the problem of graduate unemployment in India and to examine the implications of the social and political framework within which manpower and educational planning is taking place. It is a critical approach to manpower planning whose limitations are seen to arise not so much from conceptual limitations, but from the practical difficulties of operationalisation. However, the overall economic problems of the educated tribal youth in the state are specifically given below in Fig. 5.1.

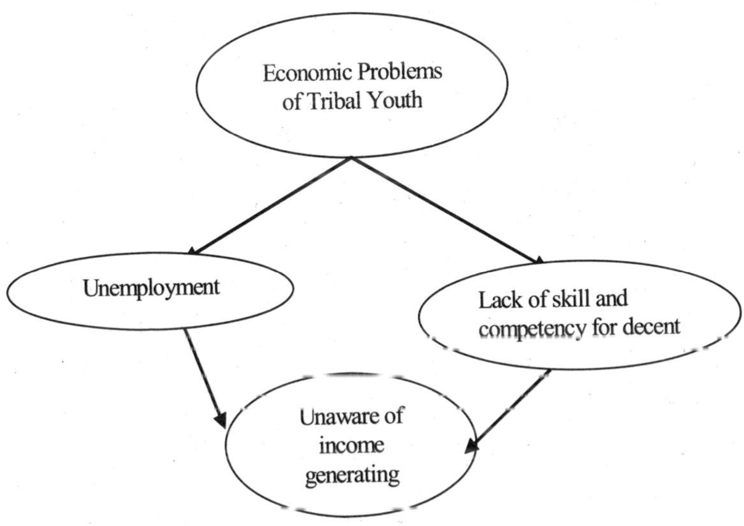

Fig. 5.1.

The above Fig. 5.1 shows that the economic problems of educated tribal youth like unemployment, lack of skill and competency for decent development and unaware of income generating opportunities are closely inter-related to each other. It also indicates that educated unemployment arises because the tribal youth were lacking skill and competency for decent development and this is leading to unaware of income generating opportunities, and which in turn is the main cause of unemployment among the educated tribal youth in the state. It is usually argued that most of the youth remain unemployed because they are unemployable. Visaria (1998:45) stated that *"the major challenge before the country is to ensure the employability of the youth by training them adequately for productive work, by imparting to them marketable skills and the flexibility to learn new things and to innovate, and by inculcating in them a proper work ethic. All these goals are necessary conditions for survival and growth in the changing economic environment in which even a large country is a small part of a global village"*.

Educated tribal youth members are growing faster than the rate of job creation, too few decent employment opportunities are available for the numbers of youth seeking them. The result is that a large number of educated youth are unemployed or underemployed. Not only do these youth lack income, they lack a means of gaining respect and a sense of belonging in their communities. Inability to find decent employment means tribal youth often find employment in the informal sector, with poor working conditions and pay. Educated tribal youth will often look to urban areas for employment and move to cities. But without training in skills suited to the urban labour market, these youth have few opportunities in urban areas. Often, unemployment may lead youth to alcohol, intoxicated, crime and make them subject to exploitation. In fact, the unemployment rates for educated tribal youth can be higher than those for tribal youth with little schooling. Often this is because these educated youth are not skilled in areas in which there is demand for their labour. But this unemployment of educated tribal youth is also a result of the lack of employment opportunities, productive jobs which educated tribal youth can apply for. The main thrust of economic activities is to enhance income from existing resources and create additional employment opportunities for the tribal with optimum allocation of local resources and skills.

Therefore, there is an urgent need to look back the strategy for tribal development particularly the youth and accordingly take specific developmental activities to their specific problems.

Education and Unemployment

Education and the educated youth, both have the strongest roles to play to achieve the *'pervasive social transformation'*. The youths of today are the assets of the country, on whom the responsibilities of socio-economic, socio-cultural, socio-political etc. transformation and change lie. Tripura is facing really a puzzling problem; on the one hand there is growing backlog of the educated unemployed, on the other there is an increasing rush to the higher educational institutions. The result has been aggravating the problem of unemployment and the deterioration in the quality of education due to increased congestion. It is clearly shows in Table 3 that the number of Scheduled Tribes (STs) students is increasing during the period of 2004-05 and 2009-10 in various colleges/institutions, i.e., increase of ST student in Degree General College from 12.9 per cent to 21.4 per cent and for SC student from 17.00 per cent to 18.00 per cent but the general student 70.00 per cent to 60.6 per cent. Therefore, it can be said that the rate of growth of STs Student is the highest in the state, i.e., by 8.5 for ST and 1.00 for SC respectively. Similar situation can be seen in most of the other institutions.

Whatever may be the growth of supply of the educated labour, if there is a corresponding growth in the demand for them in the labour market, there would not be any educated unemployment, but the problem lies with the fact that the demand for the educated in the economy falls short of their supply from the educational system. Hence, the imbalance in the state between the growth rates of the educational sector and manpower absorption in the state leads to high growth rates of educated unemployment, longer periods of waiting for jobs and large scale under-employment. In other words, it can be said that educated unemployment basically arises due to the mismatch between the supply and demand for manpower.

As evident from Table 5.4, in March 2004, more than 4 lakh persons were registered on Live Register of Employment Exchanges of the state. Most of the job seekers were belonging to unreserved categories, while proportion of STs job-seekers has been found to be

Table 5.3 Strength of student in various colleges or institutions.

Sl.No.	Item	During 2004-05				During 2009-10			
		SC	ST	Gen	Total	SC	ST	Gen	Total
1.	Degrees General Colleges	3634 (17.0)	2717 (12.9)	14859 (70.0)	21045	4530 (18.0)	5388 (21.4)	15254 (60.6)	25172
2.	Polytechnic Institute	0	0	0	0	128 (17.1)	233 (31.1)	389 (51.9)	750
3.	Women's Polytechnic	133 (17.0)	242 (31.0)	405 (51.92)	780	112 (17.0)	205 (31.0)	343 (52.0)	660
4.	Tripura Govt. Law College	17 (17.0)	31 (3.01)	52 (52.0)	100	51 (17.0)	93 (31.0)	156 (52.0)	300
5.	Govt. Music College	51 (22.0)	23 (14.3)	146 (63.48)	230	21 (9.1)	52 (22.6)	157 (68.3)	230
6.	Govt. College of Art and Crafts	15 (10.0)	3 (2.0)	132 (88.0)	150	15 (16.7)	2 (2.2)	73 (81.1)	90
7.	IASE	9 (18.0)	16 (32.0)	25 (50.0)	50	15 (16.7)	2 (2.2)	73 (81.1)	90
8.	Tripura Engineering College (Now NIT)	163 (17.0)	298 (31.0)	499 (51.98)	960	-	-	-	1515

Source:-http://www.tripuradhe.in/Education/Index.aspx, Perspective Plan 2010-2020, p. 62.

Note: Table in the parentheses denotes percentages.

Table-5.4 Job Seekers Registered on Live Registrar in Tripura (As on March 2004).

Category	*Number of Persons*		
	Male	*Female*	*Total*
Unreserved	159429	47745	257174
Scheduled Tribes	46448	24062	70510
Scheduled Castes	39412	22022	62434
Physically handicapped	1568	726	2294
OBCs	9484	4273	14057
Total	257177	149828	407005

Source: SIPARD, Government of Tripura, 2004.

high, i.e., 17.32 per cent of the total job seekers. Table 5.5 shown the position of job-seekers of educated tribal youth, the largest number were in the educational level of Madhyamik, i.e., they constitutes 24.03 per cent of the total job-seekers. The same educational level of women job-seeker constitutes 38.17 per cent for ST and which is marginally higher than that of the total job-seekers of 35.68 per cent. Many who would like to start working after secondary school find that they are neither able to get jobs nor are fit for self-employment. Thus they continue with higher education not because of a strong academic urge but rather because there is not much else they can do. Considering the magnitude of educated job-seekers flowing into the state in the job market every year, it is essential that a sizeable fraction of enterprising youth is initiated into careers of self employment. Some agreements needs to be instituted in the colleges and universities to identify the deserving cases fit to take up self employment, educate them how to proceed about the job of setting up a venture, help them through the cooperation of the concerned agencies in this sphere to prepare technically sound and economically viable.

Hence, the problem of educated unemployed among the tribal youth has become a universal phenomenon. However, the problem in Tripura seems to be more deep-rooted and multi-dimensional. Unemployment is always a curse and unemployment of the educated persons is more dangerous. Unemployment of a large section of the educated youth over a long period of time is a sheer waste. It is not only a loss of human resources and resultant output, but also a colossal loss of financial resources which have been spent on their education

Table 5.5: Statement showing category wise number of job seekers waiting in the live register of the Employment Exchanges of Tripura according to education level as on 31.03.2012

Sl.No.	*Qualification*	*Scheduled Tribe*		
		Male	*Female*	*Total*
1.	Madhyamik	17829	11010	28839
2.	H.S. + 2 stage	3941	2077	6018
3.	B.A.	1826	831	2657
4.	B.Sc	141	78	219
5.	B.Com	191	7	198
6.	M.A.	238	179	417
7.	M.Sc	15	18	33
8.	M.Com	31	1	32
9.	B.E. Civil	35	11	46
10.	B.E. Elec	21	12	33
11.	B.E. Mech	46	3	49
12.	Engg. P/G Civil	1	0	1
13.	Engg. P/G Elec	0	0	0

(Contd.)

(Contd. Table 5.5)

Sl.No.	Qualification	Scheduled Tribe		
		Male	Female	Total
14.	Engg. P/G Mech	0	0	0
15.	Diploma Civil	29	8	37
16.	Diploma Elec	8	1	9
17.	Diploma Mech	28	0	28
18.	ITI	347	28	375
19.	MBBS	5	3	8
20.	BDS	6	3	9
21.	Veterinary	3	1	4
22.	BAMS	3	0	3
23.	BHMS	7	1	8
24.	Agri B.Sc	10	0	10
25.	Agri M.Sc	10	5	15
25.	Lawyer	6	1	7
27.	Skilled/Semi skilled	2465	1300	3765
23.	Others	49913	27237	77150
29.	Total	77155	42815	119970

Source: Perspective Plan 2010-2020, Government of Tripura

Note: Here others means below class VIII, below Madhyamik etc.

and training. Further, it may cause personal family and, social dissatisfaction and tension. It is said that an *'idle mind is a devil's workshop'*. Several studies have revealed that the persistent unemployment led to deviant behaviour, frustration and violence and reduced psychological well being. In order to improve employment prospects for educated tribal youth there needs to be investment on which focus on the young and such investment should:

1. Provide leadership and organisational skills training;
2. If English Medium is necessary for good education, they should set up and encourage the medium as a compulsory in the educational system of the state and thereby; enable the youth to compete with the rest of the states or country, and
3. Youth should be encouraged to do manual jobs, as labourers to supplement their income. The young rather than being unemployed should be trained to develop an attitude to work on any odd job to gain experience or earn while learning.

As Dhar (2011) has rightly pointed out that tribal education should extend beyond literacy. Education should focus on imparting values, skills and the ability to think independently. The education must promote socially relevant education programmes with economically viable options for life which meet the tribe's need to employable. Vocational streams have to be developed and expanded to equip the tribal students with meaningful occupation centric knowledge and skills such as agro-based vocational training programmes especially post harvest technology etc. Therefore, education for employment has become the main concern for education policy makers and it becomes more challenging when the questions of employability of tribal students come in to consideration. Due to increase of employment in private sectors the nature of employment has been changed rapidly.

An Alternative Way of Educated Tribal Youth

An alternative to the educated unemployed of tribal youth in the present context in Tripura seems is to be self-employed. This strategy exerts strong influence on both the supply and demand side of the problem. On supply side self-employment strategy makes the educated more productive by imparting the skills in formal and informal ways. From the demand point of view it develops, *'self-employment'* as an independent sector where the unemployed youth could seek self-employment by providing a *'package'* of inputs or services, the educated unemployed could get at least a subsistence employment if not a gainful employment. To make self employment a success, not only requisite training be organised on a massive scale but necessary facilities for self-employment unit should also be provided. Such facilities will have to be particularly provided to matriculates, who form the bulk of the educated unemployed.

There is another way to deal with the educated unemployment. Instead of dealing with it on the supply and demand side separately, an integrated manpower planning is followed. The manpower planning is a blend of education policy and employment policy. It attempts to adjust the skills and capabilities of the labour with the needs and requirements of the society or state. By a precise manpower planning educational system would produce the skills and talents required for the economy and the economy in turn, fully utilises such skills without rendering them useless or idle. A modest attempt was made by Bhattacharya (1982) in his study to examine the extent of educated unemployment in India. He suggests that the problem of unemployment among the educated could be solved only by proper manpower planning at all levels in the economy. The education system, especially at secondary and higher secondary levels, should be re-oriented to give it a technical basis for meeting the needs of a developing economy. The slowness of the education systems caused an insufficient adaptation to the rapid change in the demand for labour. Therefore, there is an urgent need to reform and improve the education systems to provide young people with skills which are useful once they leave school/college.

Conclusion

To sum up, it can be said that the economic problems of educated tribal youth is a serious problem, which needs timely attention and solution. As many educated tribal youth are not aware of the various facilities available for starting their own ventures leading to unemployment. It is, therefore, necessary to give wide publicity to the facilities that are being provided by Government, as well as by public, cooperative and private sector enterprises in the matter of training, credit and marketing facilities and there is an urgent need to reform the education system of the state. Since, tribal youth are inseparable part of the society if they remain underdeveloped our society, state and country is also going to suffer. Therefore, sincere efforts must be made by the government and its machineries to bring them at par with the rest of the society.

References

1. Third Five Year Plan, *Planning Commission, Government of India*, 1961, p. 19.
2. The Northeast Today, *"Unemployment: Tripura Gets the 1st Position in the Country"*, July 14, 2012, http://www.northeasttoday.in/our-states/tripura/unemployment-tripura-gets-1st-position-in-the-country accessed on 9/7/2012.
3. Youth Entrepreneurship Sustainability (YES) Campaign, *"Employment for Rural Youth in Asia and the Pacific"*, Jobs and empowerment on and off farm, Opportunities in the rural non-farm sector in India, http://www.yesweb.org/docs/rdbok.pdf accessed on 10.10.2011, pp. 1-4.
4. *Planning Commission of India*, htpp://www. planning commission.nic.in/plans/... accessed on 9/7/2012
5. Atchly, Robert, C., *"The Social Forces in Later Life Miami Florida";* Scripts Foundation Granr Centre, Miami University, 1977.
6. Bajpai, P.K., *"Youth Education and Unemployment"*, APH Publishing Corporation, New Delhi, 2010, p. 15.
7. Chatterjee, R., "Role of NGOs in Tribal Development with Particular Reference to Tripura: Some Measures in Bera, G.K. (ed.); *Tribal Development in Tripura*, EBH Publishers (India), Guwahati, 2009, p. 175.
8. Bhattacharya, A.K., *"The Problem of Educated Unemployment in India"*, Meenakshi Prakashan, Meerut, 1982.
9. Bose, P.K., B.C.Sanyal and Mukerjee, S.P., *"Graduate Employment and Higher Education in West Bengal"*, International Institute for Educational Planning, Paris, 1983.
10. Dhar, T.N., *"The Politics of Manpower Planning. Graduate unemployment and the Planning of Higher Education in India"*, Minerva, Calcutta, 1979.
11. Government of India, *Planning Commission, First Five Year Plan*, New Delhi, p. 615
12. Kikhi, K., *"Educated Unemployed Youth in Nagaland: A Sociological Study"*, Akansha Publishing House, New Delhi, 2006, pp. 110-111.
13. Pratap, S. and Gupta, N.K., *"Unemployment and Psychological Well being in Professional Graduates"*, Spring, 1985, pp. 271-272.

14. Puttaswamaiah, K., *"Employment in India-Policy for Manpower";* New Delhi, Oxford and IBH Publishing Co., 1977.
15. Sahni, A., *"Stresses and Distresses in the Youth",* Health Administrator, Vol. XVII, Number 1, 2010, pp. 75-77.
16. Sarma, Mukunda, *"Problems of Youth-Tips to Research and Project",* EBH Publishers (India), Guwahati, 2010, pp. 9.
17. Saxena, J.P., "*Educated Unemployment in India, Problems and Suggestions",* Commercial Publications Bureau, New Delhi, 1979.
18. Visaria P., *'Unemployment Among Youth in India: Level, nature and Policy Implications, Employment and Training",* Geneva, Deptt. International Labour Office, 1998, p. 45.

6

Tribal Life in India: Past vs. Present

Prahelika Roy

Introduction

Humans are primates of the family Hominidae and the only living species of the genus *Homo*. They originated in Africa, where they reached anatomical modernity about 200,000 years ago and began to exhibit full behavioural modernity around 50,000 years ago. Like men and women everywhere, the daily lives of tribal people are a reflection of their beliefs and traditions. Although their lives may be simple in material terms, the task of surviving in many different environments makes them different in their approach and indigenous methods. In the remotest parts of the world, food is obtained by hunting, gathering produce from the forest, growing grains, vegetables and fruit, fishing or keeping livestock. Women tend to be in charge of most food production other than hunting. Matis women work in their gardens whilst the men spend most of their time involved in hunting activities. Women are also usually responsible for childcare. The tribal people and ethnic races throughout the world have developed their own culture, customs, cults, religious rites, taboos, totems, legends and myths, folk-lores and song, foods, medicinal practices, etc. In Indian conditions, the tribal's and forests are inseparable phenomenon and in general public understanding both are almost synonymous.

Tribal people are increasingly threatened in today's world. Dangers come in many forms, i.e., from governments and multi-national companies; banks, missionaries and guerrilla armies, sometimes in the name of economic growth and development. Mining and logging companies have destroyed whole landscapes, including vast tracts of rainforest and seriously jeopardised tribal lifestyles. As their land is appropriated and their environment destroyed, indigenous people's knowledge and identity are at risk. India is a land of multitudinous culture and peoples. Every state of India has its own culture and tradition. The different forms of people found here out numbers any country. There are certain states in India where the number of tribal population is much more than that of the other states. Due to the presence of these tribes India has received various flavours and the tribal people are the real treasures of our country. There are many acute problems of the tribal peoples that need immediate attention and early solution. The problems relate to various aspects of tribal peoples, viz., social, economical, educational, health, religion, land, law and order situation, self-centered tendency and so on. Many of these problems cannot be well understood due-to lack of necessary and adequate information.

Who are Tribal's?

The term *"Scheduled Tribes"* refers to specific indigenous peoples whose status is acknowledged to some formal degree by national legislation. A collective term in use locally to describe most of these peoples is *"Upajati"*. The Constitution of India, Article 366 (25) defines Scheduled Tribes as *"such tribes or tribal communities or part of or groups within such tribes or tribal communities as are deemed under Article 342 to the scheduled Tribes (STs) for the purposes of this Constitution"*. In Article 342, the procedure to be followed for specification of a scheduled tribe is prescribed. However, it does not contain the criterion for the specification of any community as scheduled tribe. An often used criterion is based on attributes such as:

1. *Geographical isolation:* — they live in cloistered, exclusive, remote and inhospitable areas such as hills and forests.
2. *Backwardness*: —their livelihood is based on primitive agriculture, a low-value closed economy with a low level of technology that leads to their poverty. They have low levels of literacy and health.

3. *Distinctive culture, language and religion* - communities have developed their own distinctive culture, language and religion.

4. *Shyness of contact* – they have a marginal degree of contact with other cultures and people.

Tribal people are also called as *indigenous people*. Indigenous peoples primarily refers to *ethnic groups that have historical ties to groups that existed in a territory prior to colonisation or formation of a nation state, and which normally preserve a degree of cultural and political separation from the mainstream culture and political system of the nation state within the border of which the indigenous group is located.* Indigenous peoples confront a diverse range of concerns associated with their status and interaction with other cultural groups, as well as changes in their inhabited environment. The interaction between indigenous and non-indigenous societies throughout history has been complex, ranging from outright conflict and subjugation to some degree of mutual benefit and cultural transfer. Indigenous populations are distributed in regions throughout the globe. The numbers, condition and experience of indigenous groups may vary widely within a given region.

Situation of Tribal's in India

India is the home to large number of indigenous people, who are still untouched by the lifestyle of the modern world. With more than 84.4 million, India has the largest population of the tribal people in the world. These tribal people also known as the *adivasi's* are the poorest in the country who still dependent on haunting, agriculture and fishing. Some of the major tribal groups in India include *Gonds, Santhals, Khasis, Angamis, Bhils, Bhutias and Great Andamanese*. All these tribal people have their own culture, tradition, language and lifestyle. Tribals are found in almost all the states of country. Currently there are between 258 and 540 scheduled tribe communities exists. India's tribal belts refer to contiguous areas of indigenous settlement of tribal people of India. Tribal people constitute 8.2 per cent of the nation's total population, over 84 million people according to the 2001 census. Another concentration lives in the hilly areas of central India (Chhattisgarh, Madhya Pradesh, Orissa and, to a lesser extent, Andhra Pradesh); in this belt, which is bounded by the Narmada River to the north and the Godavari River to the southeast, tribal peoples occupy the slopes of the region's mountains. Other tribal's, including the Santals; live in Jharkhand and West Bengal.

India's northeast represents a large number of diverse tribes whose unique adaptive strategy made this huge geographical space in to a cultural space. However, tribal situation in Northeast has gained huge research attention across the world because of the complexities of the issues related to bio-cultural diversities, ethnicity, historicity of the people, tribal people's response to variegated state policies and their on going negotiation processes in a globalise world. These have accelerated the process of transition/transformation among the diverse tribal population depending on their exposure to the forces of change and intricate link to the wider socio-political realities of life. Diversity is the key to understanding the tribal situation in Northeast India. Tribes in the region have diverse histories, cultures, languages, religions, social organisations, polities, economies and sizes. In *'civilising'* the tribes of North-East India the agendas of both the colonialists as well the Christian missionaries synchronised.

The Tribal Belt of Northwest India includes the states of Rajasthan, Gujarat, Maharashtra, and Karnataka. The Central India Tribal Belt stretches from Gujarat in the west up to Assam in the east across the states of Madhya Pradesh, Chhattisgarh and Jharkhand. It is among the poorest regions of the country. Over 90 per cent of the Belt's tribal population is rural, with primitive agriculture. India is home to a large number of tribes with population of about 70 million. In terms of geographical distribution about 55 per cent of tribal's lived in central India, 28 per cent in west, 12 per cent in North-East India, 4 per cent in South India and 1 per cent elsewhere. Each tribal communities are rich in there culture, folk tales, folk songs and folk stories. The northeast is India's chief tribal area, and the numerous tribes of Arunachal Pradesh, Orissa, Nagaland, Manipur and those in the rest of India make a glorious and colourful portray of Indian history through its ethnic world. Here's a list of some of the tribes in India and the areas they inhabit.

Many tribes and castes on the mainland of India live by hunting, fishing or gathering. The aboriginal inhabitants of the Andaman Islands depend upon these entirely for their livelihood. They have no trade relations with others and are so much isolated from one another that

Table 6.1 Some Prominent Tribes in India

Tribes	*Place Where They Inhabit*
Abors	Arunachal Pradesh, Assam
Adi, Apatati, Khampi, Miri, Tagin	Arunachal Pradesh
Angami, Ao, Rengma, Sema, Zeliang	Nagaland
Badagas, Todas	Tamil Nadu
Baiga, Bhils	Madhya Pradesh, Rajasthan, Gujarat
Bhutias, Mundas	Sikkim
Birhor, Mundas, Oarons	Bihar
Bodos, Chutia, Kacharis, Karbi, Mishing, Rabhas	Assam
Chenchus	Andhra Pradesh, Orissa
Dangs	Gujarat
Gaddis	Himachal Pradesh
Garos	Meghalaya

Source: Ministry of Tribal Welfare.

the Onge of Little Andaman does not understand the language of the Jarawa of the Great Andaman or of the inhabitants of the North Sentinel Island, all of which are close by. Pigs are plentiful and their meat and fat is relished by the Andamanese.

Rajasthan has a large indigenous populace Minas (Minawati) in Alwar, Jaipur, Bharatpur, and Dholpur areas. The Oswals hails from Osiyan near Jodhpur are successful traders and are predominately Jains. While the Mahajan (the trading class) is subdivided into a large number of groups, some of these groups are Jain, while others are Hindu. In the north and west, the Jat and Gujar are among the largest agricultural communities. The Gujars who are Hindus dwell in eastern Rajasthan. The nomadic Rabari or Raika are divided in two groups the Marus who breed camels and Chalkias who breed sheep and goats. Gujarat still has a number of tribes like Jats, Harijans, Ahirs, Rabaris, etc. Where the Jats are believed to be herdsmen of Sindh, Ahirs are said to be the descendants of Lord Krishna. Meghwal people were named as the Harijans by Mahatma Gandhi. Originally from Marwar, Harijans are known for their exclusive handiworks. Unlike other tribal people of Gujarat, the Rabaris are nomads and have their own unique lifestyle. The women amongst all the tribes are essentially homemakers, who spend their time taking care of their children and house.

Life of Tribal's: Historical Perspectives

The quality of life of tribal people during pre-independence period was more deplorable and their main occupation was hunting, gathering of wood and forest products and primitive shifiting cultivation. Due to destruction of forest and non availability of proper facilities, tribal were forced to lead a miserable life. After independence with the adoptation of Indian constitution in 1950 special attention was given for the upliftment of the tribal people under the *"Article 48"*— it was mandatory on the part of the state government to make all the efforts to improve economic, social, and educational standard of the tribal people. In Mahabharata, it is referred that the demise of Krishna at the hands of a Bhil Jaratha showed the existence of tribal people in India. In the ancient scriptures, considered to be sacred by the upper castes, various terms are used depicting Adivasis as almost animals. The epics of Ramayana and Mahabharata, the Puranas, Samhitas and other so-called *'sacred books'* refer to Adivasis as Rakshasa (demons), Vanara (monkeys), Jambuvan (boar men), Naga (serpents), Bhusundi Kaka (crow), Garuda (King of Eagles) etc. In medieval India, they were called derogatorily as Kolla, Villa, Kirata, Nishada, and those who surrendered or were subjugated were termed as slaves and the robbers.

Tribal areas are the remotest as well as the most secluded and generally inaccessible hilly tracts. The life in these areas is full of adventure and susceptible to natural calamities. The tribal people by and large, comprise of primitive groups who might have come to these isolated and inhospitable terrain in the past due to some historical compulsions such as seeking refuge or for fear of invaders or aggressors who exploited and tortured these people. These people are highly superstitious by nature. Most of the tribal population is desperately poor, backward, uneducated and leads a very hard and miserable life. During the colonial period, a number of merchants, money lender, landlords, petty officials etc. coming from the non-tribal community disrupted the life of tribal people by acquiring their land, disrupting their traditional way of life, exploiting them in their own business at a lower cost etc. In this particular sense, Verrier Elwin comments that *'. . .they (tribal people) suffered oppression and exploitation, for there soon came merchants and liquor-venders, cajoling, tricking, swindling them in their ignorance and simplicity until bit by bit their broad acres dwindled and they sank into the poverty in which many of them still live today. . .'*. From the above comments, it clearly shows that the tribal people suffered a lot from the non-tribal community. Therefore, the sufferings of tribal people particularly from the non-tribal led a number of uprisings and rebellion during the 19th and 20th century AD. For example, Santhal uprising, Munda uprises etc.

Hunting and honey collection are men's job and the women and children collect roots and tubers. There is a high degree of individual freedom among the sexes and monogamy is the rule. Husband-wife and parent-children relationships are based on mutual respect and deep affection. Medical and health facilities occupy a significant place in any welfare state. The health of the people in general is poor in the tribal areas due to malnutrition and lack of protein in the diet. The cold conditions of the area have restricted the habits of people in matters of bathing, washing, cleaning etc. Health education is also not effective because the people are very conservative and believe in old customs and traditions. In the tribal belt agriculture and allied pursuits being the mainstay of the people, development of animal husbandry assumes an added importance. The economy of the tribal areas is highly agro-pastoral. Such areas are industrially most backward.

The population estimated to have the deficiency is about 13 million, primarily residing in Madhya Pradesh, Maharashtra, Tamil Nadu, Orissa, and Assam states (15 per cent). The incidence is high in malaria zones. Screening kits are needed by health workers, so that identified people can be tattooed and high risk families counseled accordingly. The Onges, Jarawas, and Shompens of Andaman and Nicobar Islands are facing extinction due to endemic diseases, venereal diseases, and a shortage of women. Health workers need information on the folklore related to health of these and other tribal groups, in order to provide appropriate health and sanitary practices and to document indigenous herbs for medical use. Malnutrition is pervasive among tribals. Deficiencies have been detected in gross amounts of calcium, vitamin A, vitamin C, riboflavin, and animal protein. Southern tribes are known for their caloric and protein deficiencies. Those in rice-eating belts tend to have had higher protein intake. The workload of tribal women is heavy, long, and increasing. Maternal mortality is due to unhygienic conditions and inappropriate tribal practices.

Majority tribes live under poverty line. The tribes follow many simple occupations based on simple technology. Most of the occupation falls into the primary occupations such as hunting, gathering, and agriculture. The technology they use for these purposes belong to the most primitive kind. There is no profit and surplus making in such economy. There per capita income is very meager much lesser than the Indian average. Most of them live under miserable poverty and are in debt in the hands of local moneylenders and Zamindars. In order to repay the debt they often mortgage or sell their land to the moneylenders. Indebtedness is almost inevitable since heavy interest is to be paid to these moneylenders. In the past, many tribal groups were forced to assimilate into the dominant culture of the country. But some groups, such as the Bhils, Gonds, Santals, Oraons, Mundas, Khonds, Mizos, Nagas, and Khasis resisted change and assimilation to maintain their cultural identities and languages. According to many Indians, their continued isolation poses problems to national integration. Under the banner of national unity, the government is now bringing these minority groups into the national mainstream. The main question is whether tribal societies can enter the national mainstream while preserving their distinct social, cultural and political beliefs. Girijan tribes live on the Eastern Ghats. The Girijans follow farming practice that is eco-friendly but they are being asked to adopt the conventional methods to gain better yield.

The hilly region of North-East India can be suitably called the *home of various tribes*. The hill areas of the entire region have been occupied by different tribes since long past. These tribes came from different parts of the countries across North-East India in different points of time. These tribes have cultural diversities although some of them belong to same linguistic group. Each of them has its own historical background and mode of living. Until the coming of the British rule the hill tribes of the region remained totally unexposed to the other cultures of the country. They had little or no contact with plains peoples. The British administration also followed the policy of isolation of these tribes from the plains by adopting the *Inner Line Permit System*. The system debarred the plains people from entering the hill areas, without proper permission from the district administration, which was a difficult proposition. Although the tribes were officially under British administration, practically they were independent in socio-economic sphere. Each tribe lived according to its own social customs and traditions. The area occupied by a tribal group was considered as its homeland. The area inhabited by the Naga tribes was called *Nagaland*, the hills occupied by the Lushai (Mizo) tribes was known as *Lushai hills*, the Khashi hills were occupied by Khasi tribes and so on.

Tripura, Manipur, Nagaland, Mizoram and Arunachal Pradesh are all situated in the north-eastern end of India. The rainfall is heavy, being well over 100 inches annually in many places. In Nagaland or Arunachal Pradesh the land may be used for only one season or two; while in more crowed places like Orissa, it may be used for three seasons and then left for a number of years to recuperate. The period of recovery may very from three or four to ten years; it all depends upon the needs of the farmer and the pressure of population in the locality. This process of shifting the area of cultivation has many names. In Assam, it is known as *jhum*; in Orissa as *podu, dahi* or *kamana*; *penda* in Madhya Pradesh, and so on. The crops which are grown in these fields vary from place to place. In Nagaland millets like Job's tears and cotton are grown in abundance. In the North Cacher and Karbi Anglong districts of Assam cotton, papaya and vegetables of many kinds form the principal crops. Women in the Dimasa Kachari tribe carry these in their baskets, suspended by means of a tump-line which runs across their forehead, over long distances in order to sell them in the market of Lumding.

The benefits covered under a health contract, absence of health education, lack of national preventive programmes, and lack of health services are responsible for the poor health of the tribal's. Problems like in-sanitary food supplies, water contamination, and poor food in-take reflect on the health status of tribal's. The tropical disease like malaria is still widespread in the tribal areas. Better nutrition and good environmental health are the important aspects of village health services. Climate change is also beginning to impact indigenous habitats. Steps taken to conserve the environment sometimes end up excluding local people. The creation of a national park can mean indigenous tribes are thrown off land, or that their access is limited, or they are forced to live in settled, depressed communities.

Changing Scenario of Tribal Life

Nowadays educated trible youth are not taking interest in their own folk dances and culture due to which the gradual decline in number of institutions causes grate harm to tribal society and also the Indian culture and tradition, because the chief aim of such institutions is to impart knowledge. Due to contact with other cultures, the tribal culture is undergoing a revolutionary change. Due to influence of Christian missionaries the problem of bilingualism has developed which led to indifference towards tribal language. The tribal people are imitating western culture in different aspects of their social life and leaving their own culture. It has led to degeneration of tribal life and tribal arts such as dance, music and different types of craft.

The number of indigenous people supporting the consumer culture is rising fast. The demand for high-carbon equipment, i.e., cell phones, cars and other electronic gadgets are increasing even in the remotest of places. Exposure to development is changing perceptions. Being a forest dweller is seen as being backward, helpless and a target of exploitation, and a move to the other side is seen as the solution. The situation is pronounced even within the ranks of social movements—the line between activists and petty politicians is becoming thinner. The phenomenon of movement leaders jumping into party politics and abandoning tribal philosophy is on the rise. Grassroots activists are heavily concerned with imitating the lifestyles of middle-class activists. There is one thing which has happened to tribal folk after contact with men of other faiths. It is true that these tribes are poor, devoid of formal education and oppressed by fears which arise out of modern knowledge. But in this respect they suffer from disabilities similar to those to which the poorer classes among the non-tribal people are also subject. Christian missionaries have worked upon these for more than a century; firstly, because they are more trusting and secondly, in this respect they offer a more fertile field for developing a truly religious life than the nominally Christian and poverty-stricken classes in countries from which the missionaries themselves come. Christianity has undoubtedly brought the message of a richer life, a wider companionship and a new sense of dignity to converts. But it is interesting that the Christian religion has always been attended by the benefits of modern western civilisation.

A missionary and four church leaders after Christian groups in the state of Nagaland were accused of forcing people of other faiths to convert to Christianity. The missionaries were arrested in the neighbouring state of Arunachal Pradesh and incarcerated at Changland district jail on the pretext of participating in insurgent movements. Arunachal Pradesh was one of the first states in India to frame an anti-conversion law. A varification campaign against the people of Nagaland accusing them of being anti-patriotic and indulging in terrorism has influenced government policy against the state for a number of years. The government should promote such tribal institutions for development and preservation of tribal culture. The government should make plans and programme to connect these isolated societies with the national mainstream.

Policy of Government

The struggle for independence had little impact among the tribal's of the North-East. To quote Jawaharlal Nehru: *'the essence of our struggle for freedom was the unleashing of a liberating force in India. This force did not even affect the frontier people in one of the most important tribal areas.'* Again: *'thus, they never experienced a sensation of being in a country called India and they were hardly influenced by the struggle for freedom or other movements in India. Their chief experience of outsiders was that of British officers and Christian missionaries who generally tried to make them anti-Indian.' The tribal policy of the Government of India, inspired by Jawaharlal Nehru was therefore even more relevant to the tribal people of the North-East. 'All this North-East border area deserves our special attention,'* Nehru said in October 1952, *'not only the governments, but of the people of India. Our contacts with them will do us good and will do them good also. They add to the strength, variety and cultural richness of India'.*

A reflection of this policy was in the Sixth Schedule of the Constitution, which applied only to the tribal areas of Assam. The Sixth Schedule offered a fair degree of self-government to the tribal people by providing for autonomous districts and the creation of district and regional councils which would exercise some of the legislative and judicial functions within the overall jurisdiction of the Assam legislature and the parliament. The objective of the Sixth Schedule was to enable tribal's to live according to their own ways. The Government of India also expressed its willingness to further amend the constitutional provisions relating to the tribal people if it was found necessary to do so with a view to promote further autonomy.

Nehru's and Verrier Elwin's policies were implemented best of all in the North-East Frontier Agency or NEFA, which was created in 1948 out of the border areas of Assam. NEFA was established as a Union Territory outside the jurisdiction of Assam and placed under a special administration. From the beginning, the administration was manned by a special cadre of officers who were asked to implement specially designed developmental policies without disturbing the social and cultural pattern of the life of the people. NEFA was named Arunachal Pradesh and granted the status of a separate state in 1987, While NEFA was developing comfortably, and in harmony with the rest of the country, problems developed in the other tribal areas, which were part of Assam administratively. Growth with social justice has been the avowed objective of planned development in India. Growing disparities, both regional and social drew the attention of people all over the world arousing great concern to distributive aspects in the economic process on the one hand and to the recognition of pockets of backwardness on the other. During the First Five year plan, the programmes for tribal development were for economic and educational development, improvement of communications, health facilities etc. The fifth five year plan gave birth to *"Tribal Sub-Plan"* concept. It has been proposed that sub-plan for the geographically and administratively viable areas with 50 per cent or above tribal population concentration should be prepared with the objective of (a) narrowing down the gap between tribal and other areas, (b) improving the quality of social and economic life of the tribal communities so as to bring them at par with people in other parts of the country, and (c) achieving social and cultural integration of tribal's with the rest of the society.

After Independence, the government of India laid down certain number of provisions for the safety and preservation of the tribal peoples by incorporating into the Constitution as follows:

1. Article 46 of Indian Constitution states that the state should promote with special care the educational and economic interests of the tribal people and should protect them from social injustice and all forms of exploitation through special legislatures.

2. Article 244(2) (Sixth Scheduled) provides a self-government to the tribal peoples by making a provisions of the creation of autonomous district council, creation of districts and regional councils. The objective of Sixth Scheduled was to enable tribal peoples to live according to their own ways.
3. Article 275(1) provides special grant-in-aid for promoting the welfare of the Scheduled Tribes.
4. Article 330, 332, 335 allocates a reservation of seats for the Scheduled Tribes in Lok Sabha and in state legislatures as well as in services.

The Constitution provides a framework with a three pronged strategy to improve the situation of SCs and STs.

1. *Protective Arrangements:*—Such measures as are required to enforce equality, to provide punitive measures for transgressions, to eliminate established practices that perpetuate inequities, etc. A number of laws were enacted to operationalise the provisions in the Constitution. Examples of such laws include The Untouchability Practices Act, 1955, Scheduled Caste and Scheduled Tribe (Prevention of Atrocities) Act, 1989, The Employment of Manual scavengers and Construction of Dry Latrines (Prohibition) Act, 1993, etc.
2. *Affirmative action:*—provides positive preferential treatment in allotment of jobs and access to higher education, as a means to accelerate the integration of the SCs and STs with mainstream society. Affirmative action is also popularly referred to as Reservation.
3. *Development:*—Provide for resources and benefits to bridge the wide gap in social and economic condition between the SCs/STs and other communities.

To effectively implement the various safeguards built into the Constitution and other legislations, the Constitution, under Articles 338 and 338A, provides for two statutory commissions — the National Commission for Scheduled Castes, and National Commission for Scheduled Tribes. In the light of the historical background and social realities, the idea of granting some degree of autonomy to the tribes within the framework of the Indian Constitution was developed and according the Sixth Schedule was added to the Constitution of India under the provisions of which Autonomous District Councils could be constituted for all the hill tribes of Assam. The tribal's would have a autonomy of making decisions affecting their socio-economic life through their own elected representatives and at the same time materialising the decisions with the help and control of the State super power.

The Ministry of Tribal Affairs, constituted in October, 1999, is the nodal Ministry for overall policy, planning and co-ordination of programmes of development for the Scheduled Tribes (STs). However, sectoral programmes and schemes pertaining to development of these communities, policy, planning, monitoring, evaluation, etc., as also their coordination is the responsibility of the concerned Central Ministries/Departments, State Governments and UT Administrations. Each Central Ministry/Department is the nodal Ministry or Department concerning its sector. The Ministry of Tribal Affairs, however, supports the efforts of the line Ministries and administers schemes and programmes for focused supplementation in various areas, particularly in those in which Scheduled Tribes are under served. The National Common Minimum Programme (NCMP) of the United Progressive Alliance (UPA) Government provides specific directions for the welfare of Scheduled Tribes, which inter-alia include:

1. Legislation for conferring ownership rights in respect of minor forest produce, including tendu patta;
2. Launching of a comprehensive national programme for minor irrigation of all lands owned by dalits and adivasis;
3. Endowing STs with land through implementation of land ceiling and land redistribution legislation,
4. Reconciliation of the objectives of economic growth and environmental conservation, particularly as far as tribal communities dependent on forests are concerned;
5. Immediate review of the overall strategy and programmes for the development of tribal areas to plug loopholes and to work out more viable livelihood strategies;

6. More effective systems of relief and rehabilitation for tribal and other groups displaced by development projects including rehabilitation of tribal people alienated from land;

7. Discontinuing eviction of tribal and other forest-dwelling from forest areas; and

8. Safeguard the rights of tribal communities over mineral resources, water sources, etc., as laid down by law.

To address the problems of tribal communities who are dependent on forests and to undo the historical injustice done to them, the Ministry introduced the *"Scheduled Tribes (Recognition of Forest Rights) Bill, 2005"* in Lok Sabha on 13.12.2005 to provide for recognition of forest rights to the forest dwelling Scheduled Tribes. The Bill represents a major paradigm shift in approach in addressing the concerns of forest-dwelling tribal's by providing tenurial security, livelihood and traditional rights to those who have been living in forests for generations without legal protection. The Bill recognises the following rights:

1. Tenurial security of land providing relief against the physical and psychological alienation of forest dwelling tribal's.

2. Livelihood in terms of ownership of Minor Forest Produce including rights to collect trade and process the same.

3. Traditional and customary rights.

Lack of education is one of the important factors contributing to the ignorance and poverty of the Tribal's. Tribal Mission presently runs Nursery Schools in mission centers. For Tribal students with a view to impart high quality secular education and train them to be good, morally upright and God fearing citizens. In June 1986 an accord between the government of India and the Mizo National Front ended a 20-year-old insurgency by the Mizos, an indigenous minority group in northeast India that wanted to secede from India. In the following weeks Mizo guerrillas trekked down the hills of neighboring Bangladesh and Burma and surrendered their weapons to the Indian authorities. The successful political incorporation of dissenting minority groups by giving them significant levels of political autonomy and a major say in determining public policy is an important but relatively unrecognised part of the Indian government's minority policy in the northeast.

Conclusion

Hill and tribal are interconnected. Hilly areas are the base of tribal people. Previously they lived in isolated and simple life but their life is changing for education and social upliftment. Tribal are basically simple people and live a simple life. Interaction with outsides changes the socio-economic and religious life of tribal's. The interaction between indigenous and non-indigenous societies throughout history has been complex, ranging from outright conflict and subjugation to some degree of mutual benefit and cultural transfer. Large number of tribal's are converted to Christianity in Mizoram, Meghalaya, Nagaland and other states. They are diverging from their traditional life style to western culture. Religious conversion has changed the life pattern of tribals.

References

1. Aparna Pallavi (2012).*Tribal philosophy can not be ignored beyond a point*, Retrieved from http://www.downtoearth. org.in/content/tribal-philosophy-can-t-be-ignored-beyond-point.
2. BaruahSanjib (2010), *Indigenous peoples, cultural survivor, and minority policy in North-East India,* Retrieved from http://www.cultural survival. org/publications/cultural-survival-quarterly/india/indigenous-peoples-cultural-survival-and-minority-pol.
3. Basu, S. K. (1994). *A Health profile of tribal India*, Retrieved from http:/ /www.ncbi.nlm.nih.gov/pubmed/12287763.
4. Bhuyan, K. (2008). *Sixth schedule in North-East India*, First edition, DVS Publishers, Guwahati, pp. 1-40.
5. Bhuriya Mandal (2010). *Tribal education in India*, Retrieved from http://www.culturalsurvival.org/publications/cultural-survival-quarterly/india/tribal-education-india.
6. Bose, N. (2004). *Tribal life in India*, First reprint, National Book Trust, New Delhi, pp. 1-75.
7. Daily Life (2012). Retrieved from http://www.bbc.co.uk/tribe/topics/daily.shrml
8. Dhar, B., and Coomar, P. (2004). *Tribes of Arunachal Pradesh: History and culture*, First edition, Abhijeet Publications, New Delhi, pp.1-80.
9. Dr Malsawmliana (2012). *Integrating tribal people into Indian main stream*, Retrieved from http://www.trcollege.net/articles/50-integrating-tribal-people-into-indian-mainstream
10. *Gujarati People (2012).* Retrieved from http://www.bharatonline.com/gujarat/culture/people.html.

11. *Indian tribal People (2012)*. Retrieved from http://www. indianetzone.com/37/indian_tribal_people.htm.
12. *Indian Tribes (2012)*. Retrieved from http://www.ecoindia. com/tribes/
13. *Issues (2012)*. Retrieved from http://www.bbc.co.uk/tribe/topics/issues.shtml.
14. Jairth, M. (1991). *Tribal economy and society*, First edition, Mittal Publications, New Delhi, pp. 1-30.
15. Jagawat, H. (2012). *Tribal and Forest in Western India*, Retrieved from http://www.nmsadguru.org/TRIBAL_AND_ FORESTS _IN_WESTERN _INDIA.pdf.
16. Kumar, A. (2012). *The tribal people and ethnic races throughout the world have developed their own culture, customs, cults, religious rites, taboos, totems, legends and myths, folk-fores and song, foods, medicinal practices, etc.*, Retrieved from http://www.science20.com/humboldt_fellow_ and_science/blog/tribal_people_ and_ethnic_ races_ throughout_world_ have_developed_their_own_culture_ customs_cults_
17. *Missionaries arrested in north-east India (2003)*, Retrieved from http://www.worthynews.com/400-missionaries-arrested-in-northeast-india
18. Mullah, M., Parveen, N., and Ahshanullah, M. (2007). *Tribal people and their socio-economic characteristics in Rangamati Sadar Thana*, BRAC University Journal, Volume IV, No. 1, p. 47.
19. *Political union of North-East India (2012)*. Retrieved from http://indiansaga.com/history/postindependence/north_east.html
20. *Problems of Tribal Communities (2012)*. Retrieved from http://www.sociologyguide.com/tribal-society/problems-of-tribal.php
21. *Rajasthani People (2012)*. Retrieved from http://www.rajasthantravelportal.com/RajasthanCulture/Rajasthan-People.htm
22. Sanjoy Deka (2011). *Health and Nutrition status of the Indian Tribals of Tripura and effects on education*, Retrieved from http://www.studentpulse.com/articles/407/health-and-nutritional-status-of-the-indian-tribes-of-tripura-and-effects-on-education.
23. The Hindu (June 2, 2012). *A peek into the lives of tribal people*, Retrieved from http://www.thehindu.com/news/cities/Visakhapatnam/article3482781.ece
24. *The People (2012)*. Retrieved from http://www.webindia 123.com/territories/andaman/people/lifestyle.htm
25. *The Tribal States in India (2012)*. Retrieved from http://www.walkthroughindia.com/lifestyle/the-tribal-states-of-india/

26. *Tribal situation in India's North-east: emerging issues and ongoing anthropological attention (2012)*, Retrieved from http://www.nomadit.co.uk/iuaes/iuaes2013/panels.php5? PanelID=1527
27. Various informations are taken from wikipedia of *Avivasi, Human, India Tribal Belts, Indigenous peoples, Scheduled Castes and Scheduled Tribes.*

7

Employment Avenues in Government and Corporate Sectors for Tribal People

Tarun Kumar Bahadur

Introduction

Indian tribal people play a key part in constructing the cultural heritage of India. They occupy a major part in the history of India as they are considered as the true habitants of India. The tribal people are scattered in different parts of India and they form a considerable number of the population of India. The traditional and cultural distinction of each tribal community has made them distinguishable from each other and their cultural and traditional heritage add colour and variation to the Indian culture as a whole and form a compact culture. Indian tribal people reside in approximately fifteen percent of the country's area. They primarily live in various ecological and geo-climatic conditions ranging from plains, forests, hills and inaccessible areas that perhaps lie dotted in the panoramic Indian terrain.

From the 1850s the tribal communities were loosely referred to as the *depressed classes*. The early part of 20th century saw a flurry of activities in the British Raj to assess the feasibility of responsible self government for India. In 1935 the British passed The Government of India Act 1935, designed to give Indian provinces greater self-rule and set up a national federal structure. Reservation of seats for depressed classes was incorporated into the act, which came into force in 1937. The act brought the term *"Scheduled Caste"* into use, and defined the group as including such castes, races or tribes or part of groups within castes, races or tribes, which appear to His Majesty in Council to correspond to the classes of persons formerly known as the *depressed classes,* as His Majesty in Council may prefer.

Constitutional Status

The framers of the Constitution took note of the fact that certain communities in the country were suffering from extreme social, educational and economic backwardness arising out of age-old practice of untouchability and certain others on account of this primitive agricultural practices, lack of infrastructure facilities and geographical isolation, and who need special consideration for safeguarding their interests and for their accelerated socio-economic development. These communities were notified as Scheduled Castes and Scheduled Tribes as per provisions contained in Clause 1 of Articles 341 and 342 of the Constitution respectively. Article 46 of the Constitution stats that, *"The State shall promote, with special care, the education and economic interests of the weaker sections of the people, and in particular of the scheduled castes and schedules tribes, and shall protect them from social injustice and all forms of social exploitation."* Articles 330, 332, 335, 338 to 342 and the entire fifth and sixth schedules of the Constitution deal with special provisions for implementation of the objectives set forth in Article 46. These provisions need to be fully utilised for the benefit of these weaker sections of our society.

According to Article 342 of the Indian Constitution, at present, there exist 697 tribes as notified by the Central Government. These Indian tribal groups of people have been notified to reside in more than one State. More than half of the Indian tribal population is concentrated in the States of Madhya Pradesh, Chhattisgarh, Maharashtra, Orissa, Jharkhand and Gujarat, whereas in Haryana, Punjab, Delhi, Pondicherry and Chandigarh no community has been notified as a specific tribal group. Though the tribal people in the earlier eras were not much forward but in recent times they are

Table 7.1 Tribes in Assam

Autonomous Districts			*Non-autonomous Districts*
Chakma	(13) Hongsung	(32) Singson	Barmans in Cachar
Dimasa, Kachari	(14) Harangkhwal, Rangkhol	(33) Sithou	Bodo
Garo	(15) Jongbe	(34) Sukte	Deori
Hmar		(35) Thado	Hojai
Khasi, Jaintia, Synteng, Pnar, War, Bhoi, Lyngngam	(16) Khawchung	(36) Thangngeu	Sonowal
Any Kuki tribes including:	(17) Khawathlang, Khothalong	(37) Uibuh	Lalung
(1) Biate, Biete	(18) Khelma	(38) Vaiphei	Mech
(2) Changsan	(19) Kholhou	Hajong	Mishing
(3) Chongloi	(20) Kipgen	Lakher	Rabha-bandaru
(4) Darlong	(21) Kuki	Man (Tai speaking)	borokachari
	(22) Lengthang	Any Mizo (Lushai) tribes	
	(23) Lhangum		

(Contd.)

(Contd. Table 7.1)

Autonomous Districts			Non-autonomous districts
(5) Doungel	(24) Lhoujem	Mikir	
(6) Gamalhou	(25) Lhouvun	Any Naga tribes	
(7) Gangte	(26) Lupheng	Pawi	
(8) Guite	(27) Mangjel	Syntheng	
(9) Hanneng	(28) Misao – Negrito	Burya Sikh	
(10) Haokip, Haupit	(29) Riang	Thengal Kachari	
(11) Haolai	(30) Sairhem		
(12) Hengna	(31) Selnam		

seen in some sectors of economical, educational and social development. The history says that India was the abode of various tribal groups since the commencement period of Indian history. The term *"Scheduled Tribes"* refers to specific indigenous people whose status is acknowledged to some formal degree by national legislation. A collective term in use locally to describe most of these peoples is *"Upajati"* (literally *"clans/tribes/groups"*).

Tribes of North East India

In the north eastern part of India, there is a concentration of a number of tribes. Meghalaya is the abode of a number of tribal communities who have settled down in large numbers. The tribal people of Meghalaya are categorised in two major groups namely the *Garos* and *Hynniewtrep*. The Garo tribal community occupies a major part of tribal communities of Meghalaya. Some of the Mizoram tribes are Chakma tribes which is one of the important tribes of Mizoram. The Pawi Tribes of Mizoram are named not after the name of the clan but after the name of the place where there are residing. Another important tribe of Mizoram is Ralte tribes. Manipur houses quite a number of tribes. The tribes of Manipur are as follows *Aimol, Anal, Angami, Chiru, Chothe, Gangte, Hmar, Kabui, Kacha Naga, Koirao, Koireng, Kom, Lamgang, Mao, Maram, Maring, Lushai tribes, Monsang, Moyon, Paite, Purum, Ralte, Sema, Simte, Sukte, Tangkhul, Thadou, Vaiphei and Zou*. The largest population in Assam is that of the Tibeto Burmese descent known as the Bodo tribe and Mishing tribe. Major tribes of Assam make out their livelihood through agriculture and by selling their handicrafts. List of tribes residing in Assam enlisted in the Constitution as Scheduled tribes as given below:

Demographic Profile of Scheduled Tribes in Assam

The census 2001 reveals that Scheduled tribes constitute 12.4 per cent of the total population of the state (3,308,570 ST out of 26,655,528 state populations as per census 2001). The state has registered 15.1 per cent decadal growth of ST population in 1991-2001. Among them, Boro represents nearly half of the total ST population of the state (40.9 per cent) followed by Mri (17.8 per cent), Mikir (10.7 per cent) and Rabha (8.4 per cent). The composition of ST population in the state is furnished in the following table.

The ST population in Assam is predominantly rural with 95.3 per cent rural and only 4.7 per cent urban population. Of the eight major

Table 7.2 Population of Major STs, 2001 Census

SL. No.	*Name of the Scheduled Tribe*	*Total Population*	*Proportion to the Total ST Population*
1.	All Scheduled Tribes	3,308,570	100%
2.	Boro	1,352,771	40.9
3.	Miri	587,310	17.8
4.	Mikir	353,513	10.7
5.	Rabha	277,517	8.4
6.	Kachari	235,881	7.1
7.	Lalung	170,622	5.2
8.	Dimasa	110,976	3.4
9.	Deori	41,161	1.2

Source: Office of the Registrar General, Census of India, 2001.

STs, Dimasa have recorded the highest 10.4 per cent urban population, followed by Mikir (8.3 per cent). On the other hand Miri have recorded the lowest 1.8 per cent urban population. North Cachar Hills and Karbi Anglong the two autonomous hill districts of Assam are predominantly tribal housing two important STs of Assam, i.e., the Dimasa and Mikir (now recognised as Karbi). As per 2001 Census, the North Cachar Hills has got the highest 68.3 per cent ST population, followed by Karbi Anglong (55.7 per cent). In absolute number Karbi Anglong is on top sharing 13.7 per cent of the total ST population of the state. Hailakandi, Karimganj, and Cachar districts have a negligible presence of ST population.

The ST population of Assam has recorded 62.5 per cent literacy rate, which is well above the national average for STs (47.1 per cent). The male and female literacy rate of 72.3 per cent and 52.4 per cent respectively show that women are lagging behind by 19.9 percentage points. Kachari (Sonowal) with 81.4 per cent literacy rate are well ahead of others. On the other hand it is low among Mikir (53.7 per cent). Among Kachari (Sonowal), the female literacy rate of 74.4 per cent is quite close to male (88.2 per cent). Gender gap in literacy among Miri, however, has been recorded to be the highest. With 71.4 per cent male and 48.3 per cent female literacy, the Miri women are lagging way behind by as much as 23.1 per cent.

Work Participation Rate (WPR)

According to 2001 Census, 43.2 per cent of the STs have been registered as workers, which is below the aggregated national

Table 7.3 Distribution of Total, Main and Marginal Workers among STs

T/M/F	*Total Workers* (*Percentage to Total Population)*	*Main Workers* (*Percentage to Total Workers)*	*Marginal Workers* (*Percentage to Total Workers)*
Total	1,430,404	934,217	496,187
	(43.2%)	(65.3%)	(34.7%)
Male	847,229	685,708	161,521
	(50.5%)	(80.9%)	(19.1%)
Female	583,175	248,509	334,666
	(35.8%)	(42.6%)	(57.4%)

Source: Office of the Registrar General, Census of India, 2001.

figure for STs (49.1 per cent). Of the total workers 65.3 per cent are main workers and 34.7 per cent marginal workers. The WPR of 35.8 per cent among females is high though lower than males (50.5 per cent). Gender wise disparity is, however, distinct in case of main workers; 80.9 per cent among males and only 42.6 per cent among females are main workers.

Among the major STs in the state, Deori have recorded the highest WPR of 55.5 per cent. It is lowest among Dimasa (38.9 per cent). Deori have recorded almost equal participation of male and female in the workforce with 58 per cent male and 52.9 per cent female WPR. On the contrary the gender gap in WPR is quite significant among Rabha (male 51.2 per cent, female 30.7 per cent), Lalung (male 51.8 per cent, female 33.1 per cent), and Dimasa (male 47 per cent, female 30.4 per cent).

Category of Workers

The Scheduled Tribes of Assam are predominantly cultivators as 70.6 per cent of the total ST main workers have been recorded as cultivators, while merely 6.1 per cent as agricultural labourer. At the individual ST level, Miri have recorded a high of 85.6 per cent of their total main workers as cultivators, closely followed by Mikir (79.3 per cent) and Deori (78.2 per cent). Rabha have recorded the highest percentage of agricultural labourers, which is only 9 per cent of total main workers thereby indicating that majority of the STs in Assam are not landless.

Government and Corporate Sector Job Opportunity for ST

In response to the burden of social stigma and economic backwardness borne by persons belonging to some of India's castes, the Constitution of India allows for special provisions for members of these castes. Articles 341 and 342 include a list of castes and tribes entitled to such provisions and all those groups included in this list and subsequent modifications to this list are referred to as, respectively, *"Scheduled Castes"* (SC) and *"Scheduled Tribes"* (ST). These special provisions have taken two main forms.

1. The first is action against adverse discrimination towards persons from the SC and the ST.

2. The second is compensatory discrimination in favour of persons from the SC and the ST.

Compensatory discrimination has taken the form of guaranteeing seats in national and state legislatures and in village *panchayats*, places in educational institutions, and the reservation of a certain proportion of government jobs for the SC and the ST. In the mind of the Indian public it is job reservation that is seen as the most important of the public concessions towards the SC and the ST and it is the one which arouses the strongest of passions. On the one hand, there is the demand to extend reservation to persons who are not from the SC or the ST but who, nevertheless, belong to economic and socially backward groups - the *'other backward classes'* (OBC). On the other hand, there is the demand from the SC and the ST to extend reservation to private sector jobs. On the basis of data for the 55th round of the NSS, the distribution of 77,535 men, between the ages of 25 and 45 (*"prime-age"* males), and living in the 16 major states of India and the Union Territory of Delhi, by their educational standard, between the following categories of economic status:

1. Own account workers (self-employed);
2. Unpaid family workers;
3. Regular salaried or wage workers;
4. Casual wage labourers;
5. Employers;
6. Seeking and/or available for work.

Of these six categories, the first four were the main categories of economic status for prime-age men: 29,787 of the 77,535 men (38 per cent) were own account workers; 17,314 men (22 per cent of the total) were regular salaried or wage workers; 19,296 men (25 per cent of the total) were casual labourers; and 8,476 men (11 per cent of the total) were unpaid family workers. Being a casual labourer or an own account worker was largely the preserve of poorly educated men while regular salaried or wage workers were largely drawn from the ranks of the better educated men: of the 19,296 prime age men who were casual wage labourers, 92 per cent had an education standard less than secondary school and 49 per cent were illiterate; of the 29,787 men who were own account workers, 69 per cent had an education standard less than secondary school and 25 per cent were illiterate; on the other hand, of the 17,314 prime-age men who were regular salaried or wage workers, 61 per cent were educated to secondary (or above) and 27 per cent were graduates (or above).

Only 1,639 men (2 per cent of the total) were unemployed in the conventional meaning of the term. Moreover, job search appeared to be the prerogative of better educated men: of the 1,639 *"unemployed"* men, 76 per cent were educated to secondary level or above and 40 percent were graduates or postgraduates. If one was to establish a hierarchy of communities in terms of the *"desirability"* of the economic status of their prime-age men then, undoubtedly, SC and the non-Christian ST, a large proportion of whose (prime age) men were casual labourers, would lie at the bottom; *"forward caste"* Hindus, with one third of their men in salaried or wage employment and only one tenth of their men working as casual labourers, would be at the top; and sandwiched between them would be the OBC (non-Muslim and Muslim) and Muslims. By far, non-Christian men from the ST and men from the SC had the lowest level of educational achievement; 52 per cent of the former and 43 per cent of the latter were illiterate. They were followed by Christian men from the ST (35 per cent of whom were illiterate) and Muslims: 35 percent of Muslims from the OBC, and 33 per cent of Muslims who were not from the OBC, were illiterate. The best educated men were *"forward caste"* Hindus and Christians: only 10 per cent of Hindu, and 6 per cent of Christian, prime-age men were illiterate and 24 per cent of Hindu, and 18 per cent of Christian, prime-age men were graduates.

The above NSS data and corresponding analysis indicate that ST people of prime age are mostly engaged in temporary and casual jobs of government and corporate sectors. The category of poorly educated status of these people restricts them from getting placed on white colour jobs in these sectors.

Should there be Job Quotas in the Private Sector?

The goal of reservation in India has been to bring about an improvement in the welfare who historically has been economically and socially depressed. But, in arriving at this judgement about who should be eligible for reservation, the criterion has been a person's caste rather than his income or wealth. Consequently, groups belonging to what Article 115 of the Indian Constitution calls "socially and educationally backward classes" have benefited from reservation even though, in practice, many of these groups could not be regarded as "backward". This has meant that many of the benefits of reservation have been captured by well-off groups from the depressed classes (for example, chamars from the SC) while poorer groups from the depressed (for example, bhangis from the SC) have failed to benefit.

The government's job reservation policies placed little emphasis on improving the job-related attributes of persons from the ST. It showed that even modest improvements in the education levels of SC/ST persons could deliver significant employment gains. In a significant departure from its oft-repeated stance that implementation of quotas in private sector should be "voluntary," the UPA government is considering enactment of a law to extend job reservations to the non-government sector. The government had so far maintained that it would leave it to the private sector to consider introducing job reservations. But now they are bringing both an amendment to the Constitution, as well as enacting a new law for the purpose. Law ministry has already brushed aside the view of attorney-general Milon Banerjee that there's no room in the Constitution for getting the private sector to implement quotas.

Lastly it can be said that an alternative and more effective, way of raising the proportion of prime-age men from the SC/ST groups in regular salaried or wage employment would be to improve their employment-related attributes through training and orientation courses.

References

1. Data Highlights: The Scheduled Tribes, Census of India 2001.
2. Has Job Reservation Been Effective? Caste, Religion, and Economic Status in India - (Article), Amit Varma, Vani K. Borooah, Amaresh Dubey and Sriya Iyer. 2005 Annual Conference on Religion, Economics and Culture, The Indira Gandhi Institute of Development Research, Mumbai.
3. UPA government plans job quotas in the private sector: Times of India, 1 May, 2010.
4. Constitution of India, Durga Das Basu.

8

Social Security of Tribals in India: Needs and Government Initiatives

Fazana Alim

Introduction

The tribal population is identified as the aboriginal inhabitants of the country. They are seen in almost every State of India. For centuries, they have been living a simple life based on the natural environment and have developed cultural patterns congenial to their physical and social environment. References of such tribal groups are found even in the literature on the ancient period, right from the Ramayana and the Mahabharata periods. Broadly speaking the tribal's may be geographically located in four groups: (1) *North-east India:* Assam, Manipur, Meghalaya, Nagaland, Tripura, Mizoram; (2) *Eastern India:* West Bengal, Bihar, Orissa; (3) *Central and Western India:* Madhya Pradesh, Rajasthan, Gujarat, part of Maharashtra and Northern Andhra Pradesh; and (4) *Southern India:* The Hilly regions of Tamil Nadu, Kerala, Western and Northern Karnataka and Andhra Pradesh.

The population of Scheduled Tribes (STs) according to the 2001 census is 8.43 crores, constituting about 8.2 per cent of the country's total population grown at the rate of 24.45 per cent during 1991-2001. Of these, about 1.32 million (1.57 per cent belongs to Primitive Tribal Groups (PTGs) The percentage of population of the Scheduled Tribes varies among the states. More than half of the Scheduled Tribes population is concentrated in the states of Madhya Pradesh,

Chhattisgarh, Maharashtra, Odisha, Jharkhand and Gujarat however the tribal percentages of these states' population vary from about 8 to 22 per cent. On the other hand, several smaller states, notably in the north-east of the country, have much higher percentages (ranging from 64 to 95 per cent), but account for a small proportion of Scheduled Tribes. Agriculture is the most important economic pursuit of a vast majority of the tribal communities. With the given agro-climatic conditions and low level of technology, the productivity is low and the return supports a low quality subsistence economy. The approach to tribal developments adopted so for may be classified under three heads. Priority was accorded to protective measures and dimension of exploitation in areas of land alienation, money lending, collection of forest produce and liqueur vending. Development of infrastructure has been the major area of investment particularly of the state share of the total outlays. The small, marginal, fragmented, unirrigated and mono crop agriculture holdings and low productive livestock population do not offer adequate opportunities for their livelihood. These factors compel them for migration to nearby towns for subsistence, leaving their productive assets idle. Tribal's residing in remote areas are still devoid of common infrastructure facilities of road and communication, health and education and safe drinking water which do not allow them to absorb technological and financial facilities provided by government.

Tribal's have traditionally lived in about 15 per cent of the country's geographical areas, mainly forests, hills and undulating inaccessible terrain in plateau areas, rich in natural resources. They have lived as isolated entities for centuries, largely untouched by the society around them. This seclusion has been responsible for the slower growth, dissimilar pattern of their socio-economic and cultural development and inability to negotiate and cope with the consequences of their involuntary integration into mainstream society and economy. Tribals continue to be socio-economically backward. The Constitution of India has provided many privileges to the scheduled tribes considering their complex problems in terms of geographical isolation, socio-economic backwardness, distinctive culture, poor infrastructure facilities, language and religion, exploitation by various groups. There are many acute problems of the tribal peoples in the country that needs immediate attention and early solution. The problems relate to various aspects of tribal peoples viz. social, economical, educational, health, religion, land, law and order situation, self-centered tendency and so on. Many of these problems cannot be well understood due-to lack of necessary and adequate information.

Article 342 Scheduled Tribes

The term *'Scheduled Tribes'* first appeared in the Constitution of India. Article 366 (25) defined scheduled tribes as *"such tribes or tribal communities or parts of or groups within such tribes or tribal communities as are deemed under Article 342 to be Scheduled Tribes for the purposes of this constitution"*. Article 342, which is described below, prescribes procedure to be followed in the matter of specification of scheduled tribes.

1. The President may, with respect to any State or Union territory, and where it is a state, after consultation with the Governor there of by public notification, specify the tribes or tribal communities or parts of or groups within tribes or tribal communities which shall, for the purposes of this constitution, is deemed to be scheduled tribes in relation to that state or Union Territory, as the case may be.

2. Parliament may by law include in or exclude from the list of Scheduled tribes specified in a notification issued under clause (1) any tribe or tribal community or part of or group within any tribe or tribal community, but save as aforesaid, a notification issued under the said clause shall not be varied by any subsequent notification.

Thus, the first specification of Scheduled Tribes in relation to a particular State/Union Territory is by a notified order of the President, after consultation with the State governments concerned. These orders can be modified subsequently only through an Act of Parliament. The above Article also provides for listing of scheduled tribes State/Union Territory wise and not on an all India basis.

In exercise of the powers conferred by Clause (1) of Article 342 of the Constitution of India, the President, after consultation with the State Governments concerned have promulgated so far 9 orders specifying the Scheduled Tribes in relation to the state and union territories. Out of these, eight are in operation at present in their original or amended form. One order namely the Constitution (Goa, Daman and Diu) Scheduled Tribes order 1968 has become defunct on account of reorganisation of Goa, Daman and Diu in 1987. Under the Goa, Daman and Diu reorganisation Act 1987 (18 of 1987) the list of Scheduled Tribes of Goa has been transferred to part XIX of the Schedule to the Constitution (Scheduled Tribes) Order, 1950 and that of Daman and Diu II of the Schedule of the Constitution (Scheduled Tribes) (Union Territories) Order, 1951.

Importance of Tribal Development

Tribal development as a subject has been an important area of inquiry in the social sciences. In recent years, the subject has acquired immense importance both at the national and international level The active support and hectic campaign by a number of international Non-Governmental Organisations (NGOs) championing the cause of the *'indigenous people'* has made it a burning issue all over the world. Further, United Nations' declaration of 1993 as the *International Year for World's Indigenous People* provides ample evidence of the growing concern of the world's highest body for the development of the indigenous people all over the world. The United Nations' Working Group on Indigenous Population in its first Draft Universal Declaration on the Rights of Indigenous People in 1988 had given the call for the promotion of indigenous societies, their culture and traditions through ethno-development and comprehensive participation. Recognising the indigenous peoples' inalienable rights of ownership and possession of lands traditionally occupied by them and their right to pursue their traditional and other economic activities without adverse discrimination, it had given them the right to decide their own future development. Further, the revision of the draft in 1990 has brought issues like their right to natural endowments, treaty rights, autonomy, self-government and self-determination, which have irked many nation states including India.

Living in remote forests and hill regions, the tribal people of India have remained unrecognised and ignored and suffered a long neglect and isolation all through the centuries. Speaking over 150 languages and 225 subsidiary languages, the tribal's are scattered along the length and breadth of India from the Himalayas to the Indian Ocean and from the Arabian Sea to the Eastern Frontiers. In a land of kaleidoscopic diversity, these tribes who have contributed to the richness of our culture and heritage are at different stages of development and their problems differ from area to area and even within their own groups. The socio-economic structure in tribal communities is markedly different from that of the non-tribal or advanced groups of people. The level of tribal economy is quite uneven though their economy is largely self-sufficient, unstructured and non-specialised. On the one extreme, there are tribal communities who are at the food gathering and haunting stage and, at the other extreme; they have become undistinguishable from the moden agricultural and industrial societies. Similarly differences have arisen in their educational status. Some of these communities particularly in the north-east are far ahead of the general educational level in the country but, at the other end, there are communities which are still at a pre-literate stage.

The structure of their economy is generally based on forests and on sea and forests for those living in coastal and island areas. Small in size and operation, the use of simple and crude technology is an important structural feature of the tribal economy where the family acts as a unit of both production and consumption. The community itself acts like a co-operative unit and the tribal communities living in a village or location are economically inter-dependent. The essential characteristics of these communities are primitive traits, geographical isolation, distinctive culture, and shyness of contact with the community at large and economic backwardness.

Constitutional Safeguards for the Children

India is a welfare State, committed to the welfare and development of its people and of vulnerable sections in particular. The preamble, Directive Principles of State Policy, Fundamental Rights and specific sections, viz., Articles 38, 39 and 46 in the Constitution of India, stand testimony to the commitment of the State to its people. Socially disadvantaged groups of Scheduled Castes/Scheduled Tribes have received special focus over the years for their social and economic advancement. Government has taken several steps for framing appropriate policies needed to design and implement various welfare programmes for achieving the objective of creating favourable environment to ensure speedy socio economic development of SCs/ STs. For the well being of these communities, special target oriented programmes are being implemented by earmarking funds, providing subsidies, offering reservations in employment and educational institutions etc.

The Constitution of India incorporates several special provisions for the promotion of educational and economic interest of Scheduled Tribes and their protection from social injustice and all forms of exploitation. These objectives are sought to be achieved through a strategy known as the Tribal Sub-Plan strategy, which was adopted at the beginning of the Fifth Five Year Plan. The strategy seeks to ensure adequate flow of funds for tribal development form the State Plan allocations, schemes/programmes of Central Ministries/Departments, financial and Developmental Institutions. The cornerstone of this strategy has been to ensure earmarking of funds for TSP by States/ UTs in proportion to the ST population in those State/UTs.

Pre-independence tribal's living in forests, hills and even on the plain were isolated from the mainstream. The status of the tribal's was unsatisfactory during princely and colonial region. It was a policy of neglect and saga of exploitation. Due to this, their land and forest were slowly and gradually grabbed by the rich people like landlords and money lenders. They were turned into bonded labourers, leading a life of extreme poverty and misery. The excessive encroachment on their rights in forest land led to an expression of anger in the form of riots. Thus independent India inherited a complex tribal problem' from the British colonial system. The major thrust is to solve the tribal problem in view of our commitment to the objectives of social justice, social, economic and political equality of status and opportunity as enshrined in the preamble to the constitution. The makers of the constitution paid special attention towards the tribal problems and tried to eradicate it for ever. The concern of the constituent members of the constitution for protection and promotion of the interests of the deprived sections is amply reflected in the preamble of the constitution which was amended in 1976. It succinctly proclaims the aims and objects of the constitution, i.e., to constitute into a Sovereign, Socialist, Secular, Democratic Republic.

The Scheduled Areas and Scheduled Tribes Commission for the Tribal Welfare and Development, 1961 headed by Sri U.N. Dhebar observed that the constitution arranged for the provision of resources and provided the required institutional apparatus. Some of the safeguards for the tribal's in the constitution were initially in co-operated for ten years. The constitution deliberately laid emphases on both aspects, i.e., protective as well as developmental. The members of the constitution were keen that the tribal's join the mainstreams of the national life in order to retain their traits and cultural heritage. Keeping this in view, the tribal status in constitution made special provision for their social and economic development. The provisions are contained in Articles 46, 244, 330, 332, 334, 335,338, 339, 342 and schedules V, VI to the constitution of India. The constitution also permits for change in laws, according to the tribal situation in concerned area. Under Article 41 of the Constitution of India, it is the responsibility of the Government to provide Education. It is a joint responsibility of both the '*State*' and the '*Central*' Government. The Fifth Schedule of the Constitution provides for administration and control of Scheduled Areas and Scheduled Tribes and gives powers to the Governors to make regulations for the peace and good governance of the Scheduled Areas. Similarly, the Sixth Schedule also contains specific provisions for the administration of tribal areas in the States of Assam, Meghalaya, Tripura and Mizoram. Deriving force from these enabling provisions in the Constitution aimed at ensuring social, economic, and political equity, several specific legislations have further been enacted by the Central and the State Governments for the welfare and protection of STs and their tribal domain.

Recognising the special needs of STs, the Constitution of India made certain special safeguards to protect these communities from all the possible exploitation and thus ensure social justice. While Article 14 confers equal rights and opportunities to all, Article 15 prohibits *discrimination against any citizen on the grounds of sex, religion, race, caste etc.* Article 15(4) enjoins upon the *State to make special provisions for the advancement of any socially and educationally backward classes*; Article 16(4) empowers *the State to make provisions for reservation in appointments or posts in favour of any backward class of citizens, which in the opinion of the State, is not adequately represented in the services under the State;* Article 46 enjoins upon *the State to promote with special care the educational and economic interests of the weaker sections of the people and, in particular, ... the STs and promises to protect them from social injustice and all forms of exploitation*. Further, while Article 275(1) promises *grant-*

in-aid for promoting the welfare of STs and for raising the level of administration of the Scheduled Areas, Articles 330, 332 and 335 stipulate *reservation of seats for STs in the Lok Sabha and in the State Legislative Assemblies and in services.* Finally, the Constitution also empowers the State to appoint a Commission to investigate the conditions of the socially and educationally backward classes (Article 340) and to specify those Tribes or Tribal Communities deemed to be as STs (Article 342).

The Constitution of the India under Article 46 contemplate that a State shall promote with special care the Educational and Economic interests of the weaker sections and in particular of Scheduled Castes and Scheduled Tribes and protect them from social injustice and exploitation in all forms. Late Pandit Jawaharlal Nehru, the first Priminster of India, laid down the approach of development of Scheduled Tribes during the times of geneous of the community. Dhebar Commission appointed Article 339 of the Constitution of India also endorsed this approach and observed that the tribal's should be integrated with the rest of the Society while allowing them to continue their traditions, ethos, arts, culture and their identity. Their right on land and forest should be safeguarded and they should be trained for their administration and development. The Hon'ble President of India in their Order No. 35/36-60-TC, Government of India, dated 14-10-1961 appointed a Committee for Scheduled Areas and Scheduled Tribes headed by Sri Dhebar. In pursuance of the recommendations of the Commissioner of Scheduled Areas and Scheduled Tribes that where the ST population in all the States was ten lakhs and above and also in Scheduled Areas. The Tribal Cultural Research and Training Institute (TCR and TI) was established during 1962-63 vide G.O.Ms.No.1242, Education Department, dated 02-05-1962 with the following aims and objectives:

1. Monographic and Ethnographic Studies;
2. Socio-Economic and Benchmark Surveys;
3. Planning for Tribal Development;
4. Evaluation Studies of on going Tribal Development Programmes.

As per the recommendations of the Dhebar Commission Report a separate Tribal Welfare Directorate from Social Welfare Department was created in the year 1966 exclusively for tribal's to uplift the economic, educational and social conditions of the tribal's as the problems of Scheduled Tribes are quite different from those relating to Scheduled Castes who have lived for centuries with other castes in the plains and that the problems relating to Health, Education backwardness of STs needs special attention.

Special Central Assistance and Grants Under Article 275 (1) of the Constitution

Special Central Assistance is given to States/UTs to supplement their efforts in tribal development through Tribal Sub-Plan. This assistance is basically meant for family-oriented income-generating schemes in the sectors of agriculture, horticulture, minor irrigation, soil conservation, animal husbandry, forests, education, cooperatives, fisheries, village and small scale industries and for minimum needs programme. Grants are also given to States/UTs, under the first proviso to article 275 (1) of the Constitution to meet the costs of projects for tribal development and for raising the level of administration of Scheduled Area therein on par with the rest of the State/UT. Part of the funds is utilized for setting up of Residential Schools for providing quality education to tribal students.

Tribal Welfare

It will be very apt to refer to Pandit Jawaharlal Nehru, the first Prime Minister of Independent India who had a key role to play in planning and implementing various programmes for tribal development, and bringing them into the fold of nationalism. Pandit Jawaharlal Nehru's Panchsheel (*Five principles*) envisaged the development of people in the lines of own genius, respect of tribal rights in lands and forests, encourage self-management, work through tribal's own social and cultural institutions; indicator of success to be sought in quality of man and not in the amount of money spent remains the most important reference point in the formulation of tribal policies in India. All the five principles are like five parables protecting the rich culture, tradition and rights of the Scheduled Tribes of India. There are 573 major tribal groups in India, each one associated with a specific geographic area, some more dispersed than others. Most have their own language, which is generally different from the *'mainstream'* language of the state in which they live. There are a total of 270 such tribal languages. Tribal people tend to live in two main types of situations: (a) in *'mixed'* (tribal and nontribal) rural communities, within reach of educational and other opportunities and resources, and (b) in habitations that are small in size and located in relatively inaccessible hilly or forested areas of the country.

A number of commissions and committees were appointed in the recent past to look in to the problems of developments in the tribal areas in the country and they have recommended a number of measures to remove the socio-economic imbalances and also to break down their old psychological barrier, which existed in the tribal areas. The important commission and committees appointed so far are:

1. The Social Welfare Team of the Committee on plan projects 1959.
2. The Verrier Elwin Committee on Tribal Development.
3. The Committee on Tribal Economy in Forest Areas -1967.
4. The Schedules Areas and Scheduled Tribal Commission (Dhebar Committee 1961).
5. The Special working Group on Cooperatives for Backward Classes -1961 (Shri M.D. Bhargava as its Chairman).
6. The Task Force on Development of Tribal Areas -1972.
7. The Dube Committee -1972.
8. The Study Team on co-operative Structure in Tribal Development Project Areas -1976.
9. The Study Group on Relief of Indebtedness Land, Alienation and Restoration in Development Agency Area -1973 (Shri P.S. Appu as its Chairman).
10. The team of Marketing, Credit and Cooperation in Tribal Areas-1978 (Shri K.S. Bawa Committee).
11. The Working Group on Development of Scheduled Tribes during the 7th Five Years Plans (1985-90).

The Dhobar Commission (1961) recommended an integrated approach based on the minimum essential items like food, drinking water, employment, educational health and village road. The task force on Development of Tribal Areas constituted in 1972 suggested that the ecological, occupational and social preemptors of the tribal population should be properly assessed for formulation of a policy and its implementation so that a steady flow of benefits could be assured to the tribal people. The Dupe committee in 1972 tried to define a new strategy for tribal development and suggested that the problem of tribal development should be defined at the national level and national efforts required for tackling it, worked out. It also suggested an integrated area development approach in consonance with the genius and aspirations of the tribal people.

The Tribal Welfare Department's mandate is to safeguard the interests of STs, guarantee rights as laid down in the Constitution and ensure development of the tribal population through various programmes and policies of the department. The department also coordinates with other departments and ministries to achieve their goals. In order to protect the economic and social interests of the tribal's from industrial exploitation and to increase the pace of access to development, the department has adopted what it calls a *Tribal Sub Plan Strategy* since 1975. Under this plan, several programmes have been introduced to bring larger sections of the tribal population under the state's welfare programs. In addition, all other departments of the state are expected to allocate a certain percentage of their annual budgets towards development programmes of scheduled tribes. Among all developmental programmes, the department gives special emphasis to tribal education.

The Tribal Policy: Focus on Formal Education

Realising that Scheduled Tribes are one of the most deprived and marginalised groups with respect to education, a host of programmes and measures were initiated ever since Independence. Elementary education has remained a priority area in all the Five Year Plans and received special attention from the Tribal sub plans (TSP) from the 5th Five Year Plan onwards. Education of Scheduled Tribe children is considered important, not only because of the Constitutional obligation but also as a crucial input for total development of tribal communities.

Formal education is the key to all-round human development. Despite several campaigns to promote formal education ever since independence, the literacy rate among Scheduled Tribes has remained low and the female literacy rate still lower compared to the national female literacy rate. In order to extend the benefit of education to the Scheduled Tribes, the policies for the Scheduled Tribes envisages that Scheduled Tribes are included in the national programme of Sarva Shiksha Abhiyan run by the Ministry of Human Resource Development. Schools and hostels are opened in areas, where no such facilities exist. At least, one model residential school is located in each tribal concentration area. Education is linked with provision of supplementary nutrition. Special incentives like financial assistance, pocket allowance, free distribution of textbooks and school uniforms are provided. Teaching is imparted in the mother tongue of Scheduled Tribes, at least up to the primary level. Educated tribal youths are given employment as teachers, wherever possible. Curricula for Meta skill up gradation are to include aspects of tribal games and sports, archery, identification of plants of medicinal value, crafts art and culture, folk dance and folk songs, folk paintings etc. Not only the policies developed specially for the Scheduled Tribes have focused on education, but also the National Policies on Education 1968 and 1986 have made special mention relating to education of the Scheduled Tribes. NPE 1986 recognised the heterogeneity and diversity of the tribal areas, besides underlining the importance of instruction through the mother tongue and the need for preparing teaching/learning material in the tribal languages. This policy document specified among other things the following:

1. Priority will be accorded to opening primary schools in tribal areas.
2. There is need to develop curricula and devise instructional material in tribal language at the initial stages with arrangements for switchover to regional languages.
3. ST youths will be encouraged to take up teaching in tribal areas.
4. Ashram schools/residential schools will be established on a large scale in tribal areas.
5. Incentive schemes will be formulated for the Scheduled Tribes, keeping in view, their special need and lifestyle.

Sarva Shiksha Aviyan (SSA)

The Sarva Shiksha Abhiyan (SSA) is the flagship programme of Government of India (GoI) to achieve Universal Elementary Education

(UEE) through a time bound integrated approach in partnership with States. Launched in 2001 with a focus on decentralised planning and community ownership, SSA aims to provide useful and relevant education to all children in the 6-14 age groups by 2010. There has been an over all increase in the enrolment of children belonging to Scheduled Tribes. The infusion of the SSA programmes into the tribal habitations has greatly helped in overcoming the problems of managing the schools and reaching the unreached habitations, regular training to teachers and availability of SSA funds to the teachers for developing teaching learning material etc. The BRC/CRC facilities have been extended to tribal habitations for continuous monitoring of the schooling activities in the tribal habitations. Some of the specific interventions being promoted for tribal children under Sarva Shiksha Aviyan (SSA) are:

1. Setting up schools, education guarantee schools (EGS) and alternative schools within one kilometer of all habitations for non-enrolled children and dropouts;
2. Alternative schools provide flexibility in terms of timing, learning modalities, etc.;
3. Upgrading EGS schools to regular schools after two years;
4. Attaching Crèches and pre-school sections *(anganwadis* and *balwadis)* to schools in tribal areas to relieve girls of sibling-care responsibilities.

Physical access to schooling, especially at the upper primary stage is still an issue in some parts of the country in remote tribal areas. The targeted coverage of all éligible habitations for the upper primary school facilities will be a priority. In some remote sparsely populated areas it may be difficult to set up primary schools due to small number of children. This may necessitate residential schools/ hostels for which scope of SSA framework has been enlarged to include construction of residential schools in sparsely populated remote, hilly, desert and tribal blocks. Seasonal migration is common in several tribal areas. Facilities like seasonal hostels may need to be provided in all such blocks with high level of migration to help retain children in villages when parents migrate. Recognising this SSA framework has been amended to give focus to the issue of seasonal migration. SSA envisages a bottom-up approach of planning instead of a top-down approach, as it reflects the reality at the grassroots level. The planning process is participatory in nature and it also focuses on creating a sense of ownership among stakeholders, enhancing awareness and capacity building of programme personnel at various levels.

Ashram Schools

One of the major interventions in the field of educating the Scheduled Tribe children is that of the Ashram schools which have been in vogue for the past many years, and have been functioning in the tribal areas. The main objectives of the Ashram schools as envisaged by the various committees and commissions are:

1. To wean the children away from an atmosphere which is generally not conducive for the development of their personality and outlook;
2. To impart general formal education;
3. To impart training on socially useful vocational/crafts along with the general education;
4. To encourage tribal traditions like folk dances so that the schools are not only mere learning places but also centres of cultural activities;
5. To provide close interaction between the teacher and taught through increased individual attention; and
6. To reduce the dropout rate and to improve the retention capacity of the schools.

Ashram schools are in general residential in nature and the inmates are provided with facilities of boarding and lodging. Moreover, they function within highly structured and systematic framework. The broad policy guidelines for the Ashram schools as envisaged by various committees and study groups on tribal welfare programmes are:

1. Ashram schools should be inter village schools;
2. Ashram schools should be opened in such areas where normal schools cannot be opened; and
3. Most backward tribal groups should be covered.

The working pattern, structure and level of education in Ashram schools differ widely among states. In some of the states like

Maharashtra and Gujarat, they are mostly run by voluntary organisations as private aided schools. Whereas in the states of Andhra Pradesh, Chhattisgarh, Jharkhand, Odisha, Madhya Pradesh and Rajasthan, Ashram schools are exclusively under the Tribal Welfare Department of respective state governments. Both primary and post basic levels of education are available in Maharashtra, Gujarat and Odisha. In case of Madhya Pradesh, Ashram schools are usually up to middle stage and at the secondary stage, these are called *'Model Schools'*. In Rajasthan, all the Ashram schools cover either primary or middle school stage. In Andhra Pradesh, Ashram schools have primary, upper primary and secondary stages of education. In Maharashtra, Gujarat and Andhra Pradesh, Ashram schools are co-educational, whereas in Rajasthan, Madhya Pradesh and Odisha, the Ashram schools are separate for girls and boys. Ashram schools in Odisha are provided at primary, upper primary and secondary levels. Vocational education is imparted in some of the secondary schools. The states of Andhra Pradesh, Chhattisgarh, Kerala, Maharashtra and Odisha have Ashram schools functioning for more than four to five decades. The efforts by these state governments in creating special provisions in these scheduled areas through the TSP, MADA and SCA. The tribal development departments are working towards the development of the Scheduled Tribes and are also providing them education. Residential Ashram schools of Odisha are also managed by the Tribal Welfare Department and the State Education Department is supposed to provide the academic support. The SSA has enabled these schools to obtain certain grants/funds to the teachers and the schools, as well as the BRC/CRC personnel have started visiting these schools for providing academic support. The State government has recently embarked upon creating Model Residential Ashram schools/ Central Ashram schools by upgrading the existing Ashram schools.

The State of Chhattisgarh is one of the youngest states and was carved out from the state of Madhya Pradesh. Unlike the Ashram schools of Madhya Pradesh, where the residences are separate and the schools are separate, the Residential Ashram schools of Chhattisgarh have both the residence and the schools together as has been envisaged in the objective of the Ashram schools in the country. The Tribal Development Department of the government of Kerala has taken initiatives in providing 13 Model Residential Ashram schools (up gradation) and improving the facilities of the existing Residential Schools in the state. The SSA has also initiated process of providing academic inputs to the Ashram schools in the state. The Central Assistance for the Ashram schools which are being provided to these schools is being utilised positively. The other free ships to the children and facilities are provided as per the norms of the Ashram schools with full days food provisions etc. The state of Maharashtra has government managed Residential Ashram schools as well as aided Residential Ashram schools under the Tribal Development Department for the Scheduled Tribe Children.

Tribal Sub-plan

The tribal population habitations are located in difficult and isolated hill/forest areas and terrains. Their socio economic conditions are mostly bound with their unique nature of social and cultural heritage. It is imperative for the State to promote appropriate conditions that would enable the tribal's to have an economic stake in the resources in their area so that they can achieve adequate levels of livelihood and well being. The main tribes in Tamil Nadu are *Malayali, Toda, Kurumba, Paniya, Irular, Kattunayakan, Kanikar, Palaiyan, Sholagar, Kadar, Veddar* etc., of which *Toda, Kurumba, Kattunayakan, Paniya and Irular* are primitive Tribes. The Tribal Sub Plan was introduced to ensure that all general development sectors at the State level earmark funds in proportion to ST population so that adequate benefits from all the concerned sectors flow to the tribal groups. Tribal Sub Plan (TSP) strategy, which came into being in the Fifth Five Year Plan with the twin objectives of area and sectoral approaches, envisages protection of the interests of the Scheduled Tribes through legal and administrative measures and developmental and welfare activities through plan efforts. Empowerment of these historically disadvantaged tribal people requires more provision of the basic capabilities for integrating them into growth process. The Tribal Sub Plan has been under implementation since 1976-77 with the aim of (1) helping the Scheduled Tribe families to cross the poverty line and (2) to provide basic amenities and facilities in their areas. The size of the Tribal Sub Plan should be in proportion to Scheduled Tribe population to the State's total population. As far as Tamil Nadu is concerned, the flow to Tribal Sub Plan should be not less than 1.03 per cent of the

State Plan outlay. The objective of the Tribal Sub Plan is to assist the Tribal families in improving their socio-economic and educational status. Economic Development Programmes in the fields of horticulture, animal husbandry, soil-conservation, minor irrigation, sericulture, small industries, bee-keeping etc., and area oriented development programmes like provision of drinking water, formation of roads, electrification, providing education and health facilities, improving forestry, communication, co-operation, social services etc. are taken up. The expenditure incurred for implementing the Tribal Sub Plan including the Special Central Assistance has increased steadily from Rs 94 lakhs in 1976-77 to Rs 17.55 crores in 2000-2001.

Vocational Training in Tribal Areas

Scheduled Tribes are the most marginalised section of the society, therefore to assist their socio-economic development; there is an imperative need to provide more employment avenues and income generation opportunities. It is aimed at upgrading the skills of the tribal youths in various traditional/modern vocations depending upon their educational qualification, present economic trends and the market potential which would enable them to gain suitable employment or enable them to become self employed. Under the scheme of Vocational Training, grants will be available for organising vocational trainings in recognised institutes or in Vocational Training Centres (VTCs) subject to terms and conditions revised from time to time of the scheme. The agencies eligible for such grants are:

1. State Governments and UT Administrations;
2. Institutions or Organisations set up by Government as autonomous bodies, either under a statue, or as a society registered under the Societies Registration Act, 1860;
3. Educational and other institutions of the likes of local bodies and cooperative bodies;
4. A Public Trust registered under any law for the time being in force. The trust must have been registered for at least three years;
5. Any Private Recognised Institution, registered and conducting such vocational courses for at least three years;
6. Any industry or an association of industries like ASSOCHAM, CII, FICCI, etc., who are willing to run such skill upgradation

training centres as per the financial norms of the scheme with a proper plan for placements.

Schemes of Development of Primitive Tribal Groups

Based on pre-agricultural level of technology, low level of literacy, declining or stagnant populations, 75 tribal communities in 17 States and 1 Union Territory of Andaman and Nicobar Island, have been identified and categorised as Primitive Tribal Groups (PTGs). Considering the vulnerability of these groups, a Central Sector Scheme was introduced in the year 1998-99 for the all round development of PTGs. The scheme is very flexible, and covers housing, infrastructure development, education, health, land distribution/development, agriculture development, cattle development, social security, insurance, etc. During 2007-08, comprehensive long term *"Conservation-cum-Development (CCD) Plans"* for PTGs has been formulated for Eleventh Plan period through baseline surveys conducted by respective State Governments/Union territory. These Plans envisage a synergy between efforts of State Governments and nongovernmental organisations.

Tribal Research Institutions

Fourteen Tribal Research Institutes (TRIs) have been set up by Andhra Pradesh, Assam, Bihar, Gujarat, Kerala, Madhya Pradesh, Maharashtra, Orissa, Rajasthan, Tamil Nadu, West Bengal, Uttar Pradesh, Manipur and Tripura. These Institutes are engaged in providing planning inputs to the State Governments, conducting research and evaluation studies, collection of data, codification of customary law and conduct of training, seminars and workshops. Some of these Institutes are also having museums exhibiting tribal artifacts.

Girls/Boys Hostels for STs

Girl's hostels scheme was started in Third Five-Year Plan with the aim of providing residential facilities to tribal girls in pursuit of education. Central assistance of 50 per cent cost of construction to the States, cent percent to the Union Territories is provided under the scheme. During 1999-2000 funds were released to the States/UTs for construction of 29 Girls' Hostels and 11 Girls Hostels during 2000-2001. Boy's hostels scheme was started in 1989-90 under the same pattern as the Girls' Hostels. During 2000-2001, funds were released for construction of 15 boys' hostels.

Strengthen Education among Scheduled Tribe Girls in Low Literacy District

It is a gender scheme of the Ministry of Tribal Welfare. The scheme aims to bridge the gap in literacy levels between the general female population and tribal women, through facilitating 100 per cent enrolment of tribal girls in the identified Districts or Blocks, more particularly in naxal affected areas and in areas inhabited by Primitive Tribal Groups (PTGs), and reducing drop-outs at the elementary level by creating the required ambience for education. The scheme recognises the fact that improvement of the literacy rate of tribal girls is essential to enable them to participate effectively in and benefit from, socio-economic development. The scheme covers 54 identified districts in 12 States and one Union Territory where the ST population is 25 per cent or more, and ST female literacy rate is below 35 per cent or its fractions, as per 2001 census. In addition, any other tribal block in a district, other than aforesaid 54 identified districts, which has scheduled tribal populations 25 per cent or above and tribal female literacy rate below 35 per cent or its fractions, as per 2001 census, are also covered. The scheme primarily envisages the running and maintenance of hostels linked with schools running under Sarva Shiksha Abhiyan or other schemes of Education Department. Where such schooling facilities are not available, the scheme has provision for establishing a complete educational complex with residential and schooling facility. The scheme has provision for tuitions, incentives and periodical awards to encourage the ST girls. The scheme does not provide and construction cost.

Coaching for Scheduled Tribes

The scheduled tribe candidates coming from deprived families and disadvantaged environment find it difficult to compete with those coming from a socially and economically advantageous background. To promote a more level playing field, and give ST candidates a better chance to succeed in competitive examinations, the Ministry of Tribal Affairs supports a scheme for coaching for disadvantaged ST candidates in quality coaching institutions to enable them to successfully compete in examinations for jobs/admission to professional courses. The scheme supports free coaching to scheduled tribe students for various competitive examinations viz. Civil Services/State Civil Services/Other Exams conducted by UPSE like CDS, NDA, etc., professional courses like Medical, Engg., Business Administration/ Banking/Staff selection Commission/Railway Recruitment Boards/ insurance companies, etc. The financial norms of the scheme have been revised during 2007-08. The scheme covers coaching fees, monthly stipend @ Rs 1000 per ST student per month and boarding/ lodging charges for outstation students @ Rs 2000 per ST student per month for the period of coaching.

Grant-in-aid to Voluntary Organisations Working for Welfare of Scheduled Tribes

The prime objective of the scheme is to enhance the reach of welfare schemes of Government and fill the gaps in service deficient tribal areas, in the sectors such as education, health, drinking water, agro-horticultural productivity, social security net, etc., through the efforts of voluntary organisations (VOs)/non-governmental organisations (NGOs), and to provide an environment for socio-economic upliftment and overall development of the Scheduled Tribes (STs). Any other innovative activity having direct impact on the socio-economic development or livelihood generation of STs may also be considered through voluntary efforts. Under this scheme 90 per cent grant is provided by the ministry and 10 per cent cost is required to be borne by the non-governmental organisations from their own resources, except in Scheduled Areas where the Government bears 100 per cent cost. The scheme provides a list of categories of projects viz. residential school, non-residential schools, 10 or more bedded hospitals, mobile dispensaries, computer training centers, etc., which could be covered under the scheme, and also prescribes fixed financial norms. The scheme does not provide any construction cost. The Proposals by NGOs are required to be routed through State Government and the recommendation of the *"State Committee for Supporting Voluntary Efforts"* constituted under the chairmanship of principal Secretary/Secretary, Tribal Welfare/Development Department of the State/UT are mandatory. The recommendation of State Committee is valid for that financial year in which it is made.

Post-matric Scholarship For Scheduled Tribes Students

The objective of the scheme is to provide financial assistance to students belonging to Scheduled Tribes pursuing Post-Matriculation recognised courses in recognised institutions. The scheme covers professional, technical as well as non-professional and non-technical courses at various levels and the scheme also includes correspondence courses including distance and continuing education. The scheme is implemented by the State Government and UT Administrations, which receive 100 per cent Central Assistance over and above the committed liability which is required to be borne by them from their own budgetary provisions. The committed liability is equal to the expenditure reached in the last year of the Plan period. Accordingly, the expenditure incurred in the last year of the Xth plan period, i.e., 2006-2007, has become the committed liability of State/UTs, which is required to be borne by them during each year of the 11th Five Year Plan period. The requirement of committed liability of North Eastern State has been dispensed with from 1997-98. The Scheme is in operation since 1944-45.

The value of the existing scholarship includes maintenance allowance, reader charges of blind students, study tour charges, thesis typing/printing charges, book allowance to students pursuing correspondence course and compulsory non-refundable fees charges by the educational institutions. The maintenance allowance for hostlers is between Rs 235/- p.m. to 740/- and for day scholars from Rs 140/- p.m. to Rs 330/- p.m., depending upon the level of courses. The prescribed annual income ceiling of both the parents/guardians, under the scheme is up to Rs 1,08,000/-, as applicable w.e.f. 1-4-2007. The income ceiling has been linked with the consumer price index for industrial workers.

Upgradation of Merit of St Students

The objective of the scheme is to upgrade the merit of ST students by providing them remedial and special coaching in classes IX to XII. While remedial coaching aims at removing deficiencies in various subjects, special coaching is provided with a view to prepare the students for competitive examinations for seeking entry into professional courses like Engineering and Medical disciplines. The scheme provides for 100 per cent central assistance to the States/ UT's. A package grant of Rs 15,000 per student per year is provided and the State/UTs are not required to bear any financial burden. Besides the amount of scholarship, students with disabilities are also eligible for the following assistance:

1. Reader Allowance of Rs 100 per month for blind students in classes IX to XII.

2. Transport allowance of Rs 50 per month for the disabled student if such a student does not reside in the hostel, which is within the premises of educational institution. The disability as per the said Act is defined as blindness, low-vision, leprosy-cured, hearing impairment, locomoter disability, mental retardation and mental illness.

3. Special pay of Rs 100 per month is admissible to any employee of the hostel willing to extend help to a severely orthopedically handicapped student residing in a hostel managed by the educational or by the State Govt./Union Territory Admn. who may need the assistance of a helper.

4. Escort allowance of Rs 50 per month for severely handicapped day scholar students with lower extremity disability.

5. Allowance of Rs 100 per month towards extra coaching to mentally retarded and mentally ill students in classes IX to XII.

Rajiv Gandhi National Fellowship Scheme

This Scheme was introduced in the year 2005-06. Under the Scheme, fellowship is provided to ST students for pursuing higher studies such as M.Phil. and Ph.D. The maximum duration of a fellowship is five years. Every year 667 fellowships are to be provided to ST students. The scheme is being implemented by University Grant Commission (UGC) on behalf of the Ministry of Tribal Affairs. Any ST student who has passed post-graduation from a UGC recognised University can apply under the scheme.

National Overseas Scholarship Scheme for Scheduled Tribes

The Scheme provides financial assistance to meritorious students belonging to STs for pursuing higher studies abroad in specified fields of Master level courses, Ph.D. and Post-Doctoral research programmes, in the field of Engineering, Technology and Science. The selected candidates are given cost of tuition and other educational fees charged by the foreign university, etc., maintenance and other grants along with travel expenses. In addition passage grants are also available to candidates belonging to ST who are in receipt of merit scholarship for postgraduate studies, research or training abroad (excluding attending seminars, workshops, conferences) from a foreign government/organisation or under any other scheme where cost of passage is not provided. Scheme of NOS has been revised in 2007-08 as Plan scheme. 15 awards would be sanctioned to ST students per year.

Scheme of Top Class Education for St Students

Ministry of Tribal Affairs has introduced a new Central Sector Scholarship Scheme of Top Class Education for ST Students from the academic year 2007-08 with the objective of encouraging meritorious ST students for pursuing studies at degree and post degree level in any of the identified institutes.There are 127 institutes identified under the scheme in both the Government and private sectors covering the field of management, medicine, engineering, law and commercial courses. Each institute has been allocated five awards, with a ceiling of total 635 scholarships per year. The family income of the ST students from all the sources shall not exceed Rs 2.00 lakh per annum. The ST students will be awarded scholarship covering full tuition fee and other non-refundable dues in respect of Government/Government-funded institutions. However, there will be a ceiling of Rs 2.00 lakh per annum per student for private sector institutions and Rs 3.72 lakh per annum per student for the private sector flying clubs for Commercial Pilot Training. In addition to the above, the scholarship also provides for (i) living expenses @ Rs 2200/- per month per student subject to actuals, (ii) books and stationery @ Rs 3000/- per annum per student and (iii) cost of a latest computer system along with its accessories limited to Rs 45000/- as one time assistance during the course.

Tribal Cooperative Marketing Development Federation of India Limited

The Tribal Cooperative Marketing Development Federation of India Limited (TRIFED) was set up by the Government of India in 1987, with the prime objective of providing marketing assistance and remunerative prices to ST communities for their minor forest produce and surplus agricultural produce and to wean them away from exploitative private traders and middlemen. The federation is a National level Cooperative apex body functioning under the Multi-State Cooperative Societies Act, 1984. The authorised share capital of TRIFED is Rs 100 crore and the paid up capital is Rs 99.98 The Government of India's contribution is Rs 99.75 crore and the balance of Rs 0.23 crore has been contributed by other shareholders.

PESA

The Provisions of the Panchayats (Extension to the Scheduled Areas) Act, 1996 (PESA) came into force on 24th December, 1996 with the objective of safeguarding and preserving the traditions and customs of people living in scheduled areas, their social, religious and cultural identities and traditional management practices of community resources. PESA is an instrument for tribal's' empowerment of tribal's. To make it effective, it is necessary to (a) endow Panchayats at the appropriate level and Gram Sabhas with ownership of minor forest produce (MFP), (b) empower Gram Sabhas to approve beneficiaries under poverty alleviation programmes and the provisions relating to minor forest produce, minor minerals and settlement of land rights in forest, (c) make prior consultation with Gram Sabha or Panchayats at the appropriate level mandatory before acquisition of land for development projects, (d) make the recommendation of Gram Sabha or Panchayat at the appropriate level mandatory for granting prospecting licences or mining leases for minor minerals and (e) get State Governments to change their existing laws whenever they are inconsistent with central legislation.

For the PESA Act to be more meaningful, provisions relating to Gram Sabhas as per the Constitutional amendment and theamended Panchayat Raj Act have to be translated into local tribal dialects and made available to all Gram Panchayats in scheduled areas. Training programmes should be organised so that all Gram Sabhas members including tribal women are aware of the function, responsibilities and powers of Gram Sabhas. In reality, PESA has not become part of mainstream policy. Many state governments have passed laws not fully in conformity with the central law. While PESA remains unimplemented, tribal areas are increasingly being opened up by State Governments for commercial exploitation by national and multinational corporate bodies.

Scheme for Assistance to State Tribal Development and Finance Corporations (STFDCs)

This is a Centrally Sponsored scheme. STFDCs are functioning in States and UTs having sizeable Scheduled Tribes population. They are playing an extremely useful role in mobilisation of finances for economic development of the Scheduled Tribes. They act as promoters and catalysts for generating credit from financial institutions, providing missing inputs by way of margin money loans and subsidy to the target group. STFDCs motivate ST families to undertake suitable economic development schemes. A person belonging to Scheduled Tribes living below the poverty line is eligible for assistance under this scheme from the State Scheduled Tribes Development Corporation. Under the scheme, State Government/ UT Administration has to provide 51 per cent share for the corporation - balance 49 per cent is to be provided by the Ministry as a Central Government's share.

State/Ut Minor Forest Produce Act 2005

The tribal's are in need of forest-based sustainable livelihoods for which ownership of forest resources and management of the ecology are crucial. The Government of India has come out with the Minor Forest Produce Act (MFPA) 2005 whereby forest dependent communities should be endowed with collection, processing and trade in minor forest produce on the principle of *"Share and Care"*. Other provisions include coverage of a minimum 1/3 of area under trees, demarcation of area under Biological Diversity Act 2002 and safeguarding forest area covered under wild life (Protection) Act 1972. If these initiatives are effectively implemented, the ecological balance will be restored and tribals will have safe livelihoods with assured participation and ownership.

Development and Employment Programmes

The Government has implemented various programmes which encourage tribals to take up new ventures. The assistance for the poor households of SCs/STs under the major programmes is as follows:

National Rural Employment Guarantee Act (NAREGA)

NAREGA guarantees 100 days of employment in a financial year to any rural household whose adult members are willing to do unskilled manual work. The Act came into force in 200 selected districts on 2nd February, 2006, and an additional 130 districts from 2007-08. The Sampoorna Grameen Rozgar Yojana (SGRY) has been subsumed into NAREGA in these 330 districts. All districts will be included from April, 2008. NAREGA is a demand-driven scheme so separate earmarking of employment/resources for SCs/STs has not been provided. However, the reports of physical achievements during 2006-07 reveal that more than 61 per cent of the total man days of employment generated were for SC/ST households. During 2007-08 (up to Dec. 2007) total employment of 8557.97 lakh man days was generated out of which employment for SCs and STs was 2330.36 lakh man days (27.2 per cent) and 2648.02 lakh (30.94 per cent) man days respectively.

Sampoorna Grameen Rozgar Yojana (SGRY)

While the SGRY is open to all rural poor who are in need of wage employment, preference is given to SCs/STs and parents of child labourers withdrawn from hazardous occupations, who are below the poverty line. 22.5 per cent of the annual allocation (inclusive of food grains) at district and intermediate panchayat level is earmarked for individual/group beneficiary schemes of SC/ST families living below the poverty line. A minimum 50 per cent of the village panchayat allocation (inclusive of food grains) is for the creation of need based village infrastructure in SC/ST habitations/wards. A total employment of 1170.75 lakh man days was created during 2007-2008 (up to Dec. 2007) out of which there were 435.49 (37.2 per cent) lakh man days for SCs and 151.31 (12.9 per cent) lakh man days for STs.

Swarnjayanti Gram Swarozgar Yojana (SGSY)

The SGSY is a major self employment programme being implemented all over the country. Its guidelines stipulate that at least 50 per cent of the Swarozgaris will be SCs/STs, 40 per cent women and 3 per cent persons with disability. Subsidies will be uniform at 30 per cent of the project cost, subject to a maximum of Rs 7500. For SCs/STs and the disabled, the subsidy limit is 50 per cent of the project cost subject to a maximum of Rs 10,000 respectively. The number of swarozgaris assisted under this scheme during 2007-08 (up to Dec. 2007) was 776408. This includes the Swarozgaris of SHGs and individual swarozgaris out of which the SC Swarozgaris assisted were 267740 (34.4 per cent) and ST Swarozgaris 113215 (14.58 per cent).

Indira Awas Yojana (IAY)

The Indira Awaas Yojana (IAY) is being implemented at national level to provide dwelling units to people below the poverty line living in rural areas. Preference is given to BPL families belonging to SCs/STs. 60 per cent of the total allocation during a financial year is for construction of dwelling units for SCs and STs. The guideline provides for allotting houses in the name of the female member of household or in the joint names of husband and wife. Three per cent of the funds are reserved for the disabled below the poverty line in rural areas. Homes completed during 2007-08 (up to Dec. 2007) were 1063920 out of which 462273 (43.4 per cent) were allotted in the name of SCs and 188247 (17.69 per cent) in the name of STs.

National Rural Health Mission (2005-2012)

The Government of India launched the National Rural Health Mission (NRHM) in April 2005 to provide effective healthcare to the rural population throughout the country with special focus on 18 states, with weak public health infrastructure and poor performance in demographic and health indicators. Those states are Arunachal Pradesh, Assam, Bihar, Chhattisgarh, Himachal Pradesh, Jharkhand, J and K, Manipur, Mizoram, Meghalaya, Madhya Pradesh, Nagaland, Orissa, Rajasthan, Sikkim, Tripura, Uttarakhand and Uttar Pradesh. The NRHM will cover all villages through approximately 2.5 lakh village-based *"Accredited Social Health Activities"* (ASHA) which will act as a link between villagers and health centers. One ASHA will be formed in every village or cluster of villages to advise villagers about sanitation, hygiene, contraception and immunisation. Rs 67 billion was provided in the budget in 2005-06. A National Health Insurance Scheme has also been launched for BPL families to ensure annual health coverage of Rs 30,000 for families or individuals. Rs 100,000 will be paid to the families of those who die in accidents and in cases of disability. Rs 50,000 is paid in case of partial disability.

Tribal Forest Interface

As per the Forest Survey of India Report, 2003, about 60.04 per cent of the 63 per cent forest cover of the country and 63 per cent of the dense forests lie in 187 tribal districts, though the geographical area of these districts is just 33.6 per cent of the country's geographical area. Out of 58 districts, which have more than 67 per cent of their area under forest cover, 51 happen to be tribal districts. A comparison of the 2001 and 2003 assessments of forest cover in tribal districts shows a net increase of 321,100 ha underscoring the point of a very strong symbiotic relationship between the STs and the forests, and of the tribal's being at the forefront of the conservation regime. There is no doubt that forest as natural resources are an asset belonging to the entire country to be enjoyed by every citizen. However, it has to be considered that the costs, including opportunity costs are borne by local stakeholders while the benefits accrue to a dispersed group of stakeholders, viz. the country at large. The STs cannot be forced to view their surroundings as total externalities for the good of the nation without getting the right to possess a homestead or earn a livelihood. Due to the faulty processes of declaration of forests in the past, the rights of the tribal's over their traditional land holdings in the forests have gradually been extinguished. Insecurity of tenure and fear of eviction from these lands have led the tribal communities to feel emotionally as well as physically alienated from forests and forest lands. The conditions of the tribal's living in and around forests is becoming increasingly precarious and vulnerable day by day due to displacement threats arising out of various causes, such as increasing emphasis on conservation of forests without human beings, etc. The Scheduled Tribes living inside forests do not get the benefit of the various welfare schemes due to non-availability of land titles in their names. The consequences of not having land titles deprives them of various entitlements such as bank loans, domicile certificates, assistance under individual benefit schemes of government like dug wells, housing under the Indira Awas Yojana etc.

The collection and marketing of MFP is a major source of livelihood for most tribal families contributing around 70 per cent of their total income. Despite the transfer of ownership, control and management of MFP to the STs through the Panchayats (Extension to Scheduled Areas) Act, 1996, the collection and trade of MFP is largely monopolised by the corporations of the Forest Departments of the States, at least in case of high value products. In many cases, such as tendu leaves, the trading is done by the Forest Corporations through the contractors and the STs are employed as labourers. Non-conferment of ownership rights over the minor forest produce directly impinges on the interests and rights of the tribal people living in and around the forests. Through this policy it will be ensured that:

1. The States enact legislation to provide tenurial security by recognising the rights of forest dwelling Scheduled Tribes over forest land under self-cultivation, ownership of MFP including rights to collect, trade and process the same, provision of minimum support price for the MFP, conversion of forest villages into revenue villages, rights over water bodies including fishing rights, rights over minor minerals as per the PESA Act.

2. Scientific forestry would be reoriented to mean that wild fruits, nuts, MFPs, grasses, leaves, twigs and other environment reserves become the main intended products from forest lands and timber a by-product. The reverse of this has been the policy for over a century since the concept of production forestry came into being.

3. The monopolies of the Forest Corporations would be done away with and ownership of MFP would in the true sense of the term be passed on to the communities with institutionalised support duly backed by minimum support price.

4. Simple processing activities, such as broom making, leaf plate making, tamarind processing, mat and rope making and other simple value addition activities would be encouraged in the household/cottage sector. Small-scale forest-based enterprises would be supported by ensuring a sustainable supply of input materials, providing managerial and technological assistance, improving access to credit, providing market support to help rural people get better prices for the forest products and secure a sustainable livelihood.

5. For multiplying tribal livelihood opportunities and involving them in regeneration and protection of forests, the State will adopt strict measures to combat illicit felling of trees, form and employ Self Help Groups of STs living in and around forests in afforestation/ regeneration activities through plantation of long, medium and short term diverse species, encourage processing of MFP items locally to reduce the number of intermediaries, and bring better returns. The economic welfare of the ST people will be the first charge on usufruct and removable forestry resources by relegating revenue objectives to secondary position.

6. Research and extension will be undertaken to improve upon the current practices, increase output and incomes and eliminate adverse ecological effects.

Legal Provisions in Scheduled Areas

After independence, the Constituent Assembly appointed a Sub-committee with A.V. Thakkar as its Chairman to formulate provisions to safeguard the interests of the tribal population. The Sub-committee examined the overall situation of the tribal's and recommended that on the basis of past experience, it was necessary to provide statutory safeguards to protect the economic life of the tribal's and their traditional customs and institutions. The general position according to the Sub-committee was that the areas predominantly inhabited by tribal people should be known as the *'Scheduled Areas.'* These areas were accorded constitutional identity and formally recognised under Article 342 of the Constitution and referred to the tribal's as the *'Scheduled Tribes,'* and the areas where substantial Scheduled Tribe population resided were declared the *'Scheduled Areas'* under the Article 244(1) and the Fifth Schedule.

Following the 73rd constitution amendment, a high level Committee under the Chairmanship of Dileep Singh Bhuria, MP, was constituted in June 1994, to examine the issues relating to the extension of the provisions of Part IX of the Constitution to the Scheduled Areas and to make recommendations on the salient features of the laws for extending provisions of this part of the constitution to the Schedule Areas. The Committee discussed various issues related to Part IX and examined certain unique characteristics of tribal societies and tribal areas as many tribal societies have their own customary laws, traditional practices, community ethos, political and administrative systems, among others. The Committee submitted its report in January 1995. The Committee's Report proposed a legal framework suited to participatory democracy particularly at the grassroots level. It was contemplated that the institutions proposed to be constituted at the district level and the lower levels should have a living relationship with the self-management practices which have been in vogue in the tribal areas. The important recommendations of the committee are:

1. It is essential to give due consideration to the tribal societies mode of living, organisations, cultural mores, present day predicament of exploitation, deprivation and marginalisation. Many tribal communities have been living autonomously and they have their own traditional structures and leaders. They have exercised control over the natural resources that govern their institutions. The Gram Sabhas and village councils have been vibrant institutions in the field of local administration, religion, politics, economics, justice and so on. Therefore, it is necessary

to have a mix of traditional and modern institutions in the Panchayati Raj system.

2. While drafting the law, advantage should be taken of both the Fifth and Sixth Schedules. The Fifth Schedule should be the fountain-head of essential and beneficial legislation. The design and contents of the Sixth Schedule could serve as the reference frame for a district within the broader canvas of the Fifth Schedule.

3. The Tribal Advisory Council envisaged in the Fifth Schedule, as a consultative body at the State level, needs to be reformed into an effective organisation. The Chief Minister of the state should be its chairperson and its meetings should be held once in every three months.

4. The Central Advisory Council at the Centre should be revived. It should serve as a sounding board for tribal policies and programmes and render advice in disputes between the state government and the Tribal Advisory Council. Its advice should be normally binding. The Prime Minister should chair its meetings and the members may be the state ministers for welfare, home and rural development and the Deputy Chairperson of the Planning Commission.

5. Considering the potential and ingrained attributes, the cooperative organisations among tribals should be constituted in line with their oral traditions and social milieu.

6. The proposed institutions in the Scheduled Areas and Tribal Areas should be vested with adequate competence to deal with emerging problems among tribal people like growing indebtedness, land alienation, deforestation, ecological degradation, displacement on account of industrialisation and modernisation.

7. Scheduled Tribe members in the Lok Sabha should be associated with the intermediate Panchayat and the District Council. But the representation should not be restricted to the Schedule Tribe MLAs; even non-ST MLAs should be associated with both tiers.

8. Since the Schedule Areas and Tribal Areas are expected to have a majority of Tribal population, the different tier Panchayats therein

should have a majority of Schedule Tribe members. Further both chairpersons and vice-chairpersons should from among the STs.

9. Panchayati Raj bodies in tribal areas should be made more effective and more participative in the context of the foregoing. More than in the past they have to function as units of self-governance and development. They have to work for socioeconomic goals for removal of poverty, illiteracy, ill-health etc. among the people.

Five Year Plans and Tribal Welfare

The planning commission laid down the objectives and strategies for tribal development from time to time. The following are the account of the tribal welfare programmes in India during the various plans.

The First Five Year Plan (1951-1956)

The First Five Year Plan outlined a positive policy for assisting the tribal's as under: -

1. Assisting them to develop their natural resources and to evoke a productive economic life wherein they will enjoy the fruits of their own labour and will not be exploited by more organised economic forces from outside.
2. It is not desirable to bring about changes in their religions and social life, except at the initiative of the tribal people themselves and with their willing consent.
3. It is accepted that there are many features in tribal life which should not only be retained but also developed; and
4. The qualities of their dialects and the rich content of their arts and crafts also need to be appreciated and preserved.

Taking into consideration the conditions of the tribal people, The First Planning Commission quoted that *"There may be a good deal of justification for such (isolation) a policy of non-interference; but it is not easily practicable when tribal life has been influenced by social forces from without, and tribal communities have reached a certain degree of acculturisation accompanied by the penetration of communications in the tribal areas, and of social services for the betterment of their lives."* In the First Five Year Plan, Community Development Projects for all round development of rural areas especially the weaker sections were started.

Second Five Year Plan (1956-1961)

During this plan the Ministry of Home Affairs provided fund to the Ministry of Community Development to establish Special Multi-purpose Tribal Blocks (SMPT) in areas with prominent tribal population.

Third Five Year Plan (1961-1966)

Towards the end of the second plan, i.e., in 1959, the government of India appointed a committee under the chairmanship of Verrier Elwin to review the SMPT Blocks. According to the recommendations of this committee, during the Third Plan period, SMPT Blocks were renamed as Tribal Development Blocks (TDB) and suggested it to be opened in all areas where over 60 per cent of the population was tribal's. In addition to the normal allotment of Rs 12 lakhs to a community development block, a provision of Rs 10 lakhs for 1st stage, and Rs five lakhs for 2nd stage for TDB was also made.

Three Annual Plans (1966-1969)

During this period no special funds were provided for tribal development. However in 1969-70 a decision was taken to extent the total life of TDBs to 15 Years by incorporating a new stage three. During the 3rd stage each TDB was given Rs 10 lakhs.

Fourth Five Year Plan (1969-1974)

During the Fourth Five Year Plan, a series of programmes were conceived and addressed to specific target groups. The Small Farmers Development Agencies (SFDA) and Marginal Farmers and Agricultural Labourers Development Agencies (MFAL) were the first two in the series. In these cases, attention was shifted from area development to development of identified individuals who qualified for special attention according to certain objective criteria. Tribal Development Agencies (TDA's) were established on the pattern of SFDA which addressed themselves to the problems of the tribal population. The level of investment in the new programme was much higher compared to TD Block. Six tribal development agencies were started during the Fourth Plan. Each Tribal Development Agency covered a group of TD Blocks. Tribal Development Agencies were expected to comprise elements of economic development, social services and prospective measures.

Fifth Five Year Plan (1974-79)

During the middle of the Fourth Five Year Plan, i.e., in the year 1972, the Planning Commission set up a *"Task force on Development of Tribal Areas"* with L.P. Vidyarthi as the Chairman. In their appraisal, the task force observed that in spite of various kinds of investment by the State and Central governments for tribal development in successive plans, the problem of the tribal's reflected in primitive methods of agriculture, land alienation, indebtedness, adverse effects of industrialisation, low rate of literacy, poor health of nutrition etc., had not been solved. The committee opined that one of the important factors for the lack of impact so far was that development of Scheduled Tribes and tribal areas had been looked upon as a problem of *'welfare'* as distinguished from *'development'*. Taking into account of the recommendations of the task force and other previous committees, during the Fifth Five Year Plan, an altogether new approach was adopted towards tribal development. This was termed as Tribal Sub-plan. It envisaged the total development of the tribal areas and provided the mechanism for integrating the developmental activities of the government and the semi government organisations by financing through the Integrated Tribal Development Project (ITDP). The Sub-Plan aimed at narrowing the gap between the levels of development of tribal and other areas, and to improve the quality of life of the tribal communities in general.

Sixth Five Year Plan (1980-85)

The Sixth Plan continued the Sub-Plan approach of the Fifth Plan. This was to be supplemented by target beneficiary approach with the objective of narrowing the gap between the level of development of the tribal's and other developed communities and bringing about a qualitative change in the life of a tribal community. The strategy of development lays emphasis on consolidation of the gains of protective measures, programmes of full employment, education and health services. The programmes under different sectors of development are required to be intensified with suitable modifications to remove the present inadequacies in implementation. The States have to give due importance to the integration of programmes in the field and effective delegation of powers to the Project Authorities in ITDPs. The approach in the Sixth Plan for the development of backward areas in general was to rely, to a greater extent, on the development of agriculture, village and small-scale industries subsidiary occupations and related services and also the Minimum Need Programmes and Area Development Programmes. Improvement of economic status of the tribal's should be the first concern and suitable programmes of horticulture, cattle development, poultry and piggery, etc., were carried out.

Seventh Five Year Plan (1985-90)

The basic premises of the Tribal Sub-Plan continued in the Seventh Plan also. During the Seventh Plan, the Tribal Sub-Plan strategy are (a) Identification of the Development Blocks where tribal population is in majority and their constitution into ITDPs with a view to adopt there an integrated and project-based approach for development; (b) Marking of funds for the Tribal Sub-Plan and ensuring the flow of funds from the control of State plan, sectoral outlays and from financial institutions; and (c) Creation of appropriate administrative structures in tribal .areas and adoption of appropriate personnel policies. The programme of tribal development with ITDP pattern was continued in the Seventh Plan also without any basic or major changes in the approach, Pattern or structure, but better co-ordination was sought between various agencies, and social services were given priority. LAMPS (Large Agricultural Marketing Societies) were to be strengthened through broadening their popular base. Seventh Plan paid attention towards the rehabilitation of poor tribal's and the removal of tribal women's backwardness.

Eighth Five Year Plan (1992-97)

In the Eighth Five Year Plan, Tribal Sub-Plan (TSP) area, MADA (Modified Area Development Approach), Scattered Development Plans, and Primitive Tribe Development Plans for the tribal development approach have been stressed. Despite the effects to diversify economic activities in non-formal sectors, the predominant source of livelihood in TSP area continuous to be agriculture. The main thrust would be on the development of fisheries, sericulture, horticulture, plantation on waste land and growing vegetables. During the Eighth Plan these areas would provide supplemental income and new avenues of employment to the tribal's. Human resources development through education, vocational/craftsman training would be taken up to improve the skills of the tribal's. Expansion of irrigation facilities and electrification of tribal settlements, expansion of irrigation wells, fertilizers, improvement of cattle breed and mining activities have also been given. In this plan, family oriented schemes have been also stressed to uplift the tribal families. The community development programmes are given second priority.

Nineth Five Year Plan (1997-2002)

The approach for the Nineth Five Year Plan has drawn attention to the need for national policy for tribal development. Effects will be made to ensure that the tribal economy is protected and supported against threats from the external markets. The ownerships/patent rights of the tribal people in respect of minor forest produces vis a vis the use of medicinal plants will be protected as per the provision of intellectual property Rights (IPR). Nineth Plan is a process and it would be able to fulfill the ambition of tribal's is the initiation of 21st' century and may be able to bring them more nearer to national mainstream. A participatory planning process is an essential precondition for ensuring equity as well as accelerating the rate of growth of the economy. For approaching to this goal, the government of India enacted an amendment to the constitution of India (73rd Amendment) for ensuring representation of backward and marginalised communities e.g., Scheduled Caste, Scheduled Tribe and women in Panchayati Raj institutions. The draft report of the working group on decentralised planning and Panchayati Raj for formulation of the Nineth Five Year Plan (1997-2002) noted that "*... large parts of the country and vast section of the population have been untouched by this progress. It is now felt that the fruits of development could have been multiplied manifold with the involvement of people at the grass-root level in the process of development.*"

Reservation

The Constitution of India states in Article 15(4): "*All citizens shall have equal opportunities of receiving education. Nothing herein contained shall preclude the State from providing special facilities for educationally backward sections (not "communities") of the population.*" It also states that "*The State shall promote with special care the educational and economic interests of the weaker sections of society (in particular, of the scheduled castes and aboriginal tribes), and shall protect them from social "injustice" and all forms of exploitation.*" [Emphasis added.] The Article further states that nothing in Article 15(4) will prevent the nation from *helping* SCs and STs for their betterment ['betterment' up to the level enjoyed by the *average* member of other communities]. In 1982, the Constitution specified 15 per cent and 7.5 per cent of vacancies in public sector and government-aided educational institutes as a quota reserved for the SC and ST candidates respectively for a period of five years, *after which the quota system would be reviewed*

Ministry of Tribal Affairs

The Ministry of Tribal Affairs was constituted in October 1999 with the objective of providing more focused attention on the integrated socio-economic development of the most under-privileged sections of the Indian society namely, the Scheduled Tribes (STs), in a coordinated and planned manner. The Ministry of Tribal Affairs is the nodal Ministry for the overall policy, planning and coordination of programmes for development of STs. To this end, the Ministry of Tribal Affairs undertakes activities that flow from the subjects allocated under the Government of India (Allocation of Business) Rules, 1961.

Conclusion

Tribals are very much deprived from the initial stages. They are sore simple and hard labourer people. Social security and special care is more important for their development. In Indian Constitution there are various provisions present which support needs of social security. A number of constitutional provisions are already in place to safeguard the interests of the tribal's in the country. Some of the important ones are indicated below.

1. *Administration:* Under Clause (1) of Article 244, the Fifth Schedule applies to the administration and control of the Scheduled Areas and STs in a state.

2. *Tribal Development:* Article 275(1) provides for Grants-in-Aid of the revenues of a state to enable it to meet the cost of development schemes for the welfare of STs in that state.

3. *Promotion of Education:* Article 15(4) along with subsequent amendments empowers the state to make any special provision for the advancement of any socially and educationally backward classes including STs and also enables the state to reserve seats for them in educational institutions.

4. *Political Safeguards:* Article 330 and 332 provides for reservation of representation of SCs and STs in the Lok Sabha (Parliament) and Vidhan Sabhas (State Legislative Assemblies).

5. *Employment:* Article 16(4) empowers the state to make, "any provision for the reservation of appointments or posts in favour of any backward class of citizens (including STs) if not represented adequately in the services under the state".

6. *Reservations in Educational and Employment Opportunities:* The Constitution of India provides for reserving certain percentage of seats in all educational institutions and public employment in proportion to the tribal population. Residential or "Ashram Schools" are being run in the ITDA areas to provide primary and secondary education for the STs. According to Article 17: Civil Rights, "Untouchability" is abolished and its practice in any form is forbidden. Enforcement of any disability arising out of "Untouchability" shall be an offence punishable in accordance with law.

References

1. Avinash Samal (2001). *Tribal Development Administration: Case study of a district of Orissa*, pp.1-5, Retrieved from http://www.isec.ac.in/Tribal_development_ administration.pdf
2. B.K.Panda, *Understanding multiple disadvantages for inclusive educational development of Scheduled tribe children*, Retrieved from http://www.ejournal.aiaer.net/vol 231212/4. per cent20Panda %20 BK.pdf
3. Chapter: III, *Policies and programmes for tribal development in India*, pp.54-67, Retrieved from http://www.isec.ac.in/Tribal_development_administration.pdf
4. Chapter 4.2 *Scheduled Tribes*, Retrieved from http://planning commission.nic.in/plans/planrel/fiveyr/10th/volume2/v2_ ch4_2.pdf
5. Census of India (2001) *Population Totals*. Government of India, New Delhi.
6. Census of India (2011) *Provisional Population Totals*. Government of India, New Delhi.
7. Government of India (2006) *Selected Educational Statistics*. Author, New Delhi.
8. Government of India (2005) *Sarva Shiksha Abhiyan – Guidelines*. Author, New Delhi.

9. Government of Orissa (2007) *Information on Ashram schools (*Website of Department of Harijan and Tribal Welfare). Author, Bhubaneswar.
10. Government of Andhra Pradesh (2007) *Monitoring Report of Ashram schools (Tribal Development Department).* Author, Hyderabad.
11. Government of Kerala (2007) *Official Website of Scheduled Tribes Development Department.* Thiruvananthapuram, Kerala.
12. Government of Maharashtra (2007) *Report on Welfare of Backward Classes (Commission orate of Tribal Development)* Author, Nashik.
13. Government of Chhattisgarh (2007) *Annual Report of Tribal Welfare Department.* Author, Raipur.
14. Govinda, R. (Ed.) (2001) *India Education Report.* NIEPA and Oxford Press, New Delhi.
15. Harish P. Jagannath (2009). Measuring progress of tribal education, Conference Paper: Measuring Progress of Tribal Education—Case Study of the Tribal Welfare, Department of the Government of Andhra Pradesh, India, p. 2.
16. K.C. Baiju (2011). Tribal development under decentralised governance in Kerala: Issues and Challenge, JOAAG, Vol: 6, No.1, p. 12.
17. Kulamani Padhi (2005). *Tribal development in India: A study in human development*, pp. 73-74, Retrieved from http://orissa.gov. in/e-magazine/ Orissareview/febmar2005/englishpdf/tribal diiasihd. pdf
18. M. Gopinath Reddy and K. Anil Kumar (2010). *Political economy of tribal development: A case study of Andhra Pradesh,* Working paper of 85, pp. 36-37.
19. Ministry of tribal Welfare (2012). Retrieved from http://tribal.nic.in/
20. Muhammad Abu Shadeque Mullah, Nabila Parveen and Mohammad Ahshanullah (2007). Tribal people and their socio-economic characteristics in Ranghamati Sadar Thana, *BRAC University Journal, Vol. IV, No. 1, p. 47.*
21. Ministry of Tribal Affairs, National Tribal Policy (Draft), Retrieved from http://www.legalpundits.com/Content_ folder/tribalpolicy.pdf
22. Mohammad Awais, Tosib Alam and Mohd. Asif (2009), Socioeconomic empowerment of Tribal Women: An Indian Perspectives, *International Journal of Rural Studies*, Vol: 16, No. 1, pp. 1-11.
23. Panda, B.K. (2000) *Organisation and functioning of schools in the tribal areas. Pariprekshya (Hindi)* 7, 4, pp. 18-29.
24. Panda, B.K. (2001) An analysis of teaching learning processes followed in Ashram schools of Orissa, *Education and Social Change* 25, 21, 36-50.
25. Panda, B.K. (2008) *Development of the Scheduled Tribes – A Perspective* (Mimeo). NUEPA, New Delhi.

26. Panda, B. K. (2010) Utilisation of reservation and participation in higher education – Special focus on scheduled tribe students. *Afro Asian Journal of Anthropology and Social Policy* 1, 2, 25-42, July.
27. Patel, S. (1991) *Tribal Education in India*. Mittal Publication, New Delhi.
28. Rajashree Mohanty (2011). Impact of development project on the displaced Tribal's: A case study of a development project in Eastern India, Orissa Review, p. 67, Retrieved from http://orissa.gov.in/e-magazine/Orissareview/2011/sep-oct/engpdf/68-74.pdf
29. Sujatha, K. (1983) *An In-depth Study of Ashram schools in Andhra Pradesh* (Mimeo). NIEPA, New Delhi.
30. Sujatha, Ratho (2011). Tribal welfare through Panchayats: The Experience from PESA in Orissa, Retrieved from http://www.rgics.org/test/2012/07/tribal-welfare-through-panchayats-the-experience-of-pesa-in-orissa/
31. The major schemes/programme of the Ministry of Tribal Welfare, Retrieved from http://www.indg.in/social-sector/tribal-welfare/the-major-schemes-programme-of-the-ministry-of-tribal-affairs.pdf
32. Tribal development fund: Guideline for implementations, Retrieved from http://oldsite.nabard.org/farm_sector/pdf/Guidelines_TDF.pdf
33. Tribal development Plan, Retrieved from http://brlp.in/admin/Files/Tribal%20Development%20Plan%20(Sum-mary).pdf
34. Tribal welfare department, Departmental manual, Retrieved from http://www.aptribes.gov.in/html/dept-manual.pdf
35. Vocational training in tribal areas, Retrieved from http://trifed.nic.in/writereaddata/mainlinkfile/File1153.pdf
36. Welfare of Scheduled castes, Scheduled tribes and other backward classes.
37. Reservation in India (2012). Retrieved from http://en.wikipedia.org/wiki/Reservation_in_India#cite_note-7

9

Tribal Culture and Elementary Schooling of the Girls in the Context of Odisha

Subhash Chandra Panda

Introduction

General level of literacy in India is far from satisfactory. Education of ethnic minority and socially disadvantaged group like tribal population, which lives in difficult and inaccessible areas in a different socio-economic cultural environment, points a grim picture. Probably the worst sufferers are the tribal women and girls. They are to be understood for the holistic improvement of the Indian society. Unless these women are empowered and girls are educated effectively our tribal brethrens cannot be brought into the main stream and India would not be able to achieve her dream of full literacy. Keeping this in mind we discuss here the various social, cultural and circumstantial impediments to the education of tribal girls and how the situation can be improved, with special reference to the state of Odisha.

The number of tribal communities in Odisha is 62 distributed in all the 30 districts. The density of tribal population is comparatively thin in coastal districts but quite high in other districts. They do have distinct culture of their own which gradually losing its identity. There is no second opinion with regard to the wide gap between tribal and non-tribal cultures. There is again an intra-differentiation among the cultures of different tribes of Odisha those have been influenced historically and geographically from the time immemorial. The dictionary meaning of culture is the improvement or refinement of mind, manners etc. By education and training condition of being thus transformed and refined particularly in form or type of intellectual development and civilisation. The faiths and beliefs of different sub-tribes are distinct from each other. Their faiths, beliefs and practices have little or no similarities with non-tribals. Rather the tribal cultures have influenced a lot even the non-tribal culture of the area and vice-versa in many parts of the states depending on the sharing, caring, influence and thickness of the population in the locality.

Similarities of Culture among Different Sections of tribals

The cultures of different tribal sections are traced through the myths, legends, history, art, architecture, languages (dialects), music, dance and drama, etc., and their respective habitations and areas. The uniqueness of each subculture lies in its blending of classical and folk culture. The restricted nomadic culture, living in a small habitation on hilly terrains, adorned with common tribal traits like simple beliefs, innocence, hospitality, hard work, truthfulness and honesty etc. They do have similarities among themselves to some extent as regards their music, dance, art, myths and legends, superstitions, dependence on and faith in nature etc.

In most of the tribal sections the women hold a significant place in the society and home as well. Generally they are not addicted to liquor as their men folk. Very few of them suffer from this habit. They shoulder most of the household responsibilities. A tribal lady bears some specificity and a few of those are worth mentioning here. She does not suffer from anxiety disorders, emotions, sweating and palpitation in general. Both men and women in a tribal family are comparatively more understanding in nature, but problem starts when man is overpowered by liquor and suffer from financial constraints. The members of whole tribal family enjoy liquor together but the situation goes out of control when male chauvinism comes to the force. Tribal men and women are very much responsible for their work. If the kids are too young then they accompany their mothers to workplace or else are left under the charge of elderly girls. Even in primary schools the tribal girls of eight or nine years old are accompanied with their younger siblings of two to three years old who have not yet attended school going age. They manage their studies in schools as well as caring of the younger ones. Many tribals have planned their families mostly under the influence of poverty. Otherwise there seem to be no social or psychological pressure on them to adopt the practice. The ladies do have more foresight which is reflected in their behaviour. For example a tribal lady is out from her home in the morning session in search of collecting food materials from the forest. She fetches different types of roots, stems, leaves, fruits and other eatables. While collecting the roots by digging soil the buds and the other remnants she hides under the soil with a view to harvest it again after rainy season. During the time again the plant propagates and produces same eatables for use. Most of the ladies irrespective of their tribes develop expertise in handicraft, use of medicinal plants love flora and fauna, agriculture practice, etc., in addition to general womanly qualities. The tribals irrespective of genders do believe in dignity of labour. The casual invitee to a family even joins hands with the host to earn. The tribal boys and girls staying in residential school provided by state government many times face health problems during health hazards. They preferred to go back their respective homes to get the emotional support from their parents as well as care of health through herbal medicine from plants of the forest laid by the women folk of the family.

Tribal Literacy and Population Growth

Tribal literacy presents a very dismal picture. The percentage of tribal literates in India is 29.5 per cent (male 40.65 per cent and female 18.19 per cent). In rural India tribal literacy is 27.38 per cent (male 38.45 per cent and female 16.09 per cent). Many states in our country are having less than 10 percent literacy in rural areas, e.g., Rajasthan, the literacy percent is 4.42, in Andhra Pradesh 7.29 per cent, in Goa 7.69 per cent, in MP 9.74 per cent and in Odisha 9.30 per cent. It seems that population growth and illiteracy are influencing each other. It is difficult to imagine the amount of effort, energy and other resources that could be required to bring the rate of literacy to a satisfactory level. Moreover in the present psycho-social juncture it seems to be a reality. Sahay (1996) observes that there are many people who believe that literacy can control the population growth. But little they do realise that our population problem has now reached such a stage that it is practically difficult to eradicate illiteracy without first controlling our rapid population growth. So even if it were corrected to assume that population problem would get solved if full literacy were attained still there is every possibility for raising fingers that it may not help us. Today the country's population is about 122 crores with annual birth and death rates as 2.19 per cent and 1 per cent respectively. It shows on an average about half a lakh children are getting added per day, to our nation since 1989-90.

Maintenance of Tribal Family: The Role of the Female

In tribal economy, education is accorded the last priority that too changes in present work culture in the tribal society. In the past they were more concentrated in working in agricultural field and procuring forest product. Now, in general, they started moving towards urban location and inhabiting in slums. They get turned to a greater work force in construction sites, brick, kilns etc. Most of tribals cultivate only one crop a year, as they are totally dependent on monsoon for water. The single crop sustains family barely for 3-4 months. For remaining 8-9 months all adults and able bodied men and women are forced to migrate to far off places, from their homes in search of work mostly to urban localities, factories, brick-kiln, road and building construction sites etc. Some times the women are left behind and families are spilt up for months. Conditions are particularly worse in certain districts of Odisha such as *Mayurbhanj, Keonjhar, Sundergarh, Phulbani, Ganjam, Gajapati, Balangir and Angul* where large-scale migration of tribal populcation is a common phenomenon. This in turn created numbers of social problems like prostitution, STD, AIDS and total disintegration of tribal families. Literacy has little practical use in daily life of tribal women. She, of course, seems to be more educated than us to maintain life as she can plan, sow, reap, cook, build her own home, make her own implements, train and doctor her own cattle, compose her own songs and dances, knows trees and herbs in the forest and survives in circumstances where a city bred professional face sustenance problems. When a tribal lady roams in a forest in search of forest products along with her young daughters she shows her great sense of responsibility. Love for nature and at the same time provides education to her children. She digs up stem and roots from soil searching for edibles and put back a part of same under the soil, so that a new plant can propagate in favourable condition. In forests there are ample jackfruits, mango, mahua, sal, tendu and other seasonal fruit plants. The tribal folk depend almost completely on seasonal products like crops and fruits. Some of the grains and seeds are also preserved for use in different practices which enriches its nutritive value also. For example the jackfruit seeds, these are rich in carbohydrates and minerals are used as a staple food by them during the normal times and surplus seeds are put deep under soil for use. At the times of scarcity of food this stock is retrieved and used.

Hunger and poverty have driven most tribal women to be sterilized in return for the incentives from the government. There is no medical follow-up to those sterilized ladies who are treated physically and psychologically as cattle; unfortunately family planning in India is gradually being made the sole responsibility of women even among tribals. The percentage of tubectomy (female sterilization) to total sterilisation which is 10.4 in 1967-68 increased to 95.7 in 91-92. The condition is still more precarious in tribal families because of rampant illiteracy and male dominance in social walk of life. Despite of the high priority given to family planning in the five year plans little has been done to involve men and women for whom child spacing and pregnancy prevention are of serious concern.

India is the first country to officially launch family planning programme in 1951. For the success of the programme women education plays a dominant role. Despite the drop in crude birth rates, it is a serious concern about the continuous rise in population of our country. The reasons of not meeting the target are identified as poverty, resources and insufficient health care system and lack of education. These factors are extremely acute in areas dominated by tribal communities in our country. Now, the problem can be ignored because of prominence of AIDS (Acquired Immuno Deficiency Syndromes). AIDS prevention publicity are been made through different programmes by the respective state governments. Similar publicity need be geared up all over the country that too specially in tribal areas. AIDS has now been included in the National Population Policy (NPP 1994). For its effective implementation educational levels of both the genders needs to be enhanced. Besides AIDS, maternity care, child health and family planning etc., there is a need of stress on other dreadful diseases like malaria, tuberculosis, leprosy, blindness which are rampant in tribal areas, more so in the state of Odisha. To prevent the dreadful effect of these diseases right education need be imparted through coordinated efforts of government and non-government agencies. Hence in NPP 1994 the focus is rightly on linkages between population, ecology, and socio-economic development instead of sterilisation target. Again education has to play a pivotal role here. A woman is really the creator and destroyer of her home. If she is educated then half of the problems are solved. So definite steps are to be taken to promote girl/women education, among the poverty stricken ethnic minority tribal families. Usha Devi (1996) reported that 39 per cent of the rural population is below poverty line. According to the norm those earning less than Rs. 11000 a year are said to be below poverty line. In Odisha most of the rural tribal families are below poverty line.

Educational Status of Tribals

In northern part of Odisha among the tribals the Santals, Kolha, and Bhunyas and in the southern districts Khands, Sauras, Parajas and among the tribals of western districts the Gonds and Mundas are dominating. Though the concentration of other tribal sections is relatively thin each section maintains its special cultural identities. The percentage of tribal population to total population in Odisha is 22.21 (Census, 2001). Though there are cultural differences among themselves the children of all the sections meet together on a single educational platform along with non-tribals. There is no differential treatment in schools to different sections of tribals. The teachers transact the curriculum with out having distinction between the tribes or between the tribes and non-tribes. The government of Odisha has a separate Department for Scheduled Tribes and Scheduled Castes, which is known as ST and SC development Department (SSDD). This department has established schools in tribal dominated and advanced areas in the form of Sevashrams (919) and Residential Sevashrams, (143) Ashrams (112) and Kanyashrams (37) Boys' (163) and Girls' (55) high schools. In Sevashrams (primary schools) there is provision of hostels (1548) where boys and girls stay together. The Ashrams and Kanyashrams are of upper primary school standard, which are meant for boys and girls separately. These are completely residential in nature. The boys' and girls' high schools do have residential facilities for the tribal students (Panda, 2002) and Special tribal hostels, (7) Teachers' training schools (2) and Eklavya Model tribal senior secondary schools (11). In addition to it School and Mass Education Department (SMED) also runs school starting from primary to secondary level. In some schools SSDD has provided some hostels where only ST and SC students can reside. The government provides scholarships, reading and writing materials, uniform etc. to the tribal students for prosecuting studies on a common platform with a common syllabus.

The tribal local specific issues could not be addressed in the school system because of certain socio-economic and psychological issues. Through SSA (Sarva Shiksha Abhiyan) experiments and research it has been tried to address these issues to a great extent. The multilingual context have been identified and tried to develop primers in different tribal dialects to address the problems floating out of the issue. The incentives in terms of reading writing materials, uniform, scholarships and support materials like bicycles to students in addition to other facilities mentioned earlier could be able to develop awareness among tribal parents to send their children to school system. Even, barring a few areas in majority of localities tribal parents get involved in the school system through SSA to own education as one of their necessity.

Teaching Learning Problems of Tribal Girls

Tribal children in general and tribal girls in particular usually face the following problems in the process of learning in schools:

1. The Santals only use a definite language, which is known as *"OlChiki"*. It has its own script and literature. Rest of the tribes does have separate dialects and literatures of their own but no scripts. They follow the script of regional language (Odia).

2. The children face language problem at the initial level, but parents prefer Odiya medium because it is the official language of the State and they will be benefited in the long run. Only at the beginning stage a bi/multi lingual situation is preferred. Many are of the opinion that the bilingualism should continued at the most up to class III. This also creates a challenging situation as it is not possible to have children from same tribes in the same class. In reality at times children having different dialects are also found in the same class.

3. For a girl child it becomes difficult to come to the school regularly by foot because of the distance from her home to school. Of course the Sarva Siksha Abhiyan tries to take care of this problem.

4. The social customs, traditions and festivals associated with various tribes create problems in the education of the girls.
5. Poor socio-economic status and illiteracy of the parents.
6. Lack of parental motivation.
7. Lack of study place and atmosphere for a girl child at home.
8. A girl child provides assistance to mother in house-hold work and take care of younger siblings. Even the girl child attends the school with her younger sibling. She has to be involved in both learning and child caring activities in schools.
9. Poor hygienic conditions at the home and at the school. A common tribal family does have one multipurpose living room to be shared by the family members and their domesticated animals
10. Specific health problems of a girl child and lack of healthcare facilities.
11. Dominance of dreadful diseases like malaria, tuberculosis, leprosy, yaws etc.
12. Excess use of liquor by parents especially by the father.
13. Unfavorable attitude of some teachers towards grown up tribal girls.
14. Lack of adequate number of female teachers in schools.
15. Inappropriate curriculum for the tribal girls. A girl gets training with required life skills at home as discussed earlier. School does not provide much in this respect.
16. Non-availability of uniform and reading and writing materials in the schools in time.
17. Non-congenial transactional procedure adopted by many teachers in the school plant though constructivist approach is the call of the day. Mostly rote memory is being emphasised in schools. Many untrained teachers are engaged. Those who are trained are not able to create a sustainable difference as compared to their counterpart.
18. Inadequacy of co-scholastic activities in the school plant for girls.
19. Inferiority complex of tribal girls.
20. Early marriage of a girl child.

21. Late admission of a girl child in school.
22. Gender bias or discrimination is no that prominent in tribal culture and societies unlike the general social situations. But the same is very common in schools. This affects the girl child very adversely.

Suggestions for Improvement of Women Education Programme

1. Though the focus is diverted from quantity of schooling to both quantity and quality of schooling of girls still it could not yield spectacular improvement in quality of schooling. The quality of the schooling must be given top priority in terms of effective management, quality teachers and better residential and infra-structural facilities in the schools meant for girls.
2. Separate functional toilets and better drinking water facilities must be ensured in different levels of schools specially meant for girls. Recently honourable Supreme court have issued direction to Central and all State Government to provide safe drinking water, toilets and other basic infrastructure within six months *(Hindustan Times October 4, 2012)*.
3. The text book should have more representation of contents from tribal cultures.
4. More tribal teachers are to be trained and employed in the school meant for tribals.
5. The teacher education programme must contain contextuality on training and methodology of teaching. Of course the SSDD runs two teacher training institute where more short in-service courses for elementary teachers need be offered.
6. The in-service teacher education programmes must be need based and gender treatment input need be encouraged.
7. Curriculum has been redesigned in the light of National Curriculum Frame Work 2005. But in the contents examples for life skills pertaining to the tribal society need be emphasised.
8. A standard procedure is to be developed to recruit morally strong teachers. Undue external interference must be avoided in the recruitment process. The right social attitude towards teaching of tribal children must be given priority in addition to academic qualifications.
9. The school management must priorities to all round development of the children under its care through its curriculum transaction.

10. Motivational level of children as well as the parents need for education of the children is enhanced. Some local parents need be inducted into the school management even at secondary level as it works very effectively in many school located in the districts of Gajapati and Kalahandi etc. (Panda, 2003).
11. There should not be any gender discrimination either in the text book or in teacher behavior.
12. Definite transfer policy of teachers need be followed in the absence of which a lot of resentment is growing among the teachers working in difficult and inaccessible areas. It will discourage the practice of teacher absenteeism and proxy teaching.
13. Monitoring of school activities need be an integral part of school management.
14. Suitable action plan for teaching environmental studies need be ensured for elementary schools (Panda, 2003).
15. The incentives and privileges in terms of uniform, reading and writing materials, finance etc. need be provided in time for smooth conducting of learning activities in school.
16. Ensuring community participation in school management to provide a sense of belongingness to tribal parents. They should develop a feeling that the school belongs to them.
17. Efficient, honest, sincere, dynamic and scholarly persons need be selected as the heads of the schools. Simple seniority criterion does not help to improve the situation.
18. Adequate number of lady teachers need be appointed in elementary schools run by SSDD.
19. Quality teachers need be identified and they need be amply rewarded for their contribution in the schooling system.
20. Varieties of tribal friendly vocational courses need be introduced from upper primary level to senior secondary levelfor girls by the school system.
21. Private tuition and coaching are to be strictly banned and right classroom teaching adopting constructivist approach required to be emphasised.

22. Mastery learning strategy is better to be implemented at elementary level (Panda and Panda, 1999) with adequate training of teachers in addition to constructivist approach.
23. Above all better disciplinary measures need be emphasised so as to improve regularity, punctuality and sincerity of the teachers which will in turn automatically be imbibed by the students.
24. The SSDD should try to develop separate curriculum in the line of the NCF 2005 with ample emphasis on context based on the varying needs and interest of tribal children so as to cater to their academic, cultural, vocational and professional needs. It must include different learner friendly activities built in scholastic areas emphasising varieties of life skills.
25. Specific research projects need be undertaken on the socio-psychological and gender issues, school life, classroom interaction problems of tribal girls, issues on stress of school going girls, student teacher relation and other related educational issues.

Conclusion

It is high time that the educated and responsible citizens of the state and the national government simply need not ponder over the matter of education of ethnic minority groups specifically women seriously but act with more involvement by improving school education in general and classroom instruction in particular. It will pave the way for empowering the women-hood. Enough remedial measures at classroom interaction level in particular need be taken to check the deterioration of the tribal lives and save their families from further disintegration. Just observing birthday of some important tribal personalities, opening schools, arranging *'AdivasiMelas'* in the capital city, conducting *'ZillaMahotsavas'*, naming some institutes after some tribal personalities is certainly a mode of encouragement but not adequate. States like Sikkim, Mizoram, Meghalaya, Nagaland etc., are adopting special measures to improve the level of women education .The situation in Odisha is different and difficult because of socio-political and cultural conditions. In some southern tribal dominated districts like Gajapati, Malkangiri, Rayagada and Koraput and northern districts like Mayurbhanj, Keonjhar and Sundargarh some kind of social upheaval in the form of Naxalite movements and Peoples War Group are already in its peak. Hence it's most urgently needed that proper attention be given to tribal education in general, women education in particular and their empowerment and preserving tribal culture through education otherwise the situation may lead to serious imbalance in the structure of rural tribal society and create chaos and anarchy init which would definitely affect the rest of the country.

Moreover, after the implementation of RTE Act 2009 it becomes very urgent to emphasis on girls' education that too for socially disadvantaged group of people. The most important issue lies in front of us not only access to schooling for girls but also majors to retain in the schooling system by providing student friendly teachers and infrastructure. These two issues have got serious baring on the part of school management which automatically clears the path for better learning achievement in relation to the tribal girls in particular.

References

1. Hindustan Times, October 04, 2012, New Delhi.
2. Mathur, H. M. (1996). The Family Welfare Programmes in India. New Delhi: Vikas Publishing House Pvt. Ltd.
3. National Curriculum Frame work 2005, NCERT, New Delhi.
4. National Population Policy (1994).Government of India, New Delhi.
5. Panda, S. C., and Panda, B.N. (1999). Effect of Mastery Learning Strategy on Attainment of Selected Competencies in Mathematics of Class I and II (DPEP Research). Bhubanes war: Regional Institute of Education (NCERT)
6. Panda, S.C. (2002). Psychosocial and Pedagogical Problems of tribal Learners in Sevashrams. Bhubaneswar: Regional Institute of Education NCERT).
7. Panda, S.C. (2002). Training Package on Curriculum Transactions for teachers of Sevashrams. Bhubaneswar: Regional Institute of Education (NCERT).
8. Panda, S.C. (2003). School Community Symbiosis: Strategies adopted in Tribal Primary Schools (DPEP Research). Bhubaneswar: Regional Institute of Education (NCERT).
9. Programme of Action (1992). Government of India, New Delhi: Ministry of Human Resource Development.
10. Rai, Usha (1996). 39 per cent of rural population under poverty line. The Hindustan Times (late city).dated December 4, 1996.
11. RTE Act 2009, MHRD, India, New Delhi
12. Sahay, K.B.(1996). Full Literacy by 2005.The Hindustan Times (late city). Dated November 6, 1996.

10

Tribals in Andaman and Nicobar Islands: An Overview

Amitra Sudan Chakraborty

Introduction

Humans are primates of the family Hominidae, and the only living species of the genus *Homo*. They originated in Africa, where they reached anatomical modernity about 200,000 years ago and began to exhibit full behavioural modernity around 50,000 years ago. All human are not equal in socio status and position. Some people settled in plain area and other in hilly areas. Tribal people are settled in hilly areas. The Constitution of India, Article 366 (25) defines Scheduled Tribes as *"such tribes or tribal communities or part of or groups within such tribes or tribal communities as are deemed under Article 342 to the scheduled Tribes (STs) for the purposes of this Constitution"*. Tribal people are particularly present in Andhra Pradesh, Bihar, Chattisgarh, Gujarat, Jharkhand, Madhya Pradesh, Maharashtra, Orissa, Rajasthan, Tamil Nadu, West Bengal and some northeastern states, and the Andaman and Nicobar Islands. Many smaller tribal groups are quite sensitive to ecological degradation caused by modernisation. Both commercial forestry and intensive agriculture have proved destructive to the forests that had endured swidden agriculture for many centuries. Tribal people constitute 8.2 per cent of the nation's total population, over 84 million people according to the 2001 census. The majority of tribal practice Hinduism and

Christianity. During the last two decades tribal from Orissa, Madhya Pradesh, Jharkhand have converted to Protestant groups.

Andaman and Nicobar Islands

The Andaman Islands are a group of Indian Ocean archipelagic islands in the Bay of Bengal, between the Indian peninsula to the west and Burma to the north and east. Most of the islands are part of the Andaman and Nicobar Islands Union Territory of India, while a small number in the north of the archipelago belong to Burma. It has 325 islands which cover an area of 6,408 km^2 (2,474 sq mi), with the Andaman Sea to the east between the islands and the coast of Burma. North Andaman Island is 285 kilometres (177 mi) south of Burma, although a few smaller Burmese islands are closer, including the three Coco Islands. As the numbers of settlers from the mainland increased (at first mostly prisoners and involuntary indentured labourers, later purposely recruited farmers), these indigenous people lost territory and numbers in the face of punitive expeditions by British troops, land encroachment and the effects of various epidemic. The Jangil were soon extinct. The Nicobar Islands are an archipelagic island chain in the eastern Indian Ocean. They are located in Southeast Asia, 150 km north of Aceh on Sumatra and separated from Thailand to the east by the Andaman Sea. Great Nicobar is the largest of the Nicobar Islands of India, north of Sumatra. Indira Point, its southernmost tip is also the southernmost point of India. The Andaman and Nicobar Islands were shrouded in mystery for centuries because of their inaccessibility. These are the paragon of beauty and present a landscape full with scenic and picturesque extravaganza.

The Great Andaman group of islands is made up of North, Middle and South Andaman Islands, with Baratang Island situated between Middle and South Andaman Islands. Ritchie's Archipelago is a group of islands located to the east of Middle Andaman while the Labyrinth group of islands is situated south west of South Andaman. Nearly 90 per cent of the total land area of 6408 sq km of the Andaman group is constituted of reserve forests and protected areas. Nearly 36 per cent of this land is designated at tribal reserve. Narcondum and Barren are the two islands here which are of volcanic origin. The former is supposed to be extinct, while the latter is still active. The Nicobar group is spread over an area of 1841 sq. km of which 1542 are forests. The Nicobars are separated from the Andamans by the 10 degree channel, a wide gap of 160 km. This group consists of 24 islands in three distinct clusters. The northern group consists of Car Nicobar and Batti Malv; the central or the Nancowry group consists of Tillangchong, Chowra, Teressa, Bompoka, Trinkat, Kamorta, Katchal and Nancowry, and the southern group which consists of the two large islands of Little and Great Nicobar together with Pigeon, Megapode, Kondul, Pilo Milo, Menchal, Teris, Trak and Meroe Islands. The entire Nicobars has been declared a tribal reserve.

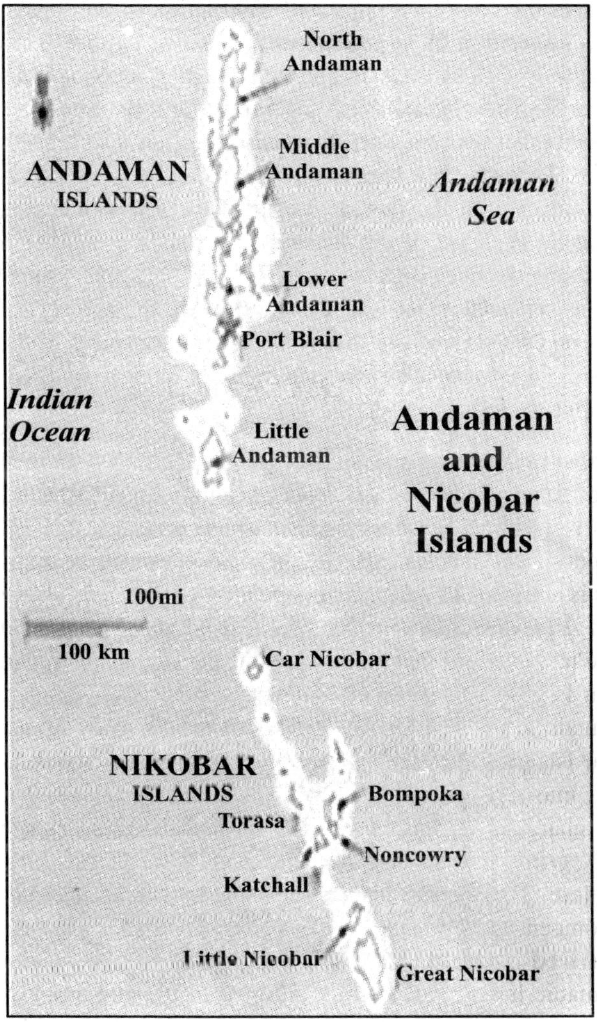

There are two distinct inhabitants of the Andaman Islands - The *'Indians'* and the *'Natives'*. The former are people from the Indian mainland especially from Punjab, West Bengal, Tamil Nadu as well as immigrants from Myanmar and Sri Lanka. The indigenous tribes are distinguished as two groups*: the Onge, Sentinelese, Jarawa and Andamanese of Negroid descent* living on the Andaman Islands and the *Shompen and Nicobarese of Mongoloid* descent living in the Nicobar Islands. Most of these tribes are on the verge of extinction because of the combined impact of destruction of the forest habitats and the imposition of an alien and insensitive culture that brought along with it various diseases and vices such as alcohol and tobacco. The two Negrito communities, the Jarawa and the Sentinelese have avoided contact with the outside world and often resorted to violence to do so. Perhaps they realise that their only way of survival is to avoid contact with the outside world. This however appears to be changing in the case of the Jarawa. Whereas the number of Great Andamanese declined because of the various epidemics, the Onge are suffering on account of the destruction of their forests and the imposition of a way of life that is alien and insensitive to them. The Nicobarese are fortunate to have found it easier to assimilate into the contemporary Indian society.

Tribes of Andaman and Nicobar Islands are known for their unique and indigenous traditions and ways of living. Andaman and Nicobar Islands is a Union Territory around which revolves several legends and modern day fancies. Steeped in history, Andaman and Nicobar Islands is home to umpteen tribal populations. The *Great Andamanese, Jarawa tribe, Sentinelese tribe, Onges tribe and Shompens tribe* are the five native tribes that mainly inhabit the islands of Andaman and Nicobar Islands. The tribes of Andaman and Nicobar Islands continue to maintain a unique lifestyle of their own. Tribes of Andaman and Nicobar Islands follow their indigenous customs and rituals. Basically divided into five groups of tribes, these aboriginal settlers have a unique character of their own. The Andaman Islands are home to four *'Negrito'* tribes, the Great Andamanese, Onge, Jarawa and Sentinelese. The Nicobar Islands are home to two *'Mongoloid'* tribes– the Shompen and Nicobarese. The *'Negrito'* tribes are believed to have arrived in the islands from Africa up to 60,000 years ago. All are nomadic hunter-gatherers, hunting wild pig and monitor lizard, and catching fish with bows and arrows. They also collect honey, roots and berries from the forest. The *'Mongoloid'* tribes probably came to the islands from the Malay-Burma coast several thousand years ago.

The Chinese knew of the Andaman and Nicobar Islands over 1000 years ago and called it the *'Yeng-t-omag'*. The Andaman and Nicobar Islands also find a place in the first map of the world drawn by Ptolemy, the Roman geographer during the 2nd Century. He called it *'Angdaman islands (Islands of good fortune)'*. During the 6th Century I'T Sing, a Buddhistmonk, named it *'Lo*-jen – kuo' (Land of the Naked). Two Arab travelers during the 8th Century referred to these islands as *'Lakhabalus or Najabulus'* (Land of the Naked). Mythologically, the name Andaman is presumed to be derived from Hanuman, who was known to the Malays as Handuman. Since pre-historic times, these islands were the home of aboriginal tribes. These emerald Islands, blessed with natural beauty, 86 per cent forest cover, world class beaches, undulating creeks, crystal clear water and unpolluted environment command the first place to visit for tourists. This archipelago of more than 572 islets and islands with 37 inhabited islands stretches over a length of more than 700 kms from North to South. The topography of the islands is hilly with exotic flora and fauna.

The diverse culture of these tribes of India is a unique feature. Men amongst the Great Andamanese tribes wear narrow belts or girdles of hibiscus fibre. They usually have a heavy body, so it suits their personality. Weapons are tucked into their belts when they go for hunting. The women folk of these tribes of India have a typical tribal dress sense. Branches of leaves cut into stripes held by belt of pandanus leaves and tail skirt amongst the girls form the dress code of women of Andamanese tribes of India. A distinctive feature of women of these tribes of India is their painted bodies. Hunting is the main source of food and occupation with these tribes of India. Moreover these tribes in India also cultivate vegetables and run poultry farm for their livelihood. The Great Andamanese tribe is settled presently on the Strait Island by the Andaman and Nicobar Administration. This was the largest tribe earlier before the establishment of Penal Settlement in Andaman Islands. These tribes of India eat almost all the variety of food. Andamanese tribes usually eat rice, wheat, dal, chapati, etc.,

Besides this, Great Andamanese tribes also prefer non vegetarian stuff such as fish, turtle eggs, crabs, roots, seeds and tubers. Pork and Andaman water monitor lizard are the prime eat up of Andamanese tribes of India. Today, they eat rice, dal chapati and other modern food articles. They can cook food with an assortment of spices. These tribes of India are generally known for three absolutely different types of language they speak. Jeru, Khora and Andamani Hindi are the major languages spoken by Andamanese tribes of India. A fortnight long festival organized by the Andaman and Nicobar Administration every year gives a festive look to the Islands. Govt. agencies and private entrepreneurs from the islands and Mainland India also attend the exhibition organized during the festival. The exhibition highlights the developmental aspects of these islands. Cultural troupes and artistes of national and international fame are invited to perform during the festival apart from performances by the talents of these islands including tribals. The various tribes of Andaman Islands are:

Great Andamanese Tribe

Great Andamanese tribal group resides in the Strait Island. This was the largest tribal group earlier in Andaman. But presently the number has decreased notably. The administration of this island has come forward to help this tribe in surviving. The people of this tribe still go for hunting and gathering. Some of them also depend upon agriculture producing different vegetables. Recently poultry farms have also been started by them. Their culture is quite different from the other tribes of this region. The great Andamanese were foragers. Their traditional food items are fish, dugong, turtle, turtle eggs, crabs, roots and tubers. In spite of the outside influences they are still carrying their age old tradition and culture. The tribe that has suffered most from contact with outsiders: nearly 99 per cent have been wiped out since the British first colonised the islands. Before the tsunami they lived in a government settlement and were dependent on government aid. They have just been moved to the islands' capital, Port Blair, as their village was badly damaged in the tsunami.

The Great Andamanese were originally divided into ten major tribes, with distinct but closely related languages comprising one of the two identified families of indigenous Andamanese languages, the Great Andamanese family. The Great Andamanese are classified by anthropologists as one of the Negrito peoples, which also include the other four aboriginal groups of the Andaman Islands (Onge, Jarawa, Jangil and Sentinelese) and a few other isolated populations of East Asia. The Andaman Negritos are thought to be the first inhabitants of the islands, having emigrated from the mainland tens of thousands of years ago. Until the late 18th century, the Andamanese peoples were preserved from outside influences by their fierce rejection of contacts and by the remoteness of the islands. Their territories spanned most of the Great Andaman islands, including Ritche's Archipelago and Rutland Island but excluding Little Andaman (inhabited by the Onge) and the Sentinel Islands (of the Sentinelese). On South Andaman the Great Andamanese coexisted with the Jarawa and on Rutland Island with the Jangil. The Great Andaman islands run in a north–south line for some 350 km but are only some 50 km wide at its widest extent. This peculiar geography meant that each tribe typically had only two or three neighbours. Indeed, until colonial times, the northern and southern tribes seemed unaware of each other's existence. Today only two tribes (Jeru and Bo) remain in significant number; the Kari tribe was on its way to extinction. There are still a few people (all elderly) with partial Kora and Pucikwar descent, but they identify themselves as either Jeru or Bo. However, the cultural and linguistic identities of the individual tribes have largely been lost; their members now speak mostly Hindi or a mixed language, a Great Andamanese creole.

Jarwa Tribe

This tribe presently resides at the Western coast of Middle Andaman and South Andaman Islands. Their esteemed population is 250-400. Administration has spread its hand to befriend the inhabitant of this tribe by gifting them bananas, coconuts and other fruits. Till 1998 they were hostile to other people but they are coming out of their inhibition and trying to mix with the local people. This nomadic tribe is surviving on hunting, fishing and gathering. The traditional food of this tribe includes wild boar, turtles and their eggs, crabs, fruits and honey. The Jarwas are healthy with smooth skin, curly hair, long and sturdy hands and legs. The Jarwa people use crude rafts to cross creeks and streams. They live on the west coast of South and Middle Andaman and are believed to have survived the tsunami. They are still completely independent and live entirely by hunting, gathering and fishing. The main threat to their existence comes from the highway running through their territory: the Indian government was ordered to close this by the Supreme Court in 2002, but it has ignored the order. Before the 19th century, the Jarawa homelands were located in the southeast part of South Andaman Island and nearby islets. With the establishment of the initial British settlement, these are suspected to have been largely depopulated by disease shortly after 1789.

Since they have largely shunned interactions with outsiders, many particulars of their society, culture and traditions are poorly understood. Along with other indigenous Andamanese peoples, they have inhabited the islands for at least several thousand years, and most likely a great deal longer. The biggest threat to the Jarawa in recent years came from the building of the Great Andaman Trunk Road through their newer western forest homeland in the 1970s. The impact of the highway, in addition to widespread encroachment, poaching and commercial exploitation of Jarawa lands, caused a lawsuit to be filed with the Calcutta High Court, which has jurisdiction over the islands. The case escalated to the Supreme Court of India as a Public Interest Litigation (or PIL). The Society for Andaman and Nicobar Ecology, the Bombay Natural History Society and Pune-based Kalpavriksh joined in the petition, resulting in a landmark High Court judgment in 2001, directing the administration to take steps to protect the Jarawa from encroachment and contact, as well as preemptively ruling out any program that involved relocating the Jarawa to a new reservation. Planned extensions of the highway were also prohibited by the court.

A major problem is the volume of sightseeing tours that are operated by private companies, where tourists view, photograph or otherwise attempt interactions with Jarawas, who are often begging by the highway. These are illegal under Indian law, and in March 2008, the Tourism Department of the Andaman and Nicobar administration issued a fresh warning to tour operators that attempting contact with Jarawas, photographing them, stopping vehicles while transiting through their land or offering them rides were prohibited under the Protection of Aboriginal Tribes Regulation, 1956, and would be prosecuted under a strict interpretation of the statute. In 2006, the Indian travel company Barefoot had established a resort three km distant from the Jarawa reserve. The development was the subject of a recent court case brought by a small section of Andaman authorities who wanted to stop the resort, and appealed against a Calcutta High Court ruling allowing it to continue.

They are now friendly and voluntary seek medical assistance. They do not have good canoes but can make rafts which they build to cross the streams. The year 1974 was a land mark in the history of Jarawas. Dropping of gifts was done in February and March 1974. After establishing this friendly mission with the Jarawas, the contact party of the Administration quite often met the Jarawas and gave them gift items like banana, coconut and other fruits. With the passage of time, the behavioral pattern of Jarawas has changed. Till the beginning of 1998, they remained hostile, but now they are coming out of the jungle quite often and are becoming friendlier. For nearly a year there is no incidence of killing of villagers by the Jarawas. On the other hand, the Jarawas are coming out from their habitat to mix with the local people. After giving them gift items like bananas, coconuts, etc., they are being sent out to live in their own natural habitat, with view not to force them to have a taste of the civilized world. Isolated so long, the Jarawas otherwise appear to be healthy, with smooth skin, deep curly hair, long and sturdy hands and legs and sturdy bones. They are physically fit for hunting, fishing.

Sentinelese Tribe

The people of this group are settled in the North Sentinel Island. They are the world's only Palaeolithic people surviving today without contact with any other group or community. The people of this tribe are considered as an off-shoot to the Onge Jarawa tribes which have acquired a different identity due to their habitation in an isolated and have lost contact with the main tribes. The Sentinelese is very hostile in nature and never leaves their Island. They mainly survive through hunting, fishing and gathering. Very little is known about these hostile tribes. Their forest home has been plundered by poachers and loggers. They were settled by the Indian administration and are dependent on food handouts. The most isolated of all the tribes, they have no peaceful contact with outsiders and fire warning arrows at those who approach. Their home, Sentinel Island, appears to have been relatively unaffected by the tsunami and some Sentinelese have been sighted since the disaster. They are completely self-sufficient hunter-gatherers.

Onges Tribe

This tribal group is one of the oldest tribe in India. They are related to the Negrito racial stock and they have been relegated to the reserved pockets both at Dugong Creek and South Bay of Little Andaman Island. Their traditional food includes turtle, fish, roots and jack fruits and etc. These people developed artistry and craft. Their present population is 105. They occasionally go for hunting and fishing. They are independent in their own ways. The people of this tribe are on the way of remarkable progress. In the 18th century the Onge were distributed across Little Andaman Island and the nearby islands, with some territory and camps established on Rutland Island and the southern tip of South Andaman Island. Originally restive, they were pacified by M.V. Portman in the 1890s. By the end of the 19th century they sometimes visited the South and North Brother Islands to catch sea turtles; at the time, those islands seemed to be the limit between their territory and the range of the Great Andamanese people further north. Today, the surviving members (less than 100) are confined to two reserve camps on Little Andaman, Dugong Creek in the northeast and South Bay. The Onge were semi-nomadic and used to be fully dependent on hunting and gathering for food. They are the semi-nomadic tribes and fully dependent on the food provided by nature. They have now experienced the impact of outsiders. At the same time efforts at befriending them have proved to be successful. They have been provided with pucca hut type houses, food, clothes, medicines, etc., by the Administration. They eat turtle, fish, roots and jack fruits and etc. They have developed artistry and craft. The Onges can make canoes. A primary school has been functioning at the Dugong Creek settlement of Onges. This tribe has become laid back and dependent in their ways. Also their rate of reproduction has become very low.

Shompens Tribe

The people of this tribe belong to the Mongoloid Group. They inhabit the Nicobar Island. This tribe has two divisions. The smaller division is *Mawa Shompens* that live very close to the coastal region along the river valleys and are very shy. However, they are friendly with the Nicobarese. The main group of Shompens is hostile and resides in Alexendra and Galathia river areas and also on the east coast of the area in the interiors. The Nicobarese tribal group is having their own set of laws and traditions. Their numbers have dwindled greatly as a result of various diseases and they are physically very weak. The number of the Shompens is estimated to be 400. The Shompens speak in a dialect of their own. A relatively isolated tribe of Great Nicobar Island, the Shompen are hunter-gatherers who have some, limited, contact with outsiders. They practice a hunter-gatherer subsistence economy. In keeping with the tropical climate of the islands, traditional attire includes only clothing below the waist. The traditional attire for men is a short, thin loincloth made of bark cloth, covering only the genitals without a *'tail'* of cloth in front. A man usually carried a bow and arrows, a spear and through his loincloth belt, a hatchet, knife and fire drill. The Shompen are a hunter-gatherer subsistence people, hunting wild game such as pigs, birds and small animals while foraging for fruits and forest foods. They also keep pigs and farm yams, roots, vegetables, and tobacco. Shompen huts are built to house 4 people, and villages are made up of four to five families. Once a child is grown enough, he makes his own hut. Studies of mitochondrial DNA have shown that the maternal lineage of Shompens is closest to that of Indonesians. Variations in DNA segments on the Y chromosome also reveal affinities to Austro-Asiatic people including the Nicobarese and Vietnamese, rather than to people from mainland India. Because of their isolated way of life in the interior of the island, the Shompens were largely protected from the 2004 Indian Ocean earthquake and tsunami that devastated the coastal regions inhabited by Nicobaris and the Indian population.

Nicobarese

Unlike the other tribes, the Nicobarese are largely horticulturalists. Most have converted to Christianity and are much more assimilated than the other Andaman and Nicobar tribes, but still maintain their own distinct culture. The Nicobarese have also suffered much more from the tsunami. All 12 villages on one island, Car Nicobar, have been washed away, and many are feared dead. The Nicobarese people are a Mon–Khmer-speaking people of the Nicobar Islands, a chain of 19 islands in the southeastern Bay of Bengal. Only 12 of the 19 islands are inhabited. The largest and main island is Great Nicobar. The term Nicobarese refers to the dominant tribes of the Nicobar Islands. On each island, the people have specific names, but together they are the Nicobarese. They call themselves Holchu, which means *"friend"*. The Nicobarese may not have been the first people to live in the islands; they appear to have shared the islands with Shompen who came to the islands earlier. On the Nicobar Islands, men and women have approximate equal status. The women have a lot to do with their own choice of husbands, and after marriage they are free to live with either of the couples parents. The Nicobarese men value the women economically. The villages on the islands consist of sporadically placed huts strewn about in designated areas. The huts are normally round with dome shaped roofs. They are typically lifted up from the ground and they have ladders that they climb up to get into the huts that they bring in at night. The Nicobarese have a traditionally horticultural economy, they base their monetary existence on the growing of coconuts, pandanus, areca nut palms, bananas, mangoes, and other fruits. They also hunt, fish, raise pigs, make pottery, and make canoes.

Tsunami

On 26 December 2004, the coast of the Nicobar Islands was devastated by a 10–15 m high tsunami following the 2004 Indian Ocean earthquake. At least 6,000 people (possibly a conservative estimate) were killed on the Andaman and Nicobar Islands during the disaster. Reports put the death toll on Katchal Island alone at 4,600. Several islands were heavily damaged with initial reports of islands broken in two or three pieces and coral reefs moved above water. Teressa Island was said to have been split into two pieces and Trinkat Island into three pieces. Some estimates said that the islands were moved as much as 100 feet (30 m) by the earthquake and tilted.

Supreme Court Judgement

After two British newspapers released a controversial video film showing scantily clad Jarawa tribal women dancing for tourists in return for food and money, the government finally acted: the Union Cabinet approved the promulgation of a law that brings into effect a buffer zone in the five km radius around the Jarawa tribal settlements in the Andaman and Nicobar Islands and provides for imprisonment up to seven years for those violating government norms for this area. The decision to promulgate *the Andaman and Nicobar Islands (Protection of Aboriginal tribes) Amendment Regulation 2012* has been taken under Article 240 of the Constitution, which empowers the President to take such measures in case of Union Territories. This regulation will cover the entire Andaman and Nicobar Islands. Tourist establishments will be prohibited and other commercial establishments will be regulated in the buffer zone, which will protect the aboriginal tribes from undesirable outside influences. The law provides for tough penal provisions to deter unauthorised entry, photography, videography, hunting, use of alcohol, inflammable material or biological germs, or even advertisements to attract tourists in the buffer zone. Any violation can attract a prison sentence of three to seven years and a fine up to Rs 10,000.

An earlier attempt by the Andaman Union Territory administration to prohibit all commercial and tourist activities, through a notification on October 30, 2007, within a designated buffer zone was quashed by the Calcutta High Court on the grounds that the principal Regulation only permitted such notifications for *"reserved areas."* A Special Leave Petition, challenging this, was subsequently filed in the Supreme Court, and it is in the pendency of this SLP that the Union Cabinet, using Article 240, has approved the promulgation of a law that will create a buffer zone. Official sources said this meant that the lacuna in the regulation that saw the Calcutta High Court quash the earlier notification has now been addressed: it was tantamount to a policy change. The Supreme Court has banned all commercial and tourism activities within a five-km radius of the Jarawa Tribal Reserve on the Andaman and Nicobar Islands with a view to protecting the indigenous people. A Bench of Justices G. S. Singhvi and S. J. Mukhopadhaya upheld an October 30, 2007 notification declaring an area up to a five-km radius of the Reserve a *'Buffer Zone'* and prohibiting entry of any person other than a member of the aboriginal tribe into it. Disposing of the appeal filed by the Andaman and Nicobar Administration against a Calcutta High Court order which had quashed the notification, the Bench said: *"Henceforth no commercial and tourism-related activities shall be carried out by the administration or any private individual in violation of the prohibition contained in the notification."* At the hearing of the appeal, the Bench had passed an order which said, *"No tourist establishment such as resorts, hotels, restaurants, bars and paying guest accommodation, except government-run guest houses, will be permitted within the Buffer Zone. No commercial establishment/ activities which may employ more than 20 persons or have an annual turnover of Rs 1 crore or more will be allowed in the Buffer Zone."*

After staying the High Court's order, the Supreme Court asked the Administration to strictly enforce the notification until it was considered by it. The Bench said: *"It shall be the duty of the Principal Secretary (Tribal Welfare) and other officers of the Administration to ensure total compliance with the prohibition contained in the notification and this order. Any breach of this order will entail punishment under the Contempt of Courts Act."*

Conclusion

Andaman and Nicobar islands are the land of various ancient tribes. The indigenous tribes are distinguished as two groups: the Onge, Sentinelese, Jarawa and Andamanese of Negroid descent living on the Andaman Islands and the Shompen and Nicobarese of Mongoloid descent living in the Nicobar Islands. Most of these tribes are on the verge of extinction because of the combined impact of destruction of the forest habitats and the imposition of an alien and insensitive culture that brought along with it various diseases and vices such as alcohol and tobacco. The two Negrito communities, the Jarawa and the Sentinelese have avoided contact with the outside world and often resorted to violence to do so. There are various islands are totally reserve for the tribal's. There should be more protection of tribal's in Andaman and Nicobar islands.

References

1. *Adivashi (2012).* Retrieved from http://en.wikipedia.org/wiki/Adivasi
2. *Andaman Islands (2012).* Retrieved from http://en. wikipedia.org/wiki/Andaman_Islands
3. *Andaman and Nicobar Islands (2012).* Retrieved from http://www.kalpavriksh.org/index.php/conservation-livelihoods1/andaman-nicobar-islands.html
4. *Andamanese tribes (2012).* Retrieved from http://www.indianmirror. com/tribes/andamanesetribe.html
5. *Andaman and Nicober Islands (2012).* Retrieved from http://calcuttahighcourt.nic.in/district_courts/andaman.htm
6. *Background of the tribes of the Andaman and Nicober islands (2005).* Retrieved from http://www. survival international. org/news/175
7. *Great Andamanese People (2012).* Retrieved from http://en.wikipedia. org/wiki/Great_Andamanese
8. *Great Nicobar Island (2012).* Retrieved from http://en.wikipedia.org/wiki/Great_Nicobar

9. *History (2012)*. Retrieved from http://www.andaman tourism.in/andamans-history-india.html
10. *Jarawa people (Andaman Islands) (2012)*. Retrieved from http://en.wikipedia.org/wiki/Jarawa_people_%28 Andaman_Islands%29
11. *Nicobar Islands (2012)*. Retrieved from http://en.wikipedia. org/wiki/Nicobar_Islands
12. *Nicobarese people (2012)*. Retrieved from http://en. wikipedia.org/wiki/Nicobarese_people
13. *Onge People (2012)*. Retrieved from http://en.wikipedia.org/wiki/Onge_people
14. *People of Andaman and Nicobar Islands (2012)*. Retrieved from http://www.journeymart.com/de/india/andaman-and-nicobar-islands-people-society.aspx
15. *Shompen People (2012)*. Retrieved from http://en. wikipedia. org/wiki/Shompen_people
16. *The Hindu (June 1, 2012). Jarawa region to have buffer zone*, Retrieved from http://www.thehindu.com/news/national/jarawa-region-to-have-buffer-zone/article 3477089. ece
17. *The Hindu (July 4, 2012). No commercial, tourism activity in Jarawa Reserve, rules Supreme court*, Retrieved from http://www.thehindu.com/news/states/other-states/no-commercial-tourism-activity-in-jarawa-reserve-rules-supreme-court/article3599426.ece
18. *Tribes of Andaman and Nicobar Islands*, Retrieved from http://www.indianetzone.com/30/tribes_ andaman_ nicobar _islands.htm
19. *Tribes of Andaman and Nicobar (2012)*. Retrieved from http://www.indialine.com/travel/andaman/tribes.html
20. *Way of Life at Andaman and Nicobar Islands (2012)*. Retrieved from http://www.andamanislandholidays.com/Way-of-Life.html

11

Tribal and Their Labour Problems (Indian Context)

Rakesh A. Joshi **and** *Falguni S. Vyas*

Introduction

The Indian sub-continent has the largest concentration of tribal population in the world and constitutes 8.2 per cent of the country's total population. During the last 60 years various steps has been taken for the welfare of the tribal, but their impact is slow. These steps have not disseminated benefits, at least for some tribal communities, who remain untouched. There is a diversity of communities in our country. Here, we find social hierarchy and stratification through the institution of caste. The British administrators pursued a policy of isolation and kept the tribal away from the mainstream of Indian life. A difficult challenge that the Government of India has been facing since independence is the proper provision of social justice to the tribal by improving their socio-economic conditions. Tribal constitute a weaker section of India's population from the social, economic and educational angles. Tribal born and grow as the children of the nature; but they are deprived of many civic facilities and isolated from modern and civilised way of living.

Who are the Tribal?

The constitution of India does not define scheduled Tribes as such. According to Article 342 of the constitution, *the scheduled tribes are the tribal communities or part of group within these communities, which have been declared as such by the President of India through a public notification.* As per 1991 census, the scheduled tribes account for 67.76 million representing 8.08 per cent of the country's population and in 2001, it increased to 8.2 per cent of the total population. They are spread across the country mainly in forest and hilly areas. As per 1991 census, 42.02 per cent of the Scheduled Tribes population was main workers of whom 54.50 per cent were cultivators and 32.69 per cent agricultural labourers. Thus, about 87 per cent of the main workers from these communities were engaged in primary sector activities. The literacy rate of scheduled tribes was around 29.60 per cent, as against the national average of 52 per cent in 1991. This disparity is compounded by higher dropout rates in formal education. The proportion of scheduled tribes below the poverty line made by Planning Commission for the year 1993-'94 shows that 51.92 per cent rural and 41.4 per cent urban scheduled tribes were living below the poverty line.

The constitution of India now here states explicitly how a *'tribe'* can be recognised and how it can be distinguished from a *'caste' or a 'non tribal'*. To the ordinary man, the word *'Tribe'* suggests simple folk living in hills and forests. To the people who are a little better informed, it signifies colourful folk famous for their dance and song. The dictionary of Anthropology mentions *a tribe, as a social group, usually with a definite area, dialect, cultural homogeneity, and unifying social organisation... it ordinarily has a leader and many have a common ancestor, as well as patron diety.* The families or small communities making up the tribe are linked through economic ,social religious, families or blood ties.T.B. Naik has proposed the following seven criteria by which a tribe can be recognised: (a) A tribe has the least functional inter-dependence within the community; (b) it is economically backward; (c) it is geographically isolated; (d) it speaks a common dialect which may, however be subject to regional variations; (e) it is politically a unit under a common tribal authority; (f) a tribe's members are averse to change; (g) A tribe has its own traditional laws which often differ from those of majority communities.

The above mentioned few important definitions show that, there are diversities as regards the essential characteristics of a tribe. In India a tribe is usually a territory group; it has a traditional territory, and immigrants always refer to it as their home. Members of an Indian tribe speak one common language, their own or that of their neighbours. Indian tribes are under the administrative control of state governments. The absence of institutional schooling; distinctive customs regarding birth, marriage and death; a moral code different from that of Hindus and Muslims; specialties of religious beliefs and rituals etc. are the other distinguishing features of tribesmen. In Gujarat, there are 28 various tribal; in which *Bhil, Dhodia, Chaudhari, Halpati, Kokana, Rathva, Gamit, Varli, Kunbi* etc. are in majority.

Problems Faced By The Tribal Labour

Many tribal areas in India are still identified as the areas of poverty, illiteracy, unemployment and exploitation. The corruption by the government officials, failures of govt. schemes, exploitation by the contractors and businessmen, land alienation, displacement and partial rehabilitation have created various socio-economic problems among the tribal people. By tradition and necessity, tribal people are forest dwellers. Most of them are living in a part of forest as the wild animals. Tribal labours are facing so many problems.

1. *Illiteracy:* The literacy rate of tribal community was 29.60 per cent as against the national average of 52 per cent in 1991. Due to low literacy rate the socio-economic conditions of tribal people are adverse. Drop out ratio of their children is 62.5 per cent. It effects on tribal labour. Most of them are illiterate, so they are unable to get good jobs.

2. *Unemployment:* Due to less education and training, most of the tribal persons don't get work in industrial and service sectors. Most of them are working as agricultural labourers in rural areas and they are also exploited by the landlords. In India, at least 67 per cent agricultural land is non-irrigated, so the tribal labour doesn't get 365 day's employment in agriculture.

3. *Poverty:* The tribal community living under poverty line is also more than the national average. Due to scarce resources, they earn a little. At least 49.5 per cent of the tribal live under the poverty line. Due to poverty, most of the tribal labour can't get proper food, proper education and proper training. It generates inefficiency for work.

4. *Indebtedness:* Though the tribal are poor, they spend large amount on various socio-religious functions. To fulfill their monetary need, they take debt. Generally, private money lenders charge a very high rate of interest from them. In some parts of Indian villages, the rate of interest is 5 per cent per month. Indebtedness has led to a degenerated system of labor known as bonded labour.

5. *Liquor habits:* Most of the tribal labour has liquor habits. Generally they take country side liquor, which is very harmful for the health. Due to liquor habits and its bad impact, tribal labour remain absent at the work place for so many days.

6. *Health Problems:* In tribal areas, it is very difficult to get safe drinking water. Dirty water causes cholera, dysentery and skin diseases to the tribal. There are very few doctors and nurses in tribal areas. So, whenever they become sick, the chances of survival are very less. There is no access to Doctors and clinics in 28.9 per cent of the tribal areas. Only 43 per cent tribal get safe drinking water.

7. *Insufficient infrastructural facilities*: Most of the tribal people live in forest and in hilly areas. In such type of geographical areas the facility of transportation, electricity, communication etc., are insufficient.

8. *Migration:* Due to low opportunities of jobs in their own native, tribal labour migrate in far distant places, but it is a seasonal migration. At the time of their festivals they come back to their own places. Even, they go for jobs in other states also, e.g. in Gujarat, so many tribal labour come from Madhya Pradesh, Maharashtra and Orissa.

These entire socio-economic constraints combine together to force the tribal labour to remain a low productive agent. In the given institutional setup they have no access to the various economic development programmes implemented by the government. A review of the tribal situation would indicate that the strategy for development requires an intensive approach to the tribal problems. A number of commissions and committees were appointed in the post - independence period to look into the problems of tribal community and they have recommended a number of steps to remove the socio-economic imbalances. The important commissions and committees appointed so far are:

1. The Social Welfare Team of the Committee on Plan Projects, 1959,
2. The Verrier Elwin Committee on Tribal Development,
3. The Committee on Tribal Economy in Forest Areas-1967,
4. The Scheduled Areas and Scheduled Tribal Commission (Dhebar Committee 1961),
5. The Special Working Group on Co-operatives for Backward Classes-1961,
6. The Task Force on Development of Tribal Areas, 1972,
7. The Dube Committee-1972,
8. The Study Team on Co-operative structure in Tribal Development Project Areas-1976,
9. The Study Group on Relief of indebtedness, land alienation and restoration in development agency area, 1973,
10. The Team on Marketing, Credit and Co-operation in Tribal Areas-1978,
11. The Working Group on Development of Scheduled Tribes during the 7th five year plan,
12. In order to give more focused attention to the development of scheduled tribes, a separate ministry known as the ministry of tribal affairs was established in October 1999. It is the noble ministry for overall policy, planning and co-ordination of programmes and schemes for the development of scheduled tribes.

Due to these types of efforts, considerable changes have taken place in various regions with respect to certain socio-economic characteristics of the tribal like their rural-urban composition, literacy rates, work participation rates etc.

Tribal Unrest

In the colonial period there were major rebellions in tribal areas, as for example, the Kol and Bhumaj revolts of the early 19th century, the Santhal hool of 1855, the Birsa Munda -led *"Ulugulam"* in the 1890s, the uprising in Bastar in 1911, the protests in Gudem-Rampa in the 1920s and the Warli revolt of 1945-46. Most of these protests were regarding alienation of land or the expropriation of forests. The first two decades after independence were a time of peace in tribal India. Over the past four decades, the tribal of central India have often expressed their public and collective discontent with the policies and the programmes of the Government. In Maharashtra, in the 1970s and in the Narmada Andolan, tribal have been mobilised by social activists from an urban middle class background. More recently, tribal disaffection has been largely expressed under the leadership of armed Maoist revolutionaries.

Suggestions for Improvement of Tribal Labour Conditions

1. Tribe's rights should be protected and better socio-economic safe guards should be provided.
2. Better training in the tribal is essential to build up a team of their own people to do the work of administration and development.
3. The small scale professions based on special skills and tribal knowledge should be encouraged.
4. The special health programmes for the tribal labour should be promoted.
5. The special counseling programmes should be started to stop the alcoholism in tribal labour.
6. Tribal people's rights regarding forest land should be respected.
7. The number of primary schools and teachers in tribal areas should be increased so that, in future, some specialised tribal labour can be prepared.
8. The infrastructural facilities like roads, electricity, transportation, water, health centers, and banks should be increased in tribal areas; so that they may come nearer to the civilized society.
9. Various agencies like N.G.O.S, Colleges, and Universities should collaborate and exchange ideas and redraw their research agendas to fulfill the national needs. The N.G.O.s should be involved in the promotion of education and literacy among the tribes.
10. Co-operative banking should be promoted in tribal areas to stop the exploitation done by the private money lenders.
11. Vocational Training Institutes should be established in the tribal areas.
12. In democratic society, each one has right for development. Some more focus should be given by the central as well as state governments on tribal areas. Some huge investment programmes

should be activated in tribal areas, so that tribal labour can get more jobs in their own places.

References

1. Bhowmik K.L., *"Tribal India, A Profile in Indian Ethnology"*, The World Press Pvt.Ltd Calcutta, 1971.
2. Bose N.K., "*Tribal life in India*", National Book Trust, Delhi, 1971.
3. Bose S. "Carrying Capacity of Land under shifting cultivation", Asiatic Society, Calcutta, 1967.
4. Chandra R., *"Forrest and Tribal Economy: some observations in tribal economy and wasteland development" (Ed.)*, Inter-India Publications, New Delhi, 1994.
5. Maharatna Arup, *"Demographic Perspectives on India's Tribes"*, Oxford University Press, New Delhi, 2005.
6. Sharma A.N. "*Physical Anthropology"*, Abhivyakti Prakashan, Allahabad, 1996.
7. Sharma A.N. "*Tribal Welfare and Development" (Ed.)*, Sarup and sons, New Delhi, 2002.
8. Shrivastav B.N. "*Exploitation in Tribal Area"*, Bharatiya Adimjati Sevak Sangha, New Delhi, 1968.

SECTION—B

AUTONOMOUS DISTRICT COUNCIL

12

Status of Autonomous District Council's in India: An Overview

D. Pulla Rao

Freedom implies not only emancipation from political bondage but also equal distribution of wealth, abolition of caste barriers and social inequities and destruction of communalism and religious intolerance.

—Netaji Subhash Chandra Bose

Introduction

Tribal areas are the remotest as well as the most secluded and generally inaccessible hilly tracts. The life in these areas is full of adventure and susceptible to natural calamities. The tribal people by and large, comprise of primitive groups who might have come to these isolated and inhospitable terrain in the past due to some historical compulsions such as seeking refuge or for fear of invaders or aggressors who exploited and toured these people. The tribal belts constitute a very significant part of backward areas of the country. The concentration of tribal's varies from area to area. In the tribal belt agriculture and allied pursuits being the mainstay of the people, development of animal husbandry assumes an added importance. The economy of the tribal areas is highly agro-pastoral. People rejoice in the form of feasting, drinking and dancing. Musical instruments are played in their dances. Many tribes and casts on the mainland of India live by hunting, fishing or gathering. Growth with social justice has been an avowed objective of planned development in India. Tribal population of the country is one such important segment which has almost been left out of the mainstream of the development process. All economic and social development activities are planned for the welfare of its people and this is truly reflected in their levels of living which is the end product of all economic effects.

Concept

An autonomous area or autonomous entity is an area of a country that has a degree of autonomy, or freedom from an external authority. Typically it is either geographically distinct from the rest of the country or populated by a national minority. Giving one a certain amount of self-government may be a way for a national government to try and defuse an existing or possible internal conflict. Countries that include autonomous areas are often federacies. The Constitution of India, Article 366(25) defines Scheduled Tribes as *"such tribes or tribal communities or part of or groups within such tribes or tribal communities as are deemed under Article 342 to the scheduled Tribes (STs) for the purposes of this Constitution"*. The Scheduled Tribe groups who were identified as more isolated from the wider community and who maintain a distinctive cultural identity have been categorised as *'Particularly Vulnerable Tribal Groups'* (PTGs) (previously known as Primitive Tribal Groups) by the Government at the Centre. So far seventy-five tribal communities have been identified as *'particularly vulnerable tribal groups'* in different States of India. There are several autonomous regions of India to which the central government has given varying degrees of autonomy within the state legislature. The establishment and functions of most of these autonomous councils are based on the sixth schedule to the Constitution of India.

Assam

Assam is located in the eastern Himalayan. Assam comprises the Brahmaputra and the Barak river valleys along with the Karbi Anglong and the North Cachar Hills with an area of 30,285 square miles (78,438 km^2). It is surrounded by six of the other *Seven Sister States*: Arunachal Pradesh, Nagaland, Manipur, Mizoram, Tripura and Meghalaya. These states are connected to the rest of India via a narrow strip in West Bengal called the Siliguri Corridor or *"Chicken's Neck"*. There the three autonomous district council in Assam, i.e., Bodoland Territorial Council, Karbi Anglong Autonomous Council and Dima Hasao Autonomous District Council.

Bodoland Territorial Council

The Bodos are an ethnic and linguistic community, early settlers of Assam in the northeast part of India. According to the 2011 census, there are nearly two million Bodos in Assam which makes for 5.5 per cent of the total population in the state. The Bodos are recognised as a plains tribe in the Sixth Schedule of the Indian Constitution. Udalguri and Kokrajhar are considered the centre of the Bodo area. The Bodo people constitute a diverse range of the Indigenous people of North-east India. The Bodoland Territorial Council (BTC) has legislative, administrative, executive and financial powers over 40 policy areas in the Bodoland Territorial Areas Districts comprising four districts of Assam. It was established in 2003 following a peace agreement between the Government of India and Bodo rebels and is functioning since 2003 under the provision of the Sixth Schedule of the Constitution of India. Bodoland is an area located in the north bank of Brahmaputra river in the state of Assam in north east region of India, by the foothills of Bhutan and Arunachal Pradesh; inhabited predominantly by the Bodo people. Currently the map of Bodoland includes the Bodoland Territorial Autonomous Districts (BTAD) administered by the autonomous Bodoland Territorial Council (BTC). The territory came into existence under the BTC Accord. The map of Bodoland overlaps with the districts of Kokrajhar, Baksa, Chirang and Udalguri in the state of Assam. At present, Kokrajhar serves as the capital of Bodoland. In the early 1960s the Plains Tribals Council of Assam (PTCA), a political party representing Bodos and other plains tribals of Assam realised that tribal belts and blocks were gradually being acquired by rich landlords or new immigrants through illegal means. Moreover, Bodos had little or no access to economic aid that was given by the central government. The official Bodoland Movement for an independent state of Bodoland started on March 2, 1987 under the leadership of Upendranath Brahma of the All Bodo Students' Union (ABSU). The ABSU created a political organisation, the Bodo Peoples' Action Committee (BPAC), to spearhead the movement.

The Bodoland Territorial Council (BTC) is a territorial privilege established according to the Memorandum of Settlement of February 10, 2003. BTC came into existence immediately after surrender of BLTF cadres. The BLTF laid down their weapons on December 6, 2003 under the leadership of Hagrama Mohilary and Hagrama was sworn in as the Chief Executive Member (CEM) on December 7, 2003. The area under the BTC jurisdiction is called the Bodo Territorial Autonomous District (BTAD).

Karbi Anglong Autonomous Council

The Karbi Anglong Autonomous Council (KAAC) is an autonomous council in the district constituted under the provision of the Sixth Schedule of the Constitution of India. The Karbi Anglong District is situated in the central part of Assam. It is bounded by Golaghat district in the east, Meghalaya and Morigaon district in the west, Nagaon and Golaghat district in the north and N.C.Hills district and Nagaland in the south. The district has three sub-divisions: Diphu, Hamren and Bokajan. Apart from Karbi, the native language of the erstwhile ruler, the Karbi language is one of the prominent languages of the district. Diphu town is the administrative headquarters of the district. Karbi Anglong District occupies an area of 10,434 square kilometres (4,029 sq mi).

Dima Hasao Autonomous District Council

The Dima Hasao Autonomous District Council (formerly North Cachar Hills Autonomous District Council) is an autonomous council constituted under the provisions of the Sixth Schedule of the Constitution of India to administer the district. Dima Hasao district (DHD) (Formerly North Cachar Hills district) is an administrative district in the state of Assam in north-eastern India. As of 2011 it is the least populous district of Assam. The district headquarters are located at Haflong. Dima Hasao district occupies an area of 4,888 square kilometres (1,887 sq mi). Dima Hasao district is an Autonomous District (Lok Sabha constituency) enjoying the Sixth Schedule status granted by the Constitution of India. The *Dima Hasao District* is administered by *Dima Hasao Autonomous Council (DHAC)*. Members of the Autonomous Council (MAC) are elected by people of Dima Hasao. The Political party who has majority MACs forms the rulling party. The Dimasa of Dima Hasao District, being agrarian people, celebrates various agricultural festivals in different ways and at different times. Mostly Dimasa inhabiting North Cachar Hills and Karbi Anglong districts are successful in preserving their age old traditional religious beliefs and practices in and through the celebration of several festivals, with some exceptions, due to being Hinduised. In 2006 the Indian government named Dima Hasao one of the country's 250 most backward districts (out of a total of 640). The major tribes inhabiting the district are Dimasas, Kukis, Zeme Nagas. Other significant ethnic groups include the Biates, Hrangkhawls, Vaipheis who are also Kuki, Karbis, Khasi-pnars and Khelmas. Dimasa are the most highly Populated Tribe in Dima Hasao, The Dimasas Constitute 43 per cent of total population where as Non-Dimasa tribes and Non Tribals like- Bengali, Jeme naga,Nepalese, Hmar, Kuki all together constitute 53 per cent of total population.

Mishing Autonomous Council

The Mishing Autonomous Council Act, 1995 provides that there shall be a village council for each block of villages or village having 50 per cent or more Mishing population. The other two Acts—Tiwa Autonomous Council Act, 1995 and the Rabha Hasong Autonomous Council Act, 1995 also stipulated similar ethnic criterion in favour of respective ethnic group.

Mizoram

Mizoram is a land of rolling hills, valleys, rivers and lakes. As many as 21 major hills ranges or peaks of different heights run through the length and breadth of the state, with plains scattered here and there. Mizo history in the 18th and 19th century is marked by many instances of tribal raids and head hunting led by the village chieftains. The great majority of Mizoram's population consists of several ethnic tribes who are either culturally or linguistically linked. These ethnic groups are collectively known as Mizos.

Chakma Autonomous District Council

Chakma Autonomous District Council (CADC) is an autonomous council for the Chakma people living in the south-western part of Mizoram. It was formed under the Sixth schedule of the Constitution of India on April 29, 1972. The Council is the replication of the state assembly and exercises executive power over specially allotted departments. The people of CADC are also enjoying special safeguard granted by the article 273-G of the Constitution of India. It is one of the three Autonomous District Councils of Mizoram state in North-East India. It is an autonomous council for ethnic Chakma people living in South-Western Mizoram bordering Bangladesh and Myanamar. The CADC has a land area of 1500 square kilometers and the population grew from 34,528 in 2001 to 40,265 (as of 2008). The headquarter of

Chakma Autonomous District Council is Kamalanagar which is also known as Chawngte.

Lai Autonomous District Council

Lai Autonomous District Council (LADC) is an autonomous council for the Lai people in the South-eastern part of Mizoram. It is an Autonomous District Council for ethnic Lai people earlier known as Pawi, living in South-eastern Mizoram bordering Myanmar and Bangladesh. The L.A.D.C. has its headquarters at Lawngtlai town, which is the District Capital of Lawngtlai District. Lawngtlai District has a population of 75,477 persons according to Mizoram Statistical Handbook 2003. The Lai Autonomous District Council occupies a strategic position in Mizoram, located in the Southern most corner of the state. It shares its political border with the erstwhile Burma (Myanmar) and MADC, the west by CADC, in the north Lunglei Administrative District and in the south by Myanmar. The Lai Autonomous District Council covers an area of 1870.75 km^2 with a population of 73,620 as on April 2008 and its density is 39 persons per km^2. The whole/entire population belonged to Schedule Tribes.

Mara Autonomous District Council

Mara Autonomous District Council (MADC) is an autonomous council for the Mara people living in the Southern part of Mizoram. Its autonomy was established as part of Lai District on 29 May 1971 and separated the next year as Lakher Autonomous District Council, and renamed to it current name in 1988. It covers 1445 square kilometers. Mara Autonomous District Council looks after many departments in her area including fisheries, schools (up to Middle school) and education, judiciary, land and revenue, forestry, Public Health Engineering (PHE), etc.

Tripura

The area of the modern Tripura was part of an independent Tripuri kingdom that ruled for several centuries, probably millennia. It was a princely state during the British rule in India. The kingdom merged with independent India in 1949 with the Tripura Merger Agreement. Ethnic strife between the tribes and Bengali population has led to tension and scattered violence since its integration to India. Scheduled tribes are about 30 per cent of the population in which Kokborok-speaking Tripuri people form the major tribe; Bengali people form the ethno-linguistic majority. The mainstream Indian cultural elements led by Bengali culture coexist along with tribal traditional practices.

Tripura Tribal Areas Autonomous District Council

The Tripura Tribal Areas Autonomous District Council (TTAADC) is an independent council administering the tribal areas of the state of Tripura. Its council and assembly are situated in Khumulwng, a town 20 km outside Agartala, the state capital. Tripura Tribal Areas Autonomous District Council (TTAADC) Act 1979 was passed by the Indian parliament after a series of democratic movements launched by the Indigenous people of Tripura, under the provision of the 6th scheduled of the Indian constitution. The principle objective behind setting up the Autonomous District Council is to empower the Indigenous people to govern themselves and also to bring all round developments of the backward people so as to protect and preserve their culture, customs and traditions. The total area of the TTAADC is 7,132.56 km^2, which covers about 68 per cent of the total area (10,491 km^2) of the state. The TTAADC is governed by a council which has 30 members. Out of 30 members, 28 members are elected through adult suffrage while 2 members are nominated by the Governor of Tripura. Out of 28 elected seats, 25 are reserved for Scheduled Tribes. Under the Sixth Schedule of the Constitution, the Tripura Tribal Areas Autonomous District Council is vested with two types of Powers. These are

1. Legislative Powers; and
2. Executive Powers.

Arunachal Pradesh

Arunachal Pradesh was created out of the frontier tribal areas of Assam. It was formerly known as North-East Frontier Agency (NEFA). It was made a union territory in 1972 and given its present name - Arunachal Pradesh (Land of the Dawn-lit Mountains). In 1987, it became a state. The state is surrounded on three sides by the international border with Bhutan to the west, China to the north and Burma to the east and Assam to the South. It is the only hill state in North-Eastern Region which introduced a Panchayat system as early as in 1969, under the NEFA Panchayati Raj Regulation 1967. The Arunachal Pradesh Assembly had passed a bill to create four Autonomous District Councils in the state in 2003 but the Parliament is yet to approve it.

Manipur

Manipur came under British rule as a princely state in 1891. The Manipur Constitution Act, 1947, established a democratic form of government with the *'Maharajah'* (King) as the executive head and a legislature constituted by election based on adult franchise. The Legislative Assembly was dissolved after the integration of the state with the Dominion of India in October 1949. It became as a part 'C' state under the Indian constitution with effect from 26-1-1950. Manipur achieved full statehood on January 21, 1972. Manipur is geographically divided into the hills and valley. The Hill areas are inhabited predominantly by the Nagas, Kukis, Paites, Gangtes, etc., with a sprinkling of the Nepalese in the immediate neighbourhood of the valley. The valley is inhabited by Meiteis, (Manipuri Hindus), Pangals (Manipuri Muslims), the Nepalese, and the Business communities like Marwaris, Punjabis, Biharis and so on. The Barak basin is inhabited by the Meiteis and the Bengalis.

The tribes of tribal inhabited areas irrespective of the Schedule Areas and the Tribal Areas are aware of the benefits of the Sixth Schedule to the Constitution of India. The tribals of the Hills areas of Manipur, some tribes from Assam, Gurkhas of Darjeeling Hills in West Bengal and Brus, Hmars, Paites and minority tribes of Uiphum mountain range of Lawngthai District of Mizoram are still demanding the inclusion of their respective areas in the Sixth Schedule provision. But the case of tribals of the Hills areas of Manipur is different from those of other tribals of tribal inhabited area of different states. Six Autonomous District Councils were introduced in the Hills areas of Manipur with the enactment of the *Manipur (Hill Areas) District Councils Act, 1971*. Manipur's Senapati district has two autonomous councils—the Manipur North Autonomous District Council (MNADC) and the Sadar Hills Autonomous District Council (SHADC). People living in the SHADC were not satisfied with the administration and since 1971 have been demanding a separate district, which according to them will improve the economic and infrastructural conditions of their area. The major tension is between the people living on the hills and those who live in the plains. Manipur's largest ethnic group is the Meiteis who primarily live in the valley. Although they account for more than half the state's population, they hold barely one-tenth of the land. These people are not counted in the Scheduled Tribe category and hence are not entitled to various government benefits meant for the STs. The second major groups, the Nagas are primarily hill-dwelling while the third major ethnic groups, the Kukis, are spread across the valley, hills as well as other areas of the Northeast. There are three kinds of insurgent movements going on in the state. Some groups of Meiteis and Nagas demand separate countries for them while the Kukis demand independence and then union of the Kuki-majority areas in India and Myanmar or the creation of a separate state or UT within India where the scattered Kuki population could live.

According to the ministry of home affairs, there are about seven major active militant groups. They are the People's Liberation Army (PLA), United National Liberation Front (UNLF), People's Revolutionary Party of Kangleipak (PREPAK), Kangleipak Communist Party (KCP), Kanglei Yaol Kanba Lup (KYKL), Manipur People's Liberation Front (MPLF) and the Revolutionary People's Front (RPF). The most recent annual report of the Union home ministry says that Meitei insurgents are mainly responsible for the violence. The Nagas, on the other hand, were responsible for major blockades. In 2010, elections were held in six autonomous district councils of the state. The Naga leaders were demanding the withdrawal of the *Manipur Hill Areas District Council (Amendment) Act* and deferment of the elections. When the demands were not met, they imposed two major blockades in 2010. The entire state of Manipur (except Imphal municipal area) is declared as a disturbed area under the Armed Forces Special Powers Act.

The Manipur (Hill Areas) District Council Act, 1971, an Act passed by the Parliament paved the way for establishment of six autonomous districts in Manipur. In accordance with the powers vested on the Governor of Manipur, following six Autonomous Districts Councils were constituted on 14 February, 1972:

1. Chandel, Autonomous District Council,
2. Churachandpur Autonomous District Council,
3. Sadar Hills Autonomous District Council,
4. Senapati Autonomous District Council,
5. Tamenglong Autonomous District Council and,
6. Ukhrul Autonomous district Council.

The first election to the autonomous district councils was held in the year 1973. So far the 1971 Act has been amended thrice; the first amendment in the year 1975, the second in the year 2006 and the third in the year 2008. The first amendment to the Act envisaged removal of the Chairman of the District Council by the Government for reasons to be recorded in writing upon passing of a resolution by the District Council by a simple majority of the total membership of the Council. The second amendment envisaged the following features: (a) Notifying areas as urban areas for the purpose of development plan and to execute the works; and (b) Allotment/transfer/lease of land by a resolution passed by the District Council. The third amendment to the Act envisaged the following:

1. Increase in membership from18 to 24;
2. Election Commission of the State to be entrusted election to HDC;
3. Constitution of Executive Committee;
4. Addition of 9 entries to the list of powers of the autonomous Hill Districts.

Nagaland

The Nagaland state comprises of the former Naga Hills district of Assam and the former Tuensang Frontier division of the North East Frontier Agency. These were made a Centrally Administered Area in 1957. In January 1961, it became the state of Nagaland. Village level institutions have been strong in Nagaland. Since time immemorial Naga villages were independent in nature. There had been two major forms of village governments in Naga society, viz. democratic and chieftain ships. For instance, the Angamis, the Aos and the Chakhesangs had democratic form of government whereas the Semas and the Konyaks practiced chieftainship type of village government. The governments were run the customary laws and usages. Even today customary laws are considered as the guiding principles of life in society. The history records that Naga villages were organised as independent small states or republics. However, there was no uniform legal system of village government in Naga society till 1970. After realising the importance of village government, the state government of Nagaland passed an Act known as *Nagaland Village, Area and Regional Council Act, 1970*. Thereafter, it was further amended in 1973 and 1978 as Nagaland

Village and Area Council Act with a view to bring uniformity in Village Council structure all over Nagaland. A Village Council consists of members chosen by villagers in accordance with the prevailing customary practices and usages, the same being approved by the state government, provided that hereditary village chiefs, Goan Booras (GBs) and Angs shall be e-officio members of such councils and shall have voting rights. The village council will choose a member as Chairman of the council. The Village council may select and appoint a Secretary who may or may not be a member of the council. If the Secretary is not a member of the council, he shall have no voting power. The Village Council has the following powers and duties:

1. to formulate village development schemes, to supervise proper maintenance of water supply, roads, forest, education and other welfare activities,
2. to help various govt. agencies in carrying out development works in the village,
3. to take development works on its own initiative or on request by the government.
4. to borrow money from the government, Banks or financial institution for application in the development and welfare work of the village and to repay the same with or without interest
5. to apply for and receive grants-in-aid, donations, susidies from the government or any agency, etc., and to control and disposal of immovable property, etc.

Meghalaya

Meghalaya is a northeast Indian state and about one third of the state is forested. The Meghalaya subtropical forests ecoregion encompasses the state; its mountain forests are distinct from the lowland tropical forests to the north and south. Shillong, the capital of the state is a popular hill station. The principal languages in Meghalaya are Khasi, Pnar and Garo with English as the official language of the state. The main tribes in Meghalaya are the Jaintias, the Khasis and the Garos. One of the unique features of the state is that a majority of the tribal population in Meghalaya follows a matrilineal system where lineage and inheritance are traced through women.

Garo Hills Autonomous District Council

The Garo Hills Autonomous District Council (GHADC) is seated at Tura and covers East Garo Hills district, West Garo Hills district and South Garo Hills. The East Garo Hills district was formed in 1976; after the erstwhile Garo Hills district of Meghalaya was re-organised with a view to bring the administration closer to the people. The district headquarter-complex of the district, christened as Williamnagar after the name of Captain Williamson A. Sangma the founder Chief Minister of the State of Meghalaya. Williamnagar is located on the vast plainlands along the bank of the Simsang River, at Simsanggre. The district occupies an area of 2603 km^2. East Garo Hills division is divided into five blocks. Tura town is the administrative headquarters of the west Garo Hills district. The district occupies an area of 3714 km^2. West Garo Hills district is located at the westernmost part of Meghalaya. As of 2011 it is the second most populous district of Meghalaya, after East Khasi Hills. West Garo Hills district is divided into eight blocks. The South Garo Hills district headquarters are located at Baghmara. The district occupies an area of 1850 km^2. South Garo Hills district is divided into four blocks.

Jaintia Hills Autonomous District Council

The Jaintia Hills Autonomous District Council (JHADC) is seated at Jowai and covers the Jaintia Hills district. Jaintia Hills is an administrative district in the state of Meghalaya in India. The present district was created in 22 February 1972 and occupies an area of 3819 km^2. The district is bounded by Assam on the east and north, East Khasi Hills district on the west and has an international border with Bangladesh on the south. Although the mainstay of the district is agriculture, however due to the abundance of Limestone, plenty of Cement factories have been set up in the district. More are set to come up. Coal mining at sites like Lad Rymbai is also one of the major activities set up here. Coal mined here is mostly exported to Bangladesh and Assam. Jaintia Hills district is divided into five blocks. Jowai is an important business and education hub of the entire district catering to students from all over the district as well as the adjacent parts of Assam and Bangladesh.

The people living in Jaintia Hills District of Meghalaya are ethno linguistic group of people and are believed to be of Indo-Mongoloid race although speaking a distinct Austric language belonging to the

Mon-Khmer group. With regard to the social origin of the Jaintia people there is an indigenous theory according to which they belonged to a common race which occupied a large area of Northern India, Burma, Indo-China and parts of South China in the Neolithic period. The people residing in the central region of Jaintia Hills are called *"Pnars"* by those living in the southern and northern regions and who are in turn called as *"Wars"* and *"Bhois"* respectively by the Pnar. All three are collectively known by the generic name: Jaintias" or *"Synteng"*. Jaintia people maintained their unique culture and religion called *Niamtre*.

Khasi Hills Autonomous District Council

The Khasi Hills Autonomous District Council (KHADC) covers West Khasi Hills district, East Khasi Hills district and Ri Bhoi district. The West Khasi Hills district was carved out of the erestwhile Khasi Hills district, which was dividied into West and East Khasi Hills districts on 28 October 1976. The district headquarters is located at Nongstoin. The district occupies an area of 5247 km^2. It is divided into six blocks. Shillong is the district headquarters of East Khasi Hills District. East Khasi Hills District forms a central part of Meghalaya and covers a total geographical area of 2,748 km^2. The northern portion of the district is bounded by the plain of Ri-Bhoi District gradually rising to the rolling grasslands of the Shillong plateau interspersed with river valleys, then falls sharply in the Southern portion forming a deep gorges and ravines in Mawsynram and Shella-Bholaganj, community and rural development block, bordering Bangladesh. The East Khasi Hills District is mostly hilly with deep gorges and ravines on the southern portion. East Khasi Hills division is divided into eight blocks. Ri-Bhoi district was upgraded from subdivisional level to a full fledged district on 4 June 1992. The new District was carved out from the erstwhile East Khasi Hills. The district headquarters are located at Nongpoh. The district occupies an area of 2378 km^2. It is bounded on the north by Kamrup District and on the East by Jaintia Hills and Karbi Anglong District of Assam and on the West by West Khasi Hills District. Ri-Bhoi district is divided into three blocks.

West Bengal

West Bengal is a state in the eastern region of India and is the nation's fourth-most populous. It is also the seventh-most populous sub-national entity in the world, with over 91 million inhabitants. The state has a total area of 88,752 square kilometres (34,267 sq mi). The Darjeeling Himalayan hill region in the northern extreme of the state belongs to the eastern Himalaya.

Gorkhaland Territorial Administration

Gorkhaland Territorial Administration (GTA) is a semi-autonomous administrative body for the Darjeeling hills in West Bengal, India. The GTA replaced the Darjeeling Gorkha Hill Council, which was formed in 1988 and administered the Darjeeling hills for 23 years. GTA presently has three hill subdivisions Darjeeling, Kalimpong, and Kurseong and some areas of Siliguri subdivision under its authority. The movement for a separate state of Gorkhaland gained serious momentum during the 1980s, when a violent agitation was carried out by Gorkha National Liberation Front (GNLF) led by Subhash Ghising. The agitation ultimately led to the establishment of a semi-autonomous body in 1988 called the *Darjeeling Gorkha Hill Council (DGHC)* to govern certain areas of Darjeeling district. However, in 2008, a new party called the *Gorkha Janmukti Morcha (GJM)* raised the demand for a separate state of Gorkhaland once again. On 18 April 2011, GJM signed an agreement with the state and central governments for the formation of Gorkhaland Territorial Administration, a semi-autonomous body that would replace the DGHC in the Darjeeling hills.

Jammu And Kashmir

Jammu and Kashmir is a northern state of India. Ladakh is a part of it. Ladakh lies between the Kunlun mountain range in the north and the main Great Himalayas to the south, inhabited by people of Indo-Aryan and Tibetan descent. It is one of the most sparsely populated regions in Jammu and Kashmir. Ladakh district was a district of the Jammu and Kashmir state of India until 1 July, 1979 when it was divided into Leh district and Kargil district. Each of these districts is governed by a Ladakh Autonomous Hill Development Council, which is based on the pattern of the Darjeeling Gorkha Autonomous Hill Council. These councils were created as a compromise solution to the demands of Ladakhi people to make Leh a union territory. The largest town in Ladakh is Leh. With an area of 45,110 km^2, Leh district is the second largest district in the country (after Kutch, Gujarat) in terms of area. Kargil lies near the Line of Control facing Gilgit–Baltistan to the west, and Kashmir valley to the south. Zanskar is part of Kargil district along with Suru, Wakha and Dras valleys. Kargil was at the center of a conflict between India and Pakistan in 1999.

Ladakh Autonomous Hill Development Council, Kargil

Kargil is a district of Ladakh, Kashmir, India. Kargil lies near the Line of Control facing Pakistan-administered Kashmir's Baltistan to the west, and Kashmir valley to the south. Ladakhi people are demanding to make the district a new Indian union territory because of its religious and cultural differences with Kashmir. The government of India formed the Ladakh Autonomous Hill Development Council (LAHDC), which governs the area with limited autonomy. Ladakh Autonomous Hill Development Council (LAHDC) Kargil election was held in September 2008. For a smooth conduct of elections for the LAHDC Kargil, as many as 892 polling staff and more than 1,000 police personnel including para military forces have been deployed in Kargil district. Kargil District has two assembly constituencies, Zanskar and Kargil. The LAHDC-K was established in 2003.

Ladakh Autonomous Hill Development Council, Leh

Leh is one of the two districts of Ladakh. Following widespread agitations to make it a Union Territory of India due to the cultural and liguistic differences with Kashmir the government of India formed the Ladakh Autonomous Hill Development Council (LAHDC), which governs this area with limited political autonomy. The council was created under the Ladakh Autonomous Hill Development Council Act 1995, following demands of Ladakhi people to make Leh District a new Indian Union Territory because of its religious and cultural differences with the rest of Jammu and Kashmir. In October 1993, the Indian government and the State government agreed to grant Ladakh the status of Autonomous Hill Council. The council came into being with the holding of elections on August 28, 1995. The inaugural meeting of the council was held at Leh on September 3, 1995. The first elections for the LAHDC were held in the year 1995. The council is composed of 30 Councillors of which 26 are directly elected and 4 are nominated members. Owing to the difficult geographical problems, the need for greater public participation in the planning and development process was all the more necessary.

De Facto Autonomous Area

North Sentinel Island

North Sentinel Island is situated in the island chain of the Andaman and Nicobar Islands which is a union territory of India. It is home to the Sentinelese, who are some of the world's last uncontacted peoples. The local government (Andaman and Nicobar Islands) has recently stated that they have no intention to interfere with the Sentinelese's lifestyle or habitat. The Sentinelese maintain an essentially hunter-gatherer society subsisting through hunting, fishing and collecting wild plants. There is no evidence of either agricultural practices or methods of producing fire. The present population of the Sentinelese is not known with any great degree of accuracy. Estimates have been produced ranging from lower than 40, through a median of around 250 and up to a maximum of 500. In the year 2001, the Census of India officials recorded 39 individuals (21 males and 18 females); however, out of necessity this survey was conducted from a distance and almost certainly does not represent an accurate figure for the population who range over the 72 km^2 (17,800 acres) island. Any medium or long-term impact on the Sentinelese population arising from the 2004 Indian Ocean earthquake and resulting tsunami remains unknown, other than the confirmation obtained that they had survived the immediate aftermath.

Officially, the island has been administered by India as part of the Andaman and Nicobar Islands Union Territory since 1947. However, because there has never been any treaty with the people of the island, nor any record of a physical occupation whereby the people of the island have conceded sovereignty, the island exists in a curious state of limbo under established international law and can be seen as a sovereign entity under Indian protection. It is, therefore, one of the *de facto* autonomous regions of India. The Andaman and Nicobar Administration has recently stated that they have no intention to interfere with the lifestyle or habitat of the Sentinelese and are not interested in pursuing any further contact with them.

Conclusion

Autonomous district council is a real fact in North-East India. In North-East India more or less every state has autonomous district council. Autonomous district council and tribal are interconnected. Autonomous district council is a way for providing more autonomy power to tribal people is their own development. It is proving under the six schedule of Constitution of India. There are three district councils (i.e. Bodoland Territorial Council, Karbi Anglong Autonomous Council and Dima Hasao Autonomous District Council) in Assam and in

Mizoram (i.e. Chakma Autonomous District Council, Lai Autonomous District Counci, and Mara Autonomous District Council) and Meghalaya (i.e. Garo Hills Autonomous District Council, Jaintia Hills Autonomous District Council and Khasi Hills Autonomous District Council). In Manipur there are six council and in Tripura only one. The Arunachal Pradesh Assembly had passed a bill to create four Autonomous District Councils in the state in 2003 but the Parliament is yet to approve it. There are various village level institutions in ground level which have more autonomy power.

References

1. Dipanjan Roy Chaudhury (2005). *Autonomous district councils and panchayati raj institutions in North-East India,* Retrieved from http://www.asthabharati.org/Dia_Jul%2005/dip.htm
2. Jairth, M. (1991). *Tribal economy and society,* First edition, Mittal publication, New Delhi, pp. 1-70.
3. L. Memo Singh (2012). *Formation of autonomous district councils as a part of administrative reforms*, Retrieved from http://kanglaonline.com/2010/08/formation-of-autonomous-district-councils-as-a-part-of-administrative-reforms/
4. NE Newsletter (July 2010). *Autonomous district council/Autonomous councils in the states of Assam, Manipur, Meghalaya, Mizoram and Tripura,* Volume XII, No. 7, Retrieved from http://mha.nic.in/pdfs/nenl0710.pdf
5. The Times of India (Dec 5, 2011). *Manipur blocked for a new district,* Retrieved from http://articles.timesofindia.indiatimes.com/2011-12-05/india/30477431_1_manipur-blockade-economic-blockade-united-naga-council.
6. *Various informations are collect from* wikipedia, like as *Adivasi, Autonomous areas, Autonomous Regions of India, Bodoland, Bodoland Territorial Council, Chakma Autonomous District Council, Dima Hansao Disrict, Jaintia Hills District, Jowai, East Garo Hills District, East Khasi Hills District, Gorkhaland, Kargil District, Ladakh, Ladakh Autonomous Hill Development Council (LAHDC), Lai Autonomous District Council, Leh district, Mara Autonomous District Council, Meghalaya, Mizoram, North Santinal Island, Ri Bhoi district, Sentinelese People, South Garo Hills District, Tripura, Tripura Tribal Areas Autonomous District Council, West Bengal, West Garo Hills District and West Khasi Hill District.*

13

Management of Forest for Sustainable Development with Reference to Dima Hasao Autonomous Council, Haflong, Assam

Jamshed Ali

Introduction

Dima Hasao district formerly North Cachar Hills district is an administrative district in the state of Assam in north-eastern India. The law relating to the power and function of Dima Hasao Autonomous Council in Assam has been specified in the sixth schedule of the constitution of India and has already been settled by Honourable High Court and the Honourable Supreme Court of India in a number of land marketing judgements. Article 244(2) of the Constitution of India provides that; as far as Dima Hasao Autonomous Council is concerned, the provisions of sixth schedule were made applicable from the year 1951. The sixth schedule to the constitution is unique in many respects. It has avowed objective of ensuring the development of the hill tribes without least interference with their customs, traditions and usages. It also provides for grass root level planning and encouraging the traditional institutions. It also gives the scope for a form of local self government in areas where the Provisions of the schedule are made applicable. These provisions as per the needs and requirements of the times have now evolved to its unique state as it is now.

North Cachar Hills (Dima Hasao) district is situated at the southern part of the state of Assam. The district is bounded on the North by Nagaon district and Hamren Sub-Division of Karbi Anglong district of Assam and on the East by Diphu Sub-Division of Karbi Anglong and the state of Manipur and Nagaland. On the south lies the Cacher district of Assam and on the West lies Jowai district of Meghalaya and Hamren sub-division of Karbi Anglong. The area presents undulating geographical features of moderate to medium and high hills with altitude varying from 100 m to 1800 m above MSL. The district is hilly, mostly on the northern slope of Borail range, extending from Patkai range and terminating in Shillong Plateau of Meghalaya. The Borail range runs along the southern boundary of the district up to the south of Haflong, from where it turns east till reaches Jaintia hills of Meghalaya. Highest peak is Tumjang peak (1866 m).The southern face of Borail range is steeper and the northern face gradually slopes down to the Brahmaputra Valley. In comparison to the adjacent areas, the hill areas of Dima Hasao are steeper, more rocky and rugged. Topographically, Dima Hasao district can be roughly divided into tree portions, the valley extending between river Diyung and Jatinga; the hilly areas of Borail and Jaintia ranges covering the east and south-eastern part of the district and plateau of Gunjung, Khorongma and Garampani areas. Climate is moist and tropical. The typical sub- tropical monsoon climate prevalent in the area is characterised by the excessive moisture content of air throughout the year. The southern face of Borail range receives considerably high precipitation. Dima Hasao is one of the less developed districts of Assam. The economy of the district is purely agrarian; hence the economic development of the district is highly dependent on agro-based activities.

Dima Hasao district is a common abode of different tribal groups with distinct ethnic culture traditions. It is inhabited by the *Dimasa, Zeme Naga, Kuki, Hmar, Biete, Hrangkhol, Khelma, Vaiphei, Karbi, Jaintia, Mizos*, and other non-tribal communities like *Bengali, Assamese, Manipuris and Nepalese*. The culture of Dima Hasao district is a rich tapestry infused with multi-coloured yarns of distinguished heritage of all the races that populate her. The superb blend of heritage extracted from numerous races have made Dima Hasao district the home to the most colourful festivals at once blazing, compelling and mesmerising. Festivals form an essential aspect of socio-cultural life of the people

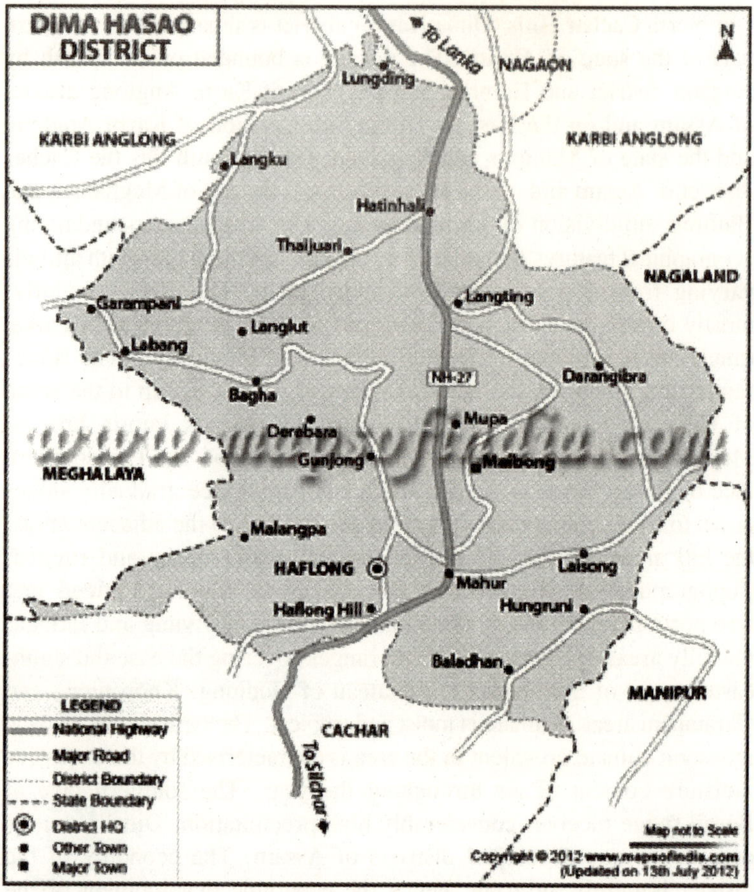

of Dima Hasao district. The festivals play an important part in promoting the traditional handicrafts of Dima Hasao district. Every community celebrates their festival according to their own customs and rituals. The commonness in the celebration is that it celebrates humanity. The real culture and tradition of the people of Dima Hasao district which is always in the tune of harmony and also acquaint the people of the plains with the socio-cultural-religious life of the hill tribes as well as for documentation of the festive mood of the people of Dima Hasao.

The natural forest is bounty with several trees species as well as other floral and faunal species. Besides agriculture, forestry is the mainstay of the thriving economy in the district. The ecological security and economic prosperity of Dima Hasao district are wholly and greatly dependent in forests. Bamboo is the major non-wood forests products in the district. Forests in Dima Hasao district from the ancient time have played in important role in social, economic and religious activities. Since the district is located in a geographically, geomorphology and ecologically fragile and sensitive areas and provides a backdrop to the plains of the Barak Valleys, management of forest areas attracts considerable significance. But the forests of Dima Hasao district still suffer severe degradation in the last few decades due to ever increasing demand of goods and services. The age old traditional practices of shifting cultivation otherwise fondly known as *'Jhumming'* has become a way of life and the only means of livelihood for many villagers. This apart, the emotional heritage, the culture and tradition, festivals and folk lore associated with the jhum cultivation has become one bottleneck that makes it difficult in the conservation and management of the fragile ecosystems of the district. The commercial exploitation of forest resource is important factor of deforestation. Illegal felling of trees is gradually increasing in many parts of the Dima Hasao district. The extraction of minor forest product is also affecting the forest wealth leading to extinguishing of various species in different scales. Due to the practice jhum cultivation system, the burning operation very often causes the spread of forest fires much beyond the jhum fields and brings considerable damage to forest wealth. The forestry scenario in Dima Hasao district emits both optimistic and pessimistic signals. The optimistic signal is that the problem plaguing the sector can be remedied by taking advantage if the relevant strengths available to support the forestry sector with planned, systematic and vigorous efforts. The pessimistic signal is that, if effective remedies are not found quickly the problems will have a disastrous effect on the forestry sector and the whole economy. The major task before the district is to rehabilitate the degraded forests and to enhance the area under forest. Forest encroachment, excessive collection of timber, fuel wood and other non-wood forests products, forests fires, pests and diseases and most important of all the extensive jhum cultivation are some of the factors which lead to the qualitative degradations of the forests. The ongoing constructions of Broad gauge railway track and four lane highways under the North-South and East-West corridor project of the central Government is another important factor for the rapid destruction of forests including biodiversity. The adverse impact of the large scale removal of forests areas and earthworks done in the hilly terrain is evident from the drying up of the Diyung River and loss of habitats to several wild animals found in the area. This trends needs to be reversed through effective action to establish the integrity of the natural forests and to control the factors which lead to deforestation and forests degradation. Natural forests are to be managed scientifically and intensively involving protection, Silvicultural treatments, aided regeneration and enrichment planting. While there have been some improvements in controlling deforestation, forest degradation or qualitative loss of natural resource appears to be still continuing. Dima Hasao district is still a neglected in the field of research for improvement of the once diverse and rich forest and this is one major setback for the people of the district.

In view of the deteriorating forests resources and their importance to the economy, environment and ecological security, the Autonomous Council has been emphasising the sustainable development of forests resources, as well as conservation of eco-systems. The Integrated Area Development programme was launched in the district with an aim to develop the jhum areas on watershed basis, rehabilitation of the degraded jhum areas, reclaiming the land affected by shifting cultivation and to upgrade the socio-economic condition of the jhumias. The forest Development Agency through its Joint Forest Management Programme shows optimism with active participation of the local villagers. Several programmes, policies and projects have been formulated and implemented by the state Government as well as by the Dima Hasao Autonomous Council. The Integrated Area Development Programme which is one such programme which gives due consideration to local tradition and culture is considered to be the mainstay in tackling the problem related to jhumming. This programme is aimed at:

1. Raising awareness among the communities about the benefits of more sedentary land use systems, in other words known as *'settled agriculture'* and;

2. Forest Development works generating sustained employment; (i) containing jhumming through short term and long term project implementations and their constant and continuous monitoring, facilitating re-orientation and improvement of the initial project parameters to suit the local requirements. (ii) Rehabilitation of shifting cultivation sites through innovative community based on afforation in forest areas.

3. Agro-forestry schemes with a significant input of horticulture and specifically approved cash crop cultivation on gentle slopes on affected community lands.

4. Steep areas are mostly used by jhumias for jhumming. Since jhumming is linked with the social customs of the local people, before imposing any regulation, the jhumias should be provided alternative source of livelihood. In this regard, brought down most of the people from the hills by paying land cost and settled them in plain areas and valley bottoms. It will help protection of forest resources and will save the people from hardship of shifting cultivation. The district Autonomous needs support of strong political will to implement regulations on clearance of streep areas.

The new participatory forest management systems being developed by the Autonomous Council and forest communities hold a great promise of a new direction in forest management. In a country of such diversity, it may not be feasible to evolve any uniform participatory forest management model. This makes the task more challenging because, depending upon the ground realities, specific model are being evolved for specific areas. It is hoped that with the willing and active participation of the village communities, co-operation of Non-Government Organisations and motivated involvement of forest departments, this challenging task will be successfully accomplished in times to come.

There is increasing pressure world-wide for improvement in the quality of forest management. Concern about environment and social issues associated with forest such as effect on bio-diversity, climate change, desertification, flooding, and conflicts over use rights and sustainable development has led to international agreements and programmes for improving forest management. Sustainable Forest Management has been described as forestry contribution to Sustainable Development. It is development which is economically viable, environmentally benign and socially beneficial and which balances present and future needs. Dima Hasao Autonomous Council efforts have been made to involve non-governmental organisations in uplifting the socio-economic condition of the rural people and involving them in the joint management, conservation, protection and preservation and also in the rehabilitation of the degraded forests. Therefore, it is needed to find out the resource potential of forest with reference to the exploration and exploitation and to study the usage and management aspect of forest in the Autonomous District of Dima Hasao for sustainable development.

Legal Status of Forest in Dima Hasao Autonomous Council

The Reserved forests were first gazetted under Section 17 of Assam forest regulation of 1891, Regulation vii of 1891. The district council has initiated action for reservation of three numbers of Un-classed state forest areas. The Un-classed state forests are non-cadastral areas and in such areas, villagers exercised their traditional right of shifting cultivation, and collection of house construction material, fuel wood, Non-Timber Forest Products (NTFP) without any hindrance. But these rights are not exercised in wanton but governed by traditional village Council/ Gaonburhas. District Council has paramount rights over the land and individual villagers, though enjoying traditional privileges have somewhat ill defined legal rights over the land. One of the most important elements or components is the compliance with the local and national regulations and various policies with all relevant legislations. Dima Hasao district have various acts and policies pertaining to the conservation and protection, usage of the national forests products. Some of the policies, Regulations and Acts are: (i) The North Cachar Hills Forest (Adoption of Assam Forest Regulation and Rules) Act-1953/1956 (ii) Bamboo and Rattan policy of Assam, (iii) Assam Forest Policy 2004 etc. Compliance with the above Acts and Policies from both the parties involved, i.e., the people as well as the governing authority will, to a great extent help the forests from further degradation. Lack of awareness among the people is a major threat looming large the district administration and the concerned Forest Department. In Dima Hasao district, the protection and conservation of the forests lies in the hands of the people. Therefore recognition of their rights will greatly help them in the conservation efforts more enthusiastically.

Management of Forest for Sustainable Development

Since the power of Management of forests is vested on the Autonomous District Council by the Sixth Schedule of the Constitution of India, management of forests in the hands of the Autonomous District Council. As such, the role of state forest department is mainly of advisory and assistance in implementation of developmental schemes/

works and under one Territorial forest division with its Head Quarter at Haflong. The division has six Territorial Ranges viz. (i) Haflong Range; (ii) Langting Range; (iii) Hatikhali Range; (iv) Diyungbra Range; (v) Garampani Range; (vi) Maibong Range. The authority must seriously address this issue to ensure sustained yield and the efficient utilisation of the resources.

Village Reserves

The North Cachar Hills District (Constitution of Village Reserves) Act, 1976 was enacted on the 24th March 1976 to provide for the constitution and management of villages Reserves in villages of North Cachar Hills. According to Section 2, Para 7 of this act, village means a revenue village having a district village boundary recorded in the Boundary Register maintained by the Land and Revenue Department of the District Council. Section 3 of the Act requires every village to constitute a village Reserve comprising of such areas as the Executive Committee may deem fit. It is the duty of the Gaonburhas to ensure protection and conservation of the village reserves failure of which will entail his dismissal from the office of the Gaonburha. The Gaonburha has the supreme power to impose penalty fine to the offenders. Most of the tribal villages in the district having their own village council set their own traditional laws and rules for proper administration of the villages. According to the village Reserves Acts of 1976, the villagers can cut and fell timber, bamboo, etc., from the reserves for their own use in house construction and other household needs, but cannot extract the forest resources from the reserves, for selling in the market.

Vegetation Profile

The natural forests of Dima Hasao district come under different sub-types approximating to the classification in the revised survey of forests types of India by Champion and Seth (1968). The whole district falls under the following broad category of forests types.

1. *Cachar Tropical Evergreen Forest-1B/C_3:* This type is generally found on the lower slopes of the Northern and Eastern aspects. The forests are largely composed of evergreen species. The upper storey is composed of *Artocarpus chaplasha* (Cham), *Mangiferra* species (Bon- am), *Alscodaphane owdenii* (Moricha sundi), *Albizia* species(sundi), etc., the middle storey is composed of *Eugenia*

fructicosa(jam), *Callophylum polyanthum* (kuta), *Kayea floribunda* (kurol), *Canarium resiniferum* (Dhuna), etc. in the lower storey *Aquilaria malaccensis* (syn. *A. agallocha*) (Agar), *Gynocordia odonaa* (chalmugra), *Holarhenna antidysentarica* (Dudhkhira) are common. Bamboo is not very common in this type but *Schizostachyum dullooa* (Dulu) and *Dendrocalamus hamiltonii* (Kako, Pecha) occur sporadically.

2. *Cachar Tropical Semi-evergreen Froest-2B/C_3:* This type of forest occurs on the hill tops, ridges and the upper slopes and in the forests areas affected by jhum in the past. The forests have both evergreen and deciduous species like *Dipterocarpus turbinatus*, *Gmelina arborea*, *Albizia procera*, *Cynometra polyandra, Amoora wallichii*, *Duabanga grandiflora*, *Terminalia species*, etc.

3. *Northern Sub- tropical Broadleaved Hill Forests-tye 8B/C_2*: In many forest of this area, repeated shifting cultivation with felling and burning have cleared and gently altered the original forests cover presumed to have been broadleaved evergreen forests without pines. There are now considerable areas of open grasslands with scattered trees adjoining broadleaved forest. In some patches almost, Oak forests are found along with Schima species. These occurrences may be viwed as degradation stage of climatic climax.

4. Tropical Moist Mixed Deciduous Forests-Type 8B (Ghogra, Oak type).

5. Cane Brakes and

6. Secondary Moist Bamboo Brakes-Type 2B/C1a.

The main Bamboo forests fall under the category of secondary moist Bamboo Brakes. This type occurs over an extensive area almost as a pure crop, either of *Melocanna bccifera* (mali) or *Oxytenanthera parviflora* (hill jati). The main species are *Teinostachyum dulloa* (Dalu), *Dendrocalamus hamiltonii* (Pecha, Kako), etc. Non-clump forming bamboo (Mali) occurs mainly in the lower hills and grows gregariously in the areas abandoned after shifting cultivation. Favourable climatic condition, rainfall, temperature, humidity and topography have helped the tropical vegetation to grow luxuriantly in the area. But heavy biotic interference, particularly shifting cultivation have in the past degenerated the characteristics tree species of evergreen and semi evergreen types into bamboo brakes over a large area of the forests.

The distribution of bamboo in the forest area is almost even and bamboo forests occupy about 90 per cent of the forest area of the Dima Hasao district. Bamboo is considered to be a unique raw material from the point of view of its growth, easy availability, straightness, smoothness etc. It is the most commonly used material in Dima Hasao district and finds multifarious uses as a basic material for low cost housing, bamboo hut, bamboo fence, fuel, bridge and also for erosion control structures in many hills areas. It also forms the basic component of many traditional musical instruments apart from its use in traditional weaving machines etc. Although bamboo is used as house hold item by the tribal community and the development of certain items having tremendous potential in handicrafts and the properties of bamboo found suitable for the construction of houses, but the local knowledge on such utilisation of bamboo resources of Dima Hasao district has not been fully appreciated and utilised from the point of view of the improvement of the socio-economic condition of the people. There is urgent need to set up bamboo based industry in the district so as to efficiently utilise the abundant resources. The recent development in the handicrafts sector is a major boost for the people of the district. The Cane and Bamboo Technology Centre at Harangajao needs to be upgraded such centre should be set up in different parts of the Dima Hasao district. But the technology and the infrastructure facilities are still major hindrance to efficient utilisation of bamboo and the artisans. The Government, particularly the Autonomous Council together with the NGOs must come forward and the needful so that, bamboo can be efficiently utilised and this will also ensure improvement in the living condition of the many tribal communities of the district.

It is revealed that the major bamboo species found in Dima Hasao district can be broadly categorised into two category, depending upon the usage and demand in the market, viz. Commercial Industrial bamboo. The commercial bamboo is mainly used for house construction and other handicrafts and day to day requirement by the local people. In the Industrial sector pulp and paper Mill is the sole consumer of bamboos from Dima Hasao district. Royalty is being paid to the Autonomous Council by the party or industry operating in the district.

Tenure and Rights

Sustainable forest management is a long term undertaking requiring investment and protection of the forest resources throughout the operation. The scheduled Tribes and other traditional forests dwellers (Recognition of Forests Rights) Act, 2007 passed by the Union Government, which will become operational from 1st January 2008 is a tremendous efforts by the Government in making the tribal and other forests dwellers, as stake holder in the forest management. According to this Act, those residing for three generations or 75 years are entitled to land rights and the right to collect and market forests products. Therefore, the protection and conservation of the forests lies in the hands of the people of Dima Hasao district.

Protection of the Environment

The varied topography ecology of the hilly terrain of the Dima Hasao district, distinctive pattern of lifestyle, isolation, different thoughts and beliefs are some of the factors for such variations. Each society has framed some sort of rules and procedures in use and management of natural resources within the jurisdiction of their habitation since long which are still adhered to by the tribesmen. This has indicated that the people are well aware of the importance development as well as preservation of natural resources for balanced economy in tradition. Forestry has a major impact on the environment, both within and outside the forest. One of the main components of forest in Dima Hasao district is the vast bamboo forests. Protection of forests includes conserving biodiversity, maintaining its ecological function, protecting soil and water resources. The environmental and ecological benefits of forests should be maximised and the adverse impacts minimised.

Consultation and Participation Process

Proper conservation and management of the forests can help the local people raise their standard of living and contribute to positive development of the district. The lack of adequate and proper management can destroy the rich forests resources. A holistic approach in consonance with the people's interests, knowledge, skills, rights or influence in forests is crucial for long-term success and sustainability of the forests. Consultation is a two-way of information between the concerned parties and it is important that Consultation and participation is done sensitively and realistically keeping in mind the culture and tradition and interests of the rural people. There is growing recognition that management of forest resources necessitates a meaningful involvement of local people living in or around the natural forests. It is revealed that when forest departments develop management agreements with local people and providing financial support for plantations which benefit both parties and result in rapid increase in biomass, genetic diversity, forest productivity and more equitable resource distribution. Therefore, joint forest management is a practical approach to get co-operation and participation of villagers in forest management.

Social Impact Assessment

A social impact assessment requires extensive consultation with the stakeholders (the affected local people), collection of information about the stakeholders and their interests, and then considering the actual or possible impacts of forests operations on these interests in order to propose mitigation measures. A thorough baseline survey and analysis of the same will help in proper planning and implementation of any programmes. Greater efforts have to be put in making the people aware and convincing them the benefits of adopting plantation planning and species selection should favour diversity at all scales that promises maximum utilisation and economic returns will inspire the people of Dima Hasao district.

Protection Forests from Illegal Activities

The forest resource must be protected from illegal harvesting and non-conformity with the prescribed felling rules. Forests encroachment in most of the reserved forests areas is likely to pose a serious threat to the long-term sustainability. Forestry crops are generally harvested at long rotations. The villagers cannot block their capital for such a long period. Some of the forestry crops which can be cultivated on short rotation are suggested to provide livelihood so that the local population can be weaned away from jhumming and forest resources can be saved from destruction which will help in improvement of environment, conservation and sustainable development of the forest resources.

Development of Cottage Industries

Majority of the local population of the district lives in the villages and proper utilisation and sustainable development of forest resources cannot be thought development of cottage industries in rural area. Economy of Dima Hasao district is mainly based on forest resources. Therefore, the cottage industries in the villages can be developed on forest products viz.; wood, bamboo, cane, etc. Since these being renewable resource and is ideal raw material for development of industries on sustainable basis. Raw material will also be available from the fields of the local people by raising crops on short rotation and they will get remunerative prices for their product and thus will have continued interest for raising forestry crops which will keep alive the tempo of conserving and growing trees which is essential for the survival of human beings and sustainable development of the forest resources.

Urgent Need

Forest management has undergone rapid change in the decades of eighties and the nineties. There is an urgent need for an increase in research activities, Geographical information system, Remote sensing techniques have the potential to provide a large amount of information on forest resource, growth, to guide management of biodiversity conservation both within and outside the protected areas and even for almost all habitat types. There is also need for chronicling traditional national resource management systems, which should be evaluated, strengthened and encouraged. Such knowledge should be exchanged or transferred between tribes for higher ecological and economic efficiencies, particularly conservation and management of forest resource for sustainable development. Conservation efforts should involve local communities by guaranteeing their land and forest right and providing them a stake in the sustainability of their natural surrounds.

There is tremendous scope for forestry development in Dima Hasao district because of low population density and the extensive forest area. But some check needs to be introduced through family planning measures. Cattle, sheep, goat and mule population is increasing at a very fast rate which has impact on regeneration of forests. Stall feeding will reduce pressure on forests. There are a number of schemes, viz., big hydro-electric projects which are adverse impact on forest resources by submerging large forest areas. Small low cost power generating units may be favoured in place of big projects. The rapid destruction of forest resources by commercial felling and illegal felling of trees should be curtailed. The forest potential could be tapped in a more rational manner to provide the necessary additional resources to help the people to improve their standard of living.

....

Conclusion

From the above discussion, we can easily draw certain interesting conclusion in relation to Managements of forest for sustainable utilization of Dima Hasao dirtrict that there is urgent need to set up forest research centre as well as industry under the jurisdiction of Dima Hasao Autonomous council so as to efficiently utilise the abundant resources. With a view to improving the social-economic condition, culture and traditions, in interest of the rural communities and the sustainable utilisation of forest resources there is need for the joint participation of the local people in order to conserve, protect and utilisation of the natural resources, prevent further degradation of the declining forests resources of Dima Hasao district. An efficient forest policy and a strong aforestation movement will not only meet increased fuel wood needs of poor, but can also compensate for the increased burning of fossil fuels and put a check on global warming. It will immensely beneficial to all those who are associated with and interested in the working of the sixth schedule.

References

1. Doungel, K, 2007: Bamboo treasure of N. C. Hills. DIPR, N.C. Hills, Haflong, Assam.
2. Shukla, S.P et al., (1997): Planet protection. Mittal Publications. New Delhi.
3. Sixth Schedule to the Constitution of India and memorandum of understanding; published, DIPR, N.C. Hills Autonomous Council, Haflong, Assam.
4. U. Kumar and M. Asija (2009): Biodiversity Principles and conservation, Second Edition, Agrobios (India), Jodhpur.

14

Karbi Anglong Autonomous District Council in Assam: Historical Perspectives

S.K. Chaudhury

Introduction

The Karbi Anglong Distrcit is situated in the central part of Assam. It is bounded by Golaghat district in the east, Meghalaya and Morigaon district in the west, Nagaon and Golaghat district in the north and N.C. Hills district and Nagaland in the south. The district with dense tropical forest covered hills and flat plains are situated between 25° 33' N to 26°35' N Latitude and 92°10' to 93°50' E Longitude. Due to variation in the topography, this hill zone experiences different climates in different parts. The winter commences from October and continues till February. The population of the district is predominantly tribal. The major tribal ethnic groups of this district are *Karbis, Bodos, Kukis, Dimasas, Hmars, Garos, Rengma Nagas, Tiwas, Man (Tai Speaking's)*. Besides, a large number of non-tribals also live together in this hill region.

Historical Perspectives

After independence, Constitution of India maintained the special status by way of provisions contained in Sixth Schedule. The district of United Mikir and North Cachar Hills district was bifurcated into two separate districts under banner as *"Mikir Hills"* and *North Cachar*

Hills district in the year 1970. The Mikir Hill district was again rechristened as *"Karbi Anglong District" w.e.f.* the 14th October, 1976 vides Govt. Notification No. TAD/R/115/74/47 Dtd. 14-10-1976. Karbi Anglong came into being as a full fledged separate district in the map of Assam with its Head quarter at Diphu. The district enjoys autonomy under the provision of Sixth Schedule of the Indian Constitution. It is the largest district of Assam with a total geographical area of 10, 434 Sq. Kilometer. The Karbi Anglong District is situated in the central part of Assam. The Karbi and Dimasa areas came to be ruled by their own District Councils. Thus came into existence the North Cachar Hills District Council on 29th April, 1952 and the Mikir Hills District Council on 23rd June, 1952. Both the District Councils were inaugurated by the then Chief Minister of Assam Bishnuram Medhi. The Mikir Hills district was again changed into Karbi Anglong vide Govt. Notification No. T.A.D./4/115/74 dated 14.10.1976. Henceforth the Council came to be called *Karbi Anglong District Council.*

The Autonomous State movement in Karbi Anglong and North Cachhar Hills districts of Assam has been a unique component of Party's practice during the last two decades. In the aftermath of the Assam movement in the late 1970s and early 1980s, the state witnessed a new awakening among the tribal communities. In Karbi Anglong district, the demand for an autonomous state as provided under Article 244A of the Indian Constitution grew into a popular movement under the leadership of the comrades. Within a short span of time, the ASDC went on to establish itself as the strongest political force not only in Karbi Anglong but also in the NC Hills. In the latter half of the 1990s ASDC not only controlled both the district councils but it also held all the five Assembly seats as well as the lone Lok Sabha seat from this region. In the 1999 Lok Sabha elections, it contested directly under the CPI (ML) banner and retained the Lok Sabha seat by polling more than 2,00,000 votes. The Congress swept the elections in the rest of Assam, but it failed once again in this region. Following the July 2000 turmoil in the Party and ASDC, the electoral scene has however undergone a dramatic change. The Congress has staged a comeback in the Assembly and council elections held in 2001.

The following measures have so far been taken to ensure a comprehensive revival of the Autonomous State movement and the Party in Karbi Anglong and NC Hills: (i) resuming the Autonomous

State movement with an extensive *"Long March"* criss-crossing the length and breadth of Karbi Anglong, (ii) launching a peasant organisation through a convention, efforts are also on to organise the peasants in reserve forest and grazing land against the eviction drive of the government, (iii) asserting the role of our members in the Autonomous Council as a consistent democratic opposition to the Congress-led council, (iv) revitalising KSA and KNCA (Karbi students' and women's organisations) and DSU and DWS (Dimasa students' and women's organisations), (v) streamlining the publication of Lotichari as a popular bilingual organ of the Party, (vi) expanding Party membership and reorganising Party structures at different levels through conferences, (vii) making bold and painstaking efforts to wean away the masses and ranks from the influence of the renegades, and (viii) restoring and strengthening our ties with the whole range of non-Party, non-Karbi sections under the banner of the Autonomous State movement.

Karbi People's Liberation Tiger (KPLT)

The Karbi People's Liberation Tiger (KPLT), earlier known as Anti-Talks Factions of Karbi Longri North Cachar Hills Liberation Front (KLNLF-ATF) was formed at an undisclosed location on January 8, 2011. The outfit was formed with 25 cadres of KLNLF-ATF who formally rechristened itself as KPLT. The KLNLF-ATF was a breakaway faction of the Karbi Longri National Liberation Front (KLNLF), which had laid down arms on February 11, 2010. KPLT has emerged as a new threat in the State. The KPLT is believed to have split towards the middle of 2011, when some of its members formed a new group, the Karbi National Protection Force (KNPF). However, not much is heard about the KNPF. KPLT is formed with an objective of carving an Autonomous Karbi State (AKS) out of Assam. The KPLT pledged to fight until the AKS is formed. Significantly, Jing Hanse, on the outfit's Foundation had declared that his party would continue subversive activities if their demands were not met. The KPLT has its base in Dima Hasao district of Assam and parts of Arunachal Pradesh. However, the outfit is most active in the Karbi Anglong district of Assam. The new outfit claims it is equipped with modern weaponry like mortars, AK-47, AK-56, M20 guns etc. The KPLT has links with the Anti-Talk faction of National Democratic Front of Bodoland (NDFB-ATF), another militant outfit of Assam and

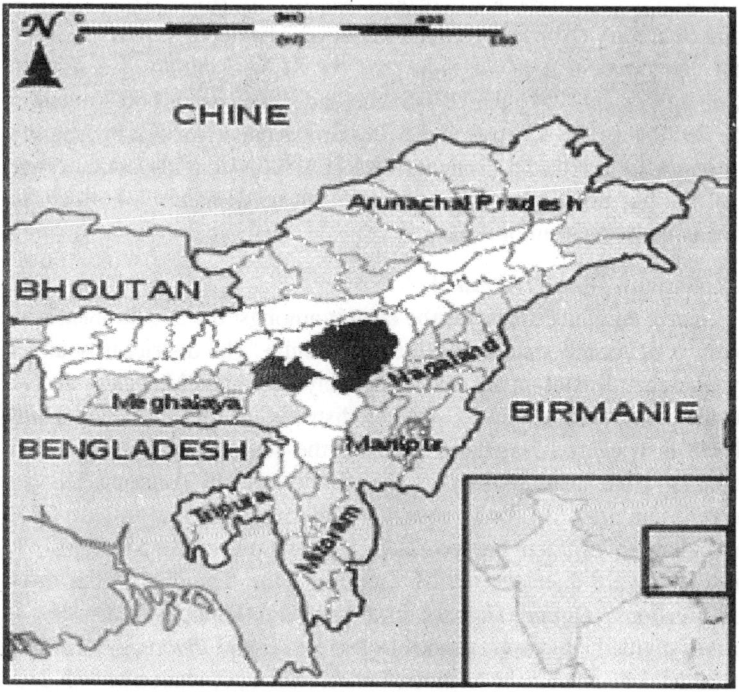

Fig. Karbi Anglong Autonomous District Council.

reportedly with Nationalist Socialist Council of Nagaland-Khaplang (NSCN-K). On July 2, 2011, around 30 militants of NDFB-ATF under the leadership of B. Narzari were reported to have built up bases inside Kaki reserve forest in the border areas of Karbi Anglong and Nagaon Districts. The NDFB-ATF is trying to secure its hold in the eastern part of Karbi Anglong with the help of KPLT. NDFB-ATF along with the KPLT is also reportedly procuring weapons and ammunitions from arms dealers operating from the Dimapur city of Nagaland. Report also stated that a batch of newly-trained 60 KPLT militants have completed their training in a NSCN-K camp near Dimapur and may join the outfit soon.

The Government rules out the possibility of talks with the outfit since it does not recognise KPLT as representative of the Karbi people and that the members of the outfit indulge in unlawful activities and are considered criminals. The Ministry of Home Affairs (MHA) only recognised United People's Democratic Solidarity (UPDS) and KLNLF as representative of the Karbi people. Ministry of Home Affairs (MHA) Joint Secretary (Northeast) Shambhu Singh stated on August 12, 2011, that *"government is of the view that the KLNLF should also sign the same agreement,"* like the UPDS who had signed accord on November 25, 2011 with the Central and State Government for Karbi Anglong Autonomous Territorial Council (KAATC). KLNLF is also under cease-fire, but has not signed any agreement on its demands, of which the core is the formation of AKS.

Autonomous District Council

Karbi Anglong district is the largest amongst the 27 administrative districts of Assam state in north-eastern India. The district is bounded by Golaghat district on the east, Meghalaya state and Marigaon district on the west, Nagaon and Golaghat districts on the north and Dima Hasao district and Nagaland state on the south. Diphu town is the administrative headquarters of the district. Karbi Anglong District occupies an area of 10,434 square kilometres (4,029 sq mi). In 2006 the Indian government named Karbi Anglong one of the country's 250 most backward districts (out of a total of 640). The district has three sub-divisions: *Diphu, Hamren* and *Bokajan.* Diphu sub-division is further divided into two revenue circles: *Diphu* and *Phuloni*. According to the 2011 census Karbi Anglong District has a population of 965,280. A number of indigenous peoples reside in this district. The Karbis are the most prominent amongst them. Other indigenous peoples residing in this district *include the Rengma Nagas, the Dimasas, the Bodos, the Kukis, the Garos, the Tiwas, the Khasis, Hmars, the Mizos and the Chakmas*. Apart from Karbi, the native language of the erstwhile ruler, the Karbi language is one of the prominent languages of the district. Other languages spoken include *Bodo, Kuki, Assamese and Aiton*, which with approximately 1500 speakers is closely related to Shan and written in the Burmese script. A hilly district of Assam Karbi Anglong is a very beautiful place in the lap of nature. It is still somewhat unknown to the tourist in spite of its enchanting natural green forests and picturesque hills.

It has the total geographical area of 10,434 sq. kms. which accounts for 13.3 per cent of the total geographical area of the State. It mostly consists of undulating and hilly terrain with numerous rivers and streams. The district can be broadly divided into two physiographic units' viz. hills and plains. About 85 per cent of the district is covered by the hills. The vast tract of hilly slopes also have been badly denuded due to practice of Jhum cultivation, as local tribals still practise this tradition though efforts are being made to permanently settle them by raising cash crop etc. through IJDP programmes. Karbi Anglong is rich in varied wild life. In areas adjoining Kaziranga National Park, one-horned rhinoceros, wild buffaloes and Bisons are very common. Tigers (Dhekiapatia), Leopard (Nahor Phutuki), Wolf (Kukurnesia) and Bears (Bhaluk) are met in almost every part of the district. The Govt. of Assam vides their Notification No. FEW. 57/99/38 dated 27-7-2000 have notified the *"Nambor Santuary"* with an area of 37 sq. km. in Silonijan Civil Circle under Bokajan Sub-Division (Civil) under Karbi Anglong East Forest Division, Diphu in Karbi Anglong District under Karbi Anglong Autonomous Council. The Wildlife Sanctuary is situated with its Northern boundary along the western and southern boundary of Garampani Wildlife Santuary upto Dhansiri River. The Government of Assam vides their Notification No. FRW. 57/99/51 dated 27-07-2000 have notified the *"East Karbi Anglong Wildlife Sanctuary"* in Silonijan Circle (Civil) under Karbi Anglong East Forest Division, Diphu in Karbi Anglong District under Karbi Anglong Autonomous Council with an area of 221.81 sq. km. The Government of Assam have notified the *"Karbi Anglong Wildlife Sanctuary"* in Duar Mauza under Bokajan Sub-Division under Karbi Anglong East Forest Division, Diphu under Karbi Anglong Autonomous council vide their Notification No. FRW. 57/99/42 dated 27/07/2000 with an area of 96 sq. km. The present Garampani Wildlife Sanctuary was notified during 1952 vide notification No, FR. 199/52 dated 10/07/52 with an area of 6 sq. km. The entire sanctuary is situated within the Karbi Anglong Autonomous Council area and is full of rare and endangered flora and fauna.

Considering the present bio-diversity of the area and recognising the need to conserve the sensitive ecosystem of this region, initial notification constituting this area as Wildlife Sanctuary was issued by Karbi Anglong District Council under Mikir Hill District Forest Act during 1997. However, in view of presence of Central Act on the subject, a proposal was forwarded to Government of Assam through Chief Conservator of Forests (Wildlife) Assam for its formal notification under Wildlife (Protection) Act, 1972. Incorporating desired modifications as requested by Chief Conservator of Forests (Wildlife)

Assam, the proposal has been resubmitted vide Council's letter No. KAC/F/M.L.WI Sanctuary/99-2000/1742 Dated 25/06/99 for formal notification by the Government of Assam through Chief Conservator of Forests (Wildlife) Assam. The proposal of Marat Longri Wildlife Sanctuary with proposed area of 451.87 sq.km. is quite rich in floral and faunal composition, and comprises of 4 (four) important Reserve Forests namely Miyungdisa (D.C.R.F.), Disama (R.F.), Kaki (R.F.) and Englongkiri (D.C.R.F.). The important wildlife species found inside proposed sanctuary include Asiatic Elephant, Royal Bengal Tiger, Binturong, Himalayan Black Bear, Barking Deer, Hoollock gibbon, etc., and a variety of avifauna. This wildlife sanctuary has adequate ecological, floral, faunal, geomorphological, natural and zoological significance and will go a long way in augmenting the conservation measures and protecting and conserving the valuable forests of this hill district. This proposed Wildlife Sanctuary is adjacent to Dhansiri Reserve Forests which is one of the largest Reserve Forests in Asia and is also quite rich in floral and faunal composition.

Karbi Anglong Autonomous Council is taking rapid strides in the scientific and sustainable management of forest resources of the district. Complete ban has been imposed on green felling since 1995. Survey of forest areas for sustainable harvesting of timbers and minor forest produces in perpetuity to meet genuine developmental and local needs has been conducted and compilation of Working Plans is under progress. More protected areas are being notified to conserve the genepool and bio-diversity of the District. Ethnobotanical studies under the guidance of Dr. S.K. Borthakur of Botany Department, Guahati University have been taken up to gather the indigenous knowledge of various tribes in Karbi Anglong who have co-existed with forests since times immemorial and a botanical garden for ex-situ conservation of these resources has been set up at Diphu. These measures will go a long way in conservation of precious flora and fauna of forests of Karbi Anglong. Let all of us join together to conserve our forest resources because *"genetic resources and bio-diversity are the national properties of each nation."*

Karbi People

The Karbis, mentioned as the Mikir in the Constitution Order of the Government of India are one of the major ethnic groups in North-east India and especially in the hill areas of Assam. Besides Karbi Anglong district, the Karbi-inhabited areas include *Dima Hasao,*

Kamrup, Marigaon district, Nagaon, Golaghat, Karimganj and Sonitpur districts of Assam; Balijan circle of Papumpare district in Arunachal Pradesh, Jaintia Hills, Ri Bhoi and East Khasi Hills districts in Meghalaya, and Dimapur District in Nagaland. Apart from Assam, the Karbis are also recognised as Scheduled Tribes in Meghalaya, Mizoram and Nagaland. With a population of around four lacs six thousand (406,000) as per 2001 Census, the Karbis constitute the third largest tribal community in Assam after the Bodos and the Mishings.

The Karbis linguistically belong to the Tibeto-Burman group. The original home of the various people speaking Tibeto-Burman languages was in western China near the Yang-Tee-Kiang and the Howang-ho rivers and from these places they went down the courses of the Brahmaputra, the Chindwin and the Irrawaddy and entered India and Burma. The Karbis, along with others entered Assam from Central Asia in one of the waves of migration. The Karbis are a patrilineal society and is composed of five major clans or Kur. They are Ingti (Lizang), Terang (Hanzang), Inghi (Ezang), Teron (Kronzang) and Timung (Tungzang) which are again divided into many sub-clans. The Karbis celebrate many festivals. Rongker is one such festival held around January–February by the entire village as thanksgiving to the various gods and for the prosperity and the well-being of the community. Most of the Karbis still practice their traditional belief system, which is animistic called *"Hemphu-Mukrang"* and there are also Karbi Christians (some 15 per cent according to census of India, 2011). The practitioners of traditional worship believe in reincarnation and honour the ancestors. The Karbi women are expert weavers and they wear home-made clothes. Their main attire consist the pekok, a piece of cloth with designs wrapped around the upper part of the body and tied into a knot on the right shoulder, the pini, similar to a sarong and a vamkok, a decorative piece of cloth tied around the waist over the pini. The Karbis traditionally practice jhum cultivation (slash and burn cultivation) in the hills. They grow variety of crops which include foodgrains, vegetables and fruits like rice, maize, potato, tapioca, beans, ginger and turmeric. From the point of view of habitation, the Karbis are divided into three groups namely *'Chinthong', 'Ronghang'* and *'Amri'*. These groups are otherwise known as Chinthong, Nilip-Ronghang and Amri Marlong. Those who live in the plains districts are called *'Dumrali'*. Fundamentally, these groups do not differ each other and they should not be confused with clans. The Karbis, like other tribes, have some traditional institutions which have been continuing from time immemorial. While some of the institutions are socio-political in nature, some are of economic character. The traditional village council of the Karbis is called *"ME"* and this council is composed of all the elderly male members of the village. The council is presided by the Sarthe or Gaonbura, the village headman. All the village disputes which are not of very grave or serious nature are settled by it.

The Karbis have **five** clans called ***"KUR"*.** These are **Terang, Teron, Enghee. Ingti** and **Timung.** Each of the five clans has a number of Sub-clans. While Enghee and Timung have (thirty) sub-clans each, Terang and Teron have (six) sub-clans each and the remaining clan Ingti has only (four) sub-clans. These clans are completely exagamous and marriage between a boy and a girl belonging to the same clan can never take place since the children of the same clan are considered as brothers and sisters. Violation of this customary law obviously leads to ex-communication of the couple involved. Even in the cremation ground called *Tipit* or *Thiri*, area is kept demarcated for each clan. Although all the five clans are socially on equality, Ingti being a priestly clan was supposed to have a higher status in former times. Although, monogamy is the prevailing practice, there is no bar to polygamy and the cases of polygamy are very rare. Cross-cousin marriage is a preferential one. Like other tribal societies, the Karbis do not have the system of bride price. After marriage, the wife continues to use the surname of her father. But the children assume the title of their father. Thus, the Karbis follow the patriarchel system of family structure.

The settlement pattern of the Karbis is in the form of a village. Each village has a headman called *Gaonbura* or *Sarthe* who is appointed by the authority of Karbi Anglong Autonomous Council. But each revenue village has a number of hamlets situated kilometers apart. Each of the hamlets has also a Gaonbura. Each Karbi village is named after the Gaonbura. The Karbis, like the other hill tribes have a tendency to live on the hill tops. But the people generally donot live in compact areas. The villages are not only smaller in size, but scattered too. In the plains portion of the Karbi Anglong District where the Karbi people practise permanent cultivation and where the village headmen are quite strong, the villages are found to be stationery. Karbi hut is neither too small nor too big. It is built on a bamboo platform using timber posts for super structure. The platform is several feet high above the ground. For roofing purpose, thatch is used. The walls made of split bamboos are mud-plastered. The house has two varandas—one at the front and the other at the rear. The house is divided into two parts lengthwise. Dance and Music play an important role in the life of the Karbi Society. Various types of dances are performed by the youths during the performances of Chomangkan, the death ceremony and other socio-religious festivals. Hacha Kekan, the dance performed at the harvesting festival is very lively and eye-catching. Their traditional songs whether folk or religious, are generally sung by experts only who are not only well conversant with their meaning but are also endowed with sweet voices. The Karbis have very limited number of musical instruments. A big drum called Cheng is their main musical instrument. It is generally played by a master drummer called Duihudi. They also use small drums called Chengbruk. They have two kinds of flutes, the wooden flute is called Muri and bamboo flute is called Pangche. In some of their dances they use war shield made of rhinocer's skin called Chong and prototype war sword called Nok.

Functions and Powers

In accordance with the provisions laid down in the Sixth Schedule to the Constitution of India the functions and powers of Karbi Anglong Autonomous Council can be divided under three main heads-Legislative, Executive and Judicial.

Legislative Powers

The Governor of Assam was pleased to make the rules in the year 1951 for the first Constitution of District Councils for the autonomous districts comprising the tribal areas specified in Part A of the tribal appended to paragraph 20 of the said schedule and these rules called the *"Assam Autonomous Districts (Constitution of District Councils) Rules, 1951"*. The Karbi Anglong Autonomous Council in respect of all areas within the district shall have the power to make laws with respect to:

1. The allotment, occupation, or use or the setting apart of land other than any land which is reserved forest, for the purpose of agriculture or grazing, or for residential or other non-agricultural purposes likely to promote the interests of the inhabitants of any village or town.

2. The management of any forest not being a reserved forest.
3. The use of any canal or water course for the purpose of Agriculture.
4. The regulation of the practice of Jhum or other forms of shifting cultivation.
5. The establishment of village or town committees or Councils and their powers
6. Any other matter relating to village or town administration includes village or town policies and public health and sanitation.
7. The appointment or succession of chief or headman.
8. The inheritance of property.
9. Marriage.
10. Social Customs.
11. The Autonomous Council has also been empowered to frame laws to regulate and control money lending and trading by persons other than the scheduled tribes.

Though the Karbi Anglong Autonomous Council has the powers to make acts, rules, but the Governor must give his assent to the acts, rules made by the Council. The Governor has the power to suspend or alter any act or resolution of the Council if he is satisfied that it is likely to endanger the safety of India.

Executive Powers

The Autonomous Council may establish, construct or manage primary schools, dispensaries, markets, cattle pounds, ferries, fisheries, road and waterways in the district and in particular may prescribe the language and manner in which primary education should be imparted in the primary schools of the district. The Autonomous Council has been allotted specific items of revenue for the efficient discharge of its functions and to meet necessary expenses. It in respect of all land within the district shall have the power to assess and collect revenue in respect of such lands in accordance with the principles for the time being followed by the Government of Assam in assessing land for the purpose of land revenue in the State of Assam generally. It shall have the power to levy and collect taxes on lands and buildings, and tolls on persons residing within such areas. It shall have the power to levy and collect all or any or the following taxes:

1. Taxes on profession, trades, callings and employment.
2. Taxes on entry of goods into a market for sale therein and tolls on passengers and goods carried in ferries.
3. Taxes for the maintenance of schools, dispensaries and roads.
4. Licenses or leases for the purpose of prospecting for, or extracting minerals. The Autonomous Council shall have the right of sharing the royalties accrued each year from licenses or leases for the purpose of prospecting for, or the extracting of minerals granted by the Government of Assam in respect of any areas within the autonomous district as may be agreed upon between the Government of Assam and the Autonomous Councils.

Judicial Powers

Para 4 of the Sixth Schedule entitles the Council to constitute Village and Council Courts in the autonomous areas to adjudicate or try cases or customary laws in which both the parties are tribal's. The District Council Court and the Regional Council Court are courts of appeal in respect of all suits and cases tried by the Village Council Courts and the Subordinate District Council Courts. No other court except the High Court and the Supreme Court of India have jurisdiction over suits and cases decided by the Council Courts.

Significance

The autonomous administrative set up of Karbi Anglong district provided by the Constitution stands as a major obstacle in protecting rhinos and other animals of Kaziranga National Park. Karbi Anglong skirts the southern border of the national park with NH-37 in between. Every year during floods, animals from the park cross the highway in search of drier highlands of Karbi Anglong. Though the state forest department wants to set up watch towers on the south of the National Highway in Karbi Anglong district, being an autonomous district, the state government has no say in the forest affairs of the district. This subject lies with the autonomous council.

The Karbi Anglong Autonomous Council (KAAC) has set up a toll gate at Sabuda, about 80 kilometers from Nongpoh, for collecting entry taxes from vehicles passing through the area. Sabuda is a disputed area. The Karbi Autonomous Council has decided to prohibit land rights to any new settlers with an immediate effect. Principal Secretary of Karbi Anglong Autonomous District Council issued an order regarding this ban a few days' back. Sale, transfer of ownership in any means including gift, lease, permission to use, mortgage or to bond out any lands owned by non tribal's in Karbi Anglong to any non tribal was banned by this order under any circumstances. By this order Karbi Anglong Autonomous District Council has categorically denied land rights to all non-tribal people, who have been living there since the formation of erstwhile Mikir Pahar district (presently Karbi Anglong) in 1951-52.

On November 25, 2011 a new beginning was made in the conflict-ridden Karbi Anglong District of Assam when the Union Home Minister P. Chidambaram signed a tripartite Memorandum of Settlement (MoS) with the United Peoples' Democratic Solidarity (UPDS). The UPDS has been fighting for a separate Karbi state within India since 1999. The MoS envisions amongst other things, the renaming of the present Autonomous District Council as the *Karbi Anglong Autonomous Territorial Council (KAATC)*; increasing seats in the Council up to 50 members of which six will be nominated by the governor (presently there are 30 seats with four being nominated by the governor); a special economic package of Rs 350 crore (Rs 70 crore per annum); improvement of road connectivity; rehabilitation of UPDS cadres; and setting up village councils for deepening the democratic process. The MoS has been received well by the Karbi population as the first concrete step towards establishing peace in Karbi Anglong since conflict broke out in 1999. For more than a decade now, the Karbi Anglong District has been afflicted by violence, especially between the UPDS and the rival ethnic Dimasa armed groups, the Dima Halam Daogah (DHD), especially the DHD (Black Widow) faction. While the MoS are a tentative step in the direction of peace, there are certain obstacles towards its implementation in letter and spirit. First, the Assam Government has shown signs of resistance to the dissolution of the current Congress-led Karbi Anglong Autonomous District Council in order to pave the way for the creation of the Territorial Council. The worst of Black Widow violence occurred in October 2005 when it ravaged the UPDS in Karbi Anglong by killing more than 30 of its cadres and supporters. Since then, the situation has calmed down but tension continues to exist even after the arrest and rehabilitation of the DHD (Black Widow) group. The other troubling issue is that while the MoS ensures that the UPDS transforms itself into a political party and joins the democratic process, the two other Karbi armed outfits responsible for most of the violence today, the Karbi Longri N C Hills Liberation Front (KLNLF) and the Karbi Peoples' Liberation Tigers (KPLT) are not covered by the MoS. According to KLNLF, the MoS is unacceptable as it says nothing on their demand for a separate Karbi state outside of Assam. The other tricky issue is the concept of *"territorial council"* itself. Karbi Anglong District is home to several tribes, prominent amongst them being the Karbi, Dimasa, Bodo, Kuki, Tiwa, Garo, Rengma, etc. The tribes do not live in contiguous areas but are instead housed in villages that are scattered across tribes. When one travels in the heavily forested district, it is noticed that a Karbi village is followed by a Dimasa village and then there is a Kuki village. The fate of the Kuki and the Dimasa villages is not clear in the MoS when the Karbi-dominated territorial council comes into existence. This is indeed a complicated issue as the Kuki and the Dimasa villages form part of the demand for a Kuki territorial council and a Dimasa state respectively.

Conclusion

The Karbis are one of the major ethnic groups in North-east India. The Karbis linguistically belong to the Tibeto-Burman group. Karbi Anglong district is the main district for them. Besides Karbi Anglong district, the Karbi-inhabited areas include Dima Hasao, Kamrup, Marigaon district, Nagaon, Golaghat, Karimganj and Sonitpur districts of Assam; Balijan circle of Papumpare district in Arunachal Pradesh, Jaintia Hills, Ri Bhoi and East Khasi Hills districts in Meghalaya, and Dimapur District in Nagaland. Apart from Assam, the Karbis are also recognised as Scheduled Tribes in Meghalaya, Mizoram and Nagaland. Karbi Anglong Autonomous district council was formed for the development of the Karbi people and at the same time for the area. It was created under six schedule of Constitution of India. Socio and economic development of tribals occurred within the autonomous council but in manytimes violence disturb the process.

References

1. Assam Times (August 7, 2007). *No Land right to non-Karbi in Karbi Anglong: Will apply to people already residing there as well.*

2. *Karbi Anglong Autonomous Council (2012)*. Retrieved from http://kaac.nic.in/
3. *Karbi Anglong Distrcit (2012)*. Retrieved from http://en.wikipedia.org/wiki/Karbi_Anglong_District
4. *Karbi Anglong District at a glance (2012)*. Retrieved from http://karbianglong.nic.in/at%20a%20glance.html
5. *Karbi People's Liberation Tiger (KPLT),* Retrieved from http://www.satp.org/satporgtp/countries/india/states/assam/terrorist_outfits/KPLT.HTM
6. Karbi People (2012). Retrieved from http://en.wikipedia.org/wiki/Karbi_people
7. The Times of India (Oct 5, 2012). *Karbi Autonomous set-up hurdle to rhino protection*, Retrieved from http://timesofindia.indiatimes.com/city/guwahati/Karbi-autonomous-set-up-hurdle-to-rhino-protection/articleshow/16690122.cms?
8. *Tribes and culture (2012)*. Retrieved from http://karbianglong.gov.in/main-web/tribes-culture.htm
9. *The Karbi Anglong and NC Hills Experience (2012),* Retrieved from http://cpiml.org/pgs/polorgreport/7.htm

15

Bodoland Territorial Council: Past vs. Present

B.K. Panda **and** ***Sukanta Sarkar***

Introduction

Scientific evidence suggests that life began on Earth approximately 3.5 billion years ago. Assam and adjoining regions have evidences of human settlements from all the periods of the Stone ages. The hills at the height of 1,500–2,000 feet (460 to 615 m) were popular habitats probably due to availability of exposed doleritic basalt useful for tool-making. Since 1947, with increasing economic problems in the region, separatist groups began forming along ethnic lines, and demands for autonomy and sovereignty grew, resulting into fragmentation of Assam. Since the mid-20th century, people from present Bangladesh have been migrating to Assam. In 1961, the Government of Assam passed a legislation making use of Assamese language compulsory. The post 1970s experienced the growth of armed separatist groups like United Liberation Front of Asom (ULFA) and National Democratic Front of Bodoland (NDFB). In November 1990, the Government of India deployed the Indian army, after which low-intensity military conflicts and political homicides have been continuing for more than a decade. Tribes of Assam found in both the valley and plain areas of Assam. They belong to the racial group of Mongoloid and Proto-Austroloid. The land of Assam is decorated with a number of Hills which include Karbi Anglong and North Cachar hills and expansive rivers like

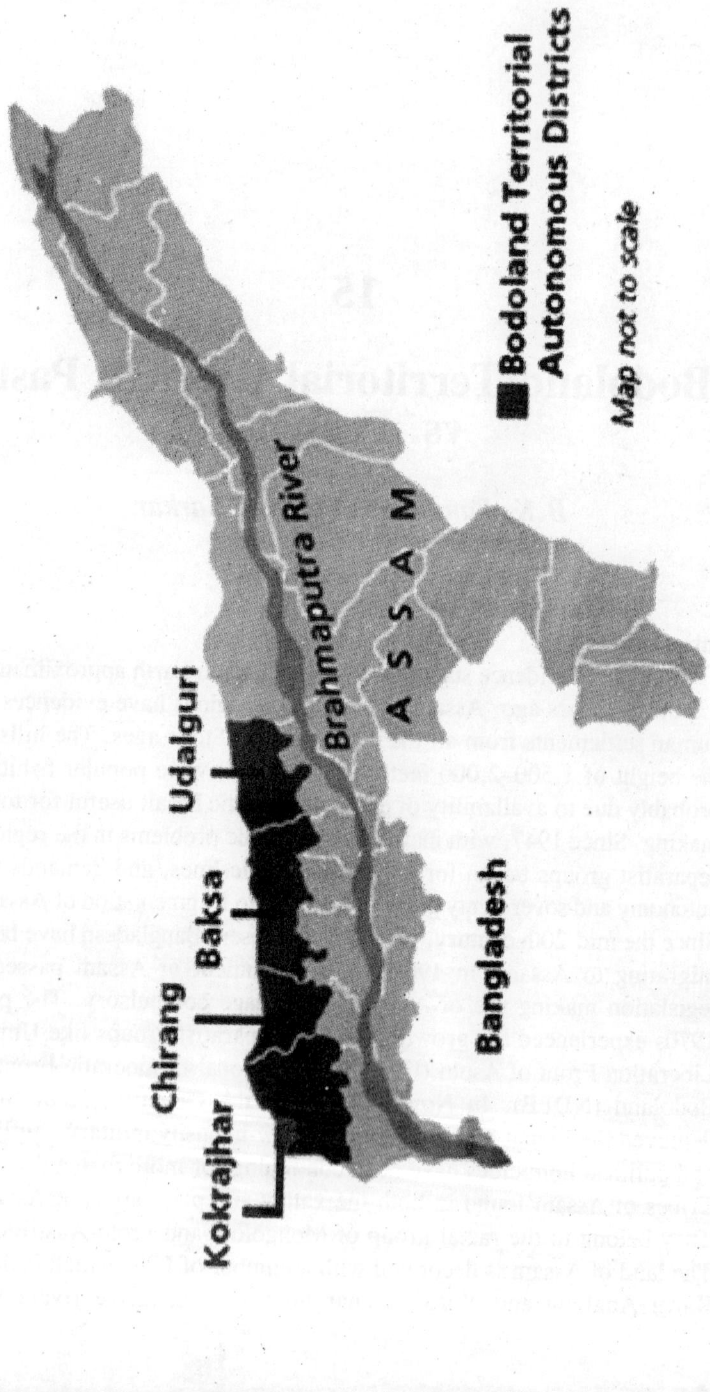
Bodoland Territorial Autonomous Districts
Map not to scale
Brahmaputra River
A S S A M
Bangladesh
Udalguri
Baksa
Chirang
Kokrajhar

Brahmaputra and Barak which create the valley of Assam. Overall the state of Assam has been important within Indian polity for it represents a large group of Indian tribes who belong to various groups of tribal origin.

Bodo People

The Bodos are an ethnic and linguistic community, early settlers of Assam in the northeast part of India. According to the 2011 census, there are nearly 2 million Bodos in Assam which makes for 5.5 per cent of the total population in the state. Bodos belong to a larger ethnic group called the Bodo-Kachari. The Bodos are recognised as a plains tribe in the Sixth Schedule of the Indian Constitution. Udalguri and Kokrajhar are considered the centre of the Bodo area. The Bodos represent one of the largest of the 18 ethnic sub-groups within the Kachari group, first classified in the 19th century. Bodos have settled in most areas of North-East India and parts of Nepal. The Bodo people constitute a diverse range of the Indigenous people of North-east India. The Bodo language is a member of the Tibeto-Burmese family. Very early on, Bodos had introduced rice cultivation, tea plantation, pig and poultry farming, and silkworm rearing in North East India. Rice is a staple food of the Bodos and is often accompanied by a non-vegetarian dish such as fish or pork. Traditionally Bodos are non-vegetarians. Bodos practice Hinduism, Christianity and Bathouism. Among Christian groups some belong to the Bodo Evangelical Lutheran Church. As of 2001, more than 90 per cent of the Bodos living in Assam were Hindus. However, the percentage of Christians is growing.

National Democratic Front of Bodoland

The National Democratic Front of Bodoland is an extremist outfit which seeks to obtain a sovereign Bodoland for the Bodo people in Assam, India. The founder of the organisation, Ransaigra Nabla Daimary, alias Ranjan Daimary has been arrested and detained by Indian authorities. The organisation came into being on October 3, 1986, in Odla Khasibari village close to Udalguri. It was originally called *Boro Security Force (BSF)* and changed its name to the present one on November 25, 1994. Majority of the cadres were Christians. This organisation is often confused with the erstwhile *Bodo Liberation Tigers Force*, which has since joined the political mainstream. The flag of the NDFB is green with a yellow star on red background on the corne. The NDFB occupied the areas to the north and northwest of the

Brahmaputra River in Assam primarily. It was also active in Bongaigaon, Chirang, Kokrajhar, Darrang, Berpeta, Nalbari, Dhubri, Sonitpur, and the Garo hills region of Meghalaya. Under an agreement on May 24, 2005 with the Government of India and the NDFB has been maintaining a ceasefire since June 1, 2005. Since the cease fire the level of threat posed by the NDFB has dropped. The agreement stated that the NDFB agree to cease hostile action against security forces and civilians. In return, the security forces would not carry out operations against the group's members. The agreement also stipulated that NDFB members would disarm and live in camps protected by the military for a year, and would refrain from assisting other militant groups.

Bodo Liberation Tigers Force

Bodo Liberation Tigers Force was an armed group operating in the Bodo dominated regions of Assam which demanded a separate state for the Bodos to be carved out of Assam. The organisation came into being on June 18, 1996 under the leadership of Prem Singh Brahma. On February 10, 2003, representatives of BLTF and the governments of Assam and India signed a Memorandum of Settlement, and 2641 cadres finally laid down arms on December 6, 2003. A vast majority of them were absorbed in the CRPF.

All Bodo Students Union

All Bodo Students' Union (ABSU) is a student's organisation (non-political) formed in 1967 in the Bodoland region of Assam, India. The ABSU under the leadership of Upendranath Brahma supported the movement for a separate state, to be called Bodoland. The Union shall make efforts, particularly to find out ways and means to: (a) Propagate the education through the mother tongue, (Bodo language) among the masses; (b) Improve and develop the Bodo language and literature through various literary activities, publication works etc; (c) Work for the welfare and development of the student's community in the educational field; (d) Safeguard and develop the culture of the Bodos; (e) Develop the Bodo nation economically by taking economic agenda and programmes from time of time; (f) Tackle and settle the political issues if and when the existence of the Bodo people is threatened, though the ABSU is a non-political organisation; (g) Struggle to achieve the rights and privileges given in the Indian Constitution through democratic process; (h) Support the principle of democratic socialism for economic emancipation. and (i) Fight for ensuring safety and security, dignity and securing Human Rights and Civil Liberty of the Bodo Nationality living around the world.

Autonomous District Council

As early as in 1930s, Gurudev Kalicharan Brahma, the then lone leader of the Bodos submitted memorandum to Simon Commission demanding for a separate political set up for the indigenous and tribal people of Assam. However, his demand for political administration was ignored by the British Raj. Even in the post Independence era, such demands were not met by the successive state government. Instead Bodos were treated as non-tribal community and force to identify as Assamese. In the 1960s, the second wave of Bodoland movement emerged. A section of educated Bodo leaders spearheaded a movement demanding a separate Union Territory called *"Udhayachal"* in 1967. However, this demand for separate Union territory failed due to lack of willingness on the part of the Central and State government to create a separate political administration for plains tribal's of Assam. Many years later, in the 1980s, the third mass struggle for Bodoland took place. The Bodos led a struggle in the name of self-determination in late 1980s under the leadership of Upendra Nath Brahma, who is now regarded as the *Father of the Bodos (Bodofa)*. In 1993, for the first time, the Assam government formed the Bodoland Autonomous Council (BAC) to fulfill socio-economic aspirations of the Bodos. But the peace accord between the leaders of All Bodo Student's Union (ABSU), Bodo People's Action Committee (BPAC) and the government of Assam failed due to non-implementation of various provisions of the Accord. The Accord collapsed in just one year of its existence. Moreover, the accord came with certain constrained resulting in administrative bottleneck. After a decade of long agitation, on 10 February 2003, the Bodos were granted the Bodoland Territorial Council (BTC), an autonomous administrative body that has within its jurisdiction the present district of Kokrajhar, Chirang, Udalguri and Baksa. The second Bodo peace award was result of negotiation between the Bodo Liberation Tiger (BLT), the Central Government and the Assam Government. Following the peace accord, BLT was required to surrender all their arms and converted into Bodoland People's Front (BPF), a political party now ruling the Council. Whereas, the National

Democratic Front of Bodoland (NDFB) another armed outfit are in ceasefire talks with the Central Government. Meanwhile, the All Bodo Student's Union (ABSU) has intensified its democratic movement for a separate state. The various district cover under Bodoland Territorial Council areduscuss below:

(a) ***Kokrajhar District:*** Kokrajhar district is an administrative district in the state of Assam in north-eastern India. The district headquarters are located at Kokrajhar town. The district occupies an area of 3,169.22 km^2. As of 2001, the district had a population of 905,764, Hindus 594,168, Muslims 184,441(20.36 per cent). It was originally a part the undivided Goalpara district. According to the 2011 census Kokrajhar district has a population of 886,999. The district has a population density of 280 inhabitants per square kilometre (730/sq mi). In 1957, under the administration of Bimala Prasad Chaliha as the Chief Minister of Assam, three sub-divisions were created one of which was Kokrajhar. It is located on the northern bank of the Brahmaputra River. It forms the gateway to the Seven Sister States. Kokrajhar shares its boundary with Bongaigaon (now known as Chirang), Dhubri, West Bengal, Barpeta and Bhutan. In 2006 the Indian government named Kokrajhar one of the country's 250 most backward districts (out of a total of 640). It is one of the eleven districts in Assam currently receiving funds from the Backward Regions Grant Fund Programme (BRGF). There are four Assam Legislative Assembly constituencies in this district: *Gossaigaon, Kokrajhar West, Kokrajhar East, and Sidli*. The district is multi-ethnic, with no majority ethnic group. Most of the Bodo and Assamese is Hindu, with a small Christian minority. Kokrajhar city is located along the bank of Gourang River. The North East Indian Railways divides the city into two sides, north and the south. Kokrajhar city is the headquarters of Kokrajhar district and the Bodoland Territorial Council (BTC).

(b) ***Chirang District:*** As of 2011 Chirang is the second least populous district in the state, after Dima Hasao. It is a relatively new district in the BTC area of the state. Chirang district has been carved out from Bongaigaon district in 2004. According to the 2011 census it has a population of 481,818. The district has a population density of 244 inhabitants per square kilometre (630/sq mi).

(c) ***Baksa District:*** Baksa was notified as one of the districts of Bodoland Territorial Council in October 2003 while it started functioning from 1 June 2004. It was created from parts of Barpeta, Nalbari, and Kamrup districts. Mushalpur town is the head quarters of the district. This district is bounded by Bhutan in the north, Udalguri district in the east, Barpeta, Nalbari and Kamrup districts in the south and Chirang district in the west. Area of the district is 2400 km^2. The district has three sub-divisions: Mushalpur, Salbari and Tamulpur. These sub-divisions are further divided into 13 revenue circles: Baksa, Barama, Tamulpur, Goreswar, Baganpara, Ghograpar, Barnagar, Bajali, Jalah, Patharighat, Rangia, Sarupeta and Tihu. According to the 2011 census Baksa district has a population of 953,773. The district has a population density of 475 inhabitants per square kilometre (1,230 /sq mi).

(d) ***Udalguri District:*** Udalguri district was formed on June 14, 2004 as one of the four districts under the Bodoland Territorial Autonomous District. This district was carved out by bifurcating Darrang district. The territory of the present district was earlier Udalguri sub-division of the undivided district. There are Hindu, Christians and Muslim population living together in the district. The main composition of people there are Assamese (Borpetia), Boro Kachari, Saotal, Marwari, Bengali Hindu and Muslims, Nepali, Garo and other tribes. This was a very peaceful place till mid 80s but various communal clashes took place from time to time. This district is bounded by Bhutan and West Kameng district of Arunachal Pradesh state in the north, Sonitpur district in the east, Darrang district in the south and Baksa district in the west. Area of the district is 1852.16 km^2. The district has two sub-divisions: Udalguri and Bhergaon. These two sub-divisions are further divided into nine revenue circles: Udalguri, Majbat, Harishinga, Kalaigaon, Khoirabari, Dalgaon, Patherighat, Mangaldai and Dhekiajuli. According to the 2011 census Udalguri district's population is 832 769, an increase of 9.8 per cent over 2001. In 1990 Udalguri district became home to Manas National Park, which has an area of 500 km^2 (193.1 sq mi). Udalguri town is the headquarters of the district. The major communities include Bodo Kachari, Assamese, Tea-tribes, Nepali and Bengali. There are also a small population of Muslim, Bihari, Nishi, Garo and

Rabha. Bihu or Bwisagu is the most celebrated festival and it falls in the month of April.

Bodo vs Bengali Violence

Large numbers of Bangladeshi Muslims are migrated in various parts of Assam. Those people have no any legal documents, i.e., illegally they entered in India. It is also a common phenomenon in Bodoland. From middle of 2012 conflict starts in Bodoland. On July 23, a murderous mob attacked the village of Bodo tribal's, reducing it to charred rubble. In that village about 250 households are lives. About 50 kilometres away in neighbouring Chirang district, about 3,000 people from three villages have taken sanctuary in a madrasa in Chatipur village. They fled on July 25, when about 100 men with automatic firearms attacked their villages, Chatipur, Bortola Part I and Bortola Part II. Kokrajhar and Chirang are part of Bodoland Territorial Autonomous Districts (BTAD), an autonomous area for the Bodo tribal's created in western Assam under the Sixth Schedule of the Constitution. The region is a tinderbox that needs only a spark to implode. The past two decades have seen at least four bloody and violent confrontations between the Bodo tribal's and Bengali Muslims, considered illegal immigrants from Bangladesh. A report by non-profit Norwegian Refugee Council published in November 2011, this is Our Land: ethnic violence and internal displacement in north-east India, estimates that close to 0.5 million people were displaced between 1993 and 1998 in three different violent events, all involving the Bodo. Of these, close to 50,000 are still living in refugee camps and need rehabilitation. In 1993, the violence between the Bodo and Bengali Muslims had claimed about 50 lives and displaced about 250,000 people. This time, the riot which erupted in mid-July, had claimed 65 lives and displaced 400,000 people till the time this magazine went to print.

The Bodoland Territorial Council (BTC) distributed utensils among relief camp inmates in Kokrajhar district who are going back to their respective villages. The utensils, which include all basic pots, pans and ladles, required in a family kitchen, were given to 483 families in Silgara and 288 families who are taking shelter at Gaide-Helena Nursing Training School, Habrubari, in Kokrajhar. The kitchen set takes in 19 items for each family, including a trunk to hold them. An important power project, which can bail out the power-starved state, has hit a roadblock since the July riots in the Bodoland Territorial Autonomous

Districts areas of lower Assam as almost half of the workforce of the construction site continues to stay away from work. Work at the 750-MW Bongaigaon Thermal Power Station (BTPS) being built by the NTPC at an estimated cost of Rs 4375.55 cr at Salakati, spread over Kokrajhar and Bongaigaon districts came to a halt when the prolonged riots ravaged lower Assam. Around 3,500 workers were working on the project but since the outbreak of violence, 1,000-1,200 of them have stopped coming to work. This has impacted the progress of the work. The report adds the outbreak of subsequent violence and imposition of curfew in August 12 worsened the situation in Kokrajhar. *"The workers' turnout at the Bongaigaon site drastically reduced and the work in different areas has come to a halt as the supply lines for essential construction material such as aggregates, sand, industrial gas, electrodes, diesel etc., are affected."*

The Assam government sounded high alert in the entire Bodoland Territorial Autonomous District (BTAD) area that comes under the control of the Bodoland Territorial Council following fresh violence. The three districts of Kokrajhar, Dhubri and Chirang, which witnessed violent clashes between Bodos and Muslims in July, still have 39,459 displaced persons taking shelter in 97 relief camps. The army, which was already engaged in counter-insurgency operations in lower Assam, was deployed for riot control duties from July 25, 2012. Additional army companies were also called in to assist the district administration. As the situation returned to normal by September, the army was taken out of riot control duties and put back on counter-insurgency operations. Most of the people displaced during the riots have returned to their homes, but there are still about 39,000 of them living in relief camps and waiting for rehabilitation. A total of 4, 46,296 persons were displaced during the July riots.

A demand for the creation of a separate Bodoland state, carved out of Assam was raised in the Lok Sabha. The UPA-II has announced a policy decision for creation of separate states like Telangana. The demand for bringing about a lasting solution to the Bodoland problem has been long overdue and urgent steps should be taken to resolve this issue. The All Bodo Students' Union (ABSU) staged a three-hour sit-in demonstration at Jantar Mantar in New Delhi against unabated influx in the Bodoland Territorial Council (BTC) area in Assam. They demanded detection and deportation of Bangladeshis. Representatives from Telengana also took part in the demonstration. After 1960, political parties encouraged influx to build a vote bank to win elections. Barbed fence was supposed to be erected as per the Assam Accord, 1985, but till date it has not been completed. Successive governments, both at the Centre and state, ignored the issue of influx. The demand for Bodoland has gained fresh momentum with several Congress workers from the Bodo heartland extending support to the All Bodo Student Union's cry for a separate state for the Bodos. Thousands of Bodoland Pradesh Congress Committee (BPCC) workers are supporting the All Bodo Students' Union in the latter's movement for a separate state of Bodoland. During the movement for Bodoland in the late Eighties, several Bodo leaders, including ABSU members, became martyrs in their armed struggle. Considering the legitimate demand for a separate Bodoland in Assam, the Centre signed a peace accord and formed the Bodoland Territorial Council (BTC) under the Sixth Schedule of the Constitution.

The Indian Confederation of Indigenous and Tribal Peoples North East Zone (ICITP-NEZ) has extended support to the demand of a separate Bodoland state. An umbrella organization of 56 indigenous and tribal organisations in the northeast, the ICITP-NEZ said the demand for a separate Bodoland state was *"legitimate"* and the delay in its creation was *"an injustice to the aspirations of the Bodos"*. ICITP-NEZ president J R Muchahary said, *"It's unfortunate to witness the historic injustice to delay in fulfilling the most legitimate and genuine 44-year demand of a separate state of Bodoland—an aspiration of most Indigenous people of Assam. The Boroland movement is contemporary with the Jharkhand movement. The demand for Jharkhand was conceded in 2000. But the demand of Bodoland has been sidelined."* The organisation also extended its support for the creation of Dimaraji—a separate state for the people living in Dima Hasao. Expressing solidarity with the groups fighting for Bodoland and Dimaraji, the ICITP functionary said it would garner support from other tribal groups in the region for the purpose. The ICITP will support the democratic movement for separate states as these are legitimate demands. They will garner moral support to all indigenous and tribal people across the country. NDFB (P) delegation was in New Delhi to seek support from the tribal members of parliament on the creation of a separate Bodoland. The NDFB (P), which is currently under a ceasefire agreement with Centre, has threatened that the ongoing peace process might be derailed if New Delhi did not take a *"pragmatic and sympathetic"* approach to solve the *"Vexed Bodoland"* issue.

Samajwadi Party (SP) has asked the Centre to initiate dialogue with Bangladesh for accepting the Bangladeshi illegal immigrants who entered the state after the cut-off date of March 25, 1971. The SP, which is trying to strengthen its base in the state, said that unless there is an agreement with Bangladesh on taking back the immigrants, the entire exercise of deportation would be meaningless. Samajwadi Party respects the broad understanding reached regarding the cut-off date for the detection and deportation of illegal migrants, but even for those people who have to be deported, the human values (rights) must be respected as India is a signatory to the International Covenant on international human rights.

Even as the movement for a separate Bodoland state is gaining momentum, non-Bodo organisations have opposed any further bifurcation of Assam. The Ana-Bodo Surakhya Samity (ABSS), a non-Bodo forum of 27 organisations in Lower Assam, threatened to intensify its stir against creating a separate Bodoland. During the May 17, 2012 Assam bandh called by ABSS, clashes erupted between non-Bodos and supporters of separate Bodoland state at Goreswar. Supporters of separate Bodoland state allegedly tried to lift the bandh called by ABSS on May 17. Rights of non-Bodos are going to be curtailed once a separate state is created. Many frontline bodo organisations have not taken kindly to the centre's invitation to *'non-bodo'* groups for peace talks on the *'bodoland'* issue in Delhi and said it could be solved only by bodos and not *'aliens'*. A special convention in lower Assam was organised by the powerful all bodo students union and coordination committee of bodoland movement at Rangiya after the centre's invitation to *'non-bodo'* groups for peace talks among the centre, the state government and the militant Bodo Liberation Tiger.

Rebels of the Bodo Liberation Tigers (BLT), now overground following a ceasefire with the Centre have decided to reconsider their decision of continuing their dialogue with the centre. Besides its demand for the inclusion of the Bodo language in the eighth schedule of the Constitution and the establishment of a university in the proposed Bodoland areas, the BLT had termed the Assam government's stand on the boundary demarcation of the proposed Bodoland Territorial Council area as *"humiliating"*. The Supreme Court allowed two weeks time to the Assam government to reply to a petition filed by the Bodoland Autonomous Council (BAC) seeking setting aside of a tripartite memorandum of settlement between Bodoland Liberation Tigers (BLT), Union government and the state. The bench also made BLT a party in the matter and directed hearing of the petition along with another filed earlier by the Bodoland Autonomous Boundary Protection Association (BABPA) challenging the state government notification of 1999 demarcating the area of BAC. The apex court on April 17 had admitted for hearing a petition filed by BAC seeking quashing of the much hyped tripartite settlement seeking to create Bodo Territorial Council (BTC). Challenging the legality and constitutional validity of the February 2003 accord, BAC said the Centre and the state governments entered into an agreement with a small terrorist group of few Bodos who have surrendered to the government and have no representative character among the people of Bodoland. BABPA had challenged the 1999 notification on the ground that the Assam government had excluded 347 villages from the boundary of Bodoland Autonomous area.

References

1. *All Bodo Students' Union (ABSU)*, Retrieved from http://en.wikipedia.org/wiki/All_Bodo_Students per cent27_Union.
2. *Arnab Pratim Dutta (2012)*. Land of discord, Retrieved from http://www.downtoearth.org.in/content/land-discord.
3. *Assam (2012)*. Retrieved from http://en.wikipedia.org/wiki/Assam.
4. *Baksa district (2012)*. Retrieved from http://en.wikipedia.org/wiki/Baksa_District.
5. *Bodo people (2012)*. Retrieved from http://en.wikipedia.org/wiki/Bodo_people.
6. *Bodo Liberation Tigers Force (2012)*. Retrieved from http://en.wikipedia.org/wiki/Bodo_Liberation_Tigers_Force.
7. *Chirang district (2012)*. Retrieved from http://en.wikipedia.org/wiki/Chirang_district.
8. *Kokrajhar (2012)*. Retrieved from http://en.wikipedia.org/wiki/Kokrajhar.
9. *Kokrajhar district (2012)*. Retrieved from http://en.wikipedia.org/wiki/Kokrajhar_district.
10. *Life (2012)*. Retrieved from http://en.wikipedia.org/wiki/Life

11. *National Democratic Front of Bodoland (2012).* Retrieved from http://en.wikipedia.org/wiki/National_Democratic_Front_of_Bodoland
12. The Hindu (November 11, 2012). *High alert as two killed in Bodoland*, Retrieved from http://www.thehindu.com/news/states/other-states/high-alert-as-two-killed-in-bodoland/article4085737.ece
13. The Times of India (May 17, 2012). *Bodo rebels threaten to reconsider talk issue*, Retrieved from http://articles.timesofindia.indiatimes.com/2002-05-17/india/27140479_1_bodo-language-bodo-liberation-tigers-bodo-rebels
14. The Times of India (May 22, 2012). *Non-Bodos oppose bifurcation of Assam*, Retrieved from http://articles.timesofindia.indiatimes.com/2012-05-22/guwahati/31813681_1_bodos-assam-bandh-lower-assam
15. The Times of India (July 14, 2012). *SC gives 2 weeks to Assam on BLT accord dispute*, Retrieved from http://articles.timesofindia.indiatimes.com/2003-07-14/india/27189839_1_assam-government-bodoland-autonomous-council-petition
16. The Times of India (July 24, 2012). *Division bell rings in congress camp over Bodoland stir*, Retrieved from http://articles.timesof india.indiatimes.com/2011-07-24/guwahati/29809737_1_bodoland-state-absu-separate-state
17. The Times of India (August 11, 2012).*Tribal forum drums up support for separate Bodo land state*, Retrieved from http://articles.timesof india.indiatimes.com/2011-08-11/guwahati/29875549_1_dimaraji-bodoland-tribal-people
18. The Times of India (August 12, 2012). *Demand for Bodoland state raised in Lok Sabha,* Retrieved from http://articles.timesofindia.indiatimes.com/2011-08-12/india/29880119_1_bodoland-creation-of-separate-states-demand.
19. The Times of India (October 29, 2012). *Centre warned against talks with non-Bodos*, Retrieved from http://articles.timesofindia.indiatimes.com/2001-10-29/india/27233236_1_bodo-blt-absu
20. The Times of India (November 3, 2012). *Bongaigaon power project stalled due to BTC riots,* Retrieved from http://articles.timesof india. indiatimes.com/2012-11-03/guwahati/34892398_1_power-project-kokrajhar-bodoland-territorial-autonomous-districts
21. Times of India (November 5, 2012).*Talk to Bangladesh about taking back migrants,* Retrieved from http://articles.timesofindia.indiatimes.com/2012-11-05/guwahati/34926307_1_btad-samajwadi-party-congress-party
22. The Times of India (November 8, 2012). *Bodoland territorial council distributes utensils among camp inmates*, Retrieved fromhttp://articles.timesofindia.indiatimes.com/2012-11-08/guwahati/34993445_1_bodoland-territorial-council-btc-chief-hagrama-mohilary-utensils

23. The Times of India (November 10, 2012). *All Bodo students Union stages stir in New Delhi,* Retrieved from http://articles.timesofindia. indiatimes.com/2012-11-10/guwahati/35033805_1_union-stages-bodo-students-union-absu
24. The Times of India (November 12, 2012). *Army steps up vigil after fresh violence in Bodoland,* Retrieved fromhttp://articles.timesofindia. indiatimes.com/2012-11-12/guwahati/35068120_1_counter-insurgency-kokrajhar-chirang
25. *Tribes of Assam (2012).* Retrieved from http://www.indianetzone.com/37/tribes_assam.htm
26. *Odalguri (2012).* Retrieved from http://en.wikipedia.org/wiki/Udalguri
27. *Udalguri District (2012).* Retrieved from http://en.wikipedia.org/wiki/Udalguri_district

16

Situation of Tribal's and Economic Transition in Nagaland

Dinesh Sarmah

Introduction

North-Eastern region of India has got its definite identity due to its peculiar physical, economic and socio-cultural characteristics. The region comprises of eight states namely, Arunachal Pradesh, Assam, Manipur, Meghalaya, Mizoram, Nagaland, Sikkim and Tripura having foreign boundary with Bangladesh in the west, Myanmar in the east and Tibet region of China and Bhutan in the north. The region may be safely divided into two broad division—Plain region which comprise of 27 per cent (i.e. 68.96 lakh hectares) of the total geographical area of NER and Hill region which comprise of the states like Arunachal Pradesh Meghalaya, Mizoram, Manipur, Sikkim, Nagaland and Karbi Anglong and North Cachar hills of Assam. The valley of the river Bramhaputra in the state of Assam is the most expansive plains area in North East India. North East India is the homeland of a large number of ethnic groups who came from different directions at different historical times. These groups belong to different racial stocks, speak different languages and have varied socio-cultural traditions. This region has been occupied by different streams of the Mongoloid people who came from the north and the east at different periods. The migration of people from ancient to present time and from various directions to North East India have significantly contributed towards the growth of ethnic diversities. Besides the tribal groups, a few other non-tribal groups have also come into existence as a consequence of prolong interactions between the cultures of the migrants and those of the indigenous people. The spread of Hinduism; invasions of different outside ruler sat different historical periods; integration of the north eastern region with the rest of India in the nineteenth century and migrations that took place as late as the last century have resulted spectacular social, cultural, economic and political transformations in this region.

Nagaland, state in extreme northeastern India, bordered on the west and north by Assam state, on the east by Myanmar, on the north by Arunachal Pradesh state, and on the south by Manipur state. Nagaland is one of India's smallest states; with a total area of 16,579 sq km. Nagaland is the 16th state of the Indian Union was established on December 1, 1963. It is divided into eleven districts: Kohima, Phek, Mokokchung, Wokha, Zunheboto, Tuensang, Mon, Dimapur, Kiphire, Longleng and Peren. It is a largely mountainous state. The Naga Hills run through this small state, which has Saramati as its highest peak at a height of 12,600 ft. The main rivers that flow through Nagaland are Dhansiri, Doyang, Dikhu and Jhanji. The terrain is mountainous, thickly wooded and cut by deep river valleys. There is a wide variety of plant and animal life. Nagaland has a monsoon climate with generally high humidity; rainfall averages between 1800 and 2500 a year. Agriculture is the most important economic activity in Nagaland. Principal crops include rice, corn, millets, pulses, tobacco, oilseeds, sugarcane, potatoes and fibres. Other economy boosters are forestry, cottage industries, insurance, real estate and tourism. Nagaland is a rural state; more than four-fifths of the population lives in small, isolated villages. Built on the most prominent points along the ridges of the hills, these villages were once stockaded, with massive wooden gates approached by narrow, sunken paths. The villages are usually divided into khels, or quarters, each with its own headmen and administration. Dimapur, Kohima, Mokokchung, and Tuensang are the only urban centres with more than 20,000 people.

The Tribes in Nagaland

The population of Nagaland is entirely tribal belong to the Indo-Mongoloid family. Available documented history about the Naga tribes is very sketchy. Ancient Indian literature, at the time the Veda Books were being compiled, makes mention of *"Kiratas"*, golden skinned people who lived in the East. In the words of J.H. Hutton, *"those tribes who are termed as Nagas have something in common with each other which distinguish them from many other tribes found in Assam and other neighbouring regions,* and *entitle them to be regarded as a racial unit in themselves."* The state at present consists of eleven administrative districts, inhabited by 16 major tribes along with other sub-tribes. Each village of Nagaland has its own definitive population, area and administration. Each tribe is distinct in character from the other in terms of customs, language and dress. The linguistic situation of Nagaland is marked by numerous complicated dialectical variations. Before the advent of the British, the Nagas belonging to different communities used to communicate with one another in Nagamese or broken Assamese. The major Naga tribes are the *Angami, Ao, Chakhesang, Chang, Khemungan, Konyak, Lotha, Phom, Pochury, Rengma, Sangtam, Sema, Yimchunger* and *Zeliang*. The Chakhesangs were earlier known as Eastern Angamis and are a combination of the Chakri, Khezha and Sangtam sub-tribes. Now the Chakhesang tribe is spilt further; Pochury's who were earlier a part of it now claim a distinct entity. Each tribe has their own languages and cultural features.

The Nagas are a handsome and friendly people. High cheek bones, almond eyes, sparkling teeth and bronzed skin set the Nagas apart. In colourful tribal outfits, with bamboo shields sheathed in bear skin and decorated spears, the Nagas are simple people, almost entirely tribal. The social position of a Naga is borne out by the number of bone necklaces he wears. Weaving is a traditional art handed down through generations in Nagaland. Each of the major tribes has its own unique designs and colours. Warm and colourful Naga shawls, hand-woven shoulder bags, decorative spears, table mats, wood carvings and bamboo works make magnificent souvenirs. Tribal dances of the Nagas give us an insight into the inborn reticence of these people. War dances and dances belonging to distinctive tribes form the major art form in Nagaland. In colorful costumes and jewellery, the dancers go through amazing mock war motions, which could prove very dangerous, if one were to be a little careless. Festivals, marriages, harvests, or just the joy of the moment are occasions for the Nagas to burst into dance. Some of the important festivals are Sekrenyi, Moatsu, Tuluni and Tokhu Emong.

It could broadly be said that Nagas are straight forward people, honest, hardworking, sturdy and with a high standard of integrity. They are lacking in humility and are inclined to equate a kind and sympathetic approach with weakness. As J.H. Hutton said *"Naga have fine qualities. They are simple, cheerful, colourful, humorous, courteous and hospitable. Nagas are people with a sense of humor and generosity at home, at work and gathering; laughter is the food of the society and truthful people, stealing is not common.... And they have respect for elders. Naga are generous but begging is an abomination. They are healthy, active, vigorous and brave people. The Nagas are well built and enthusiastically looking for a true God* and *also religious."* The Nagas have a very strong sense of self respect and would not submit to anyone riding roughshod over their sentiments. A striking characteristic of the Naga tribes is their hospitality and cheerfulness. To be greeted with a smiling face while traveling on the roads is a common experience. A visitor to Naga village is heartily received and entertained with a surfeit of rice-beer which is generally served by the lady of the house or her young daughter with warmth which is unforgettable. The way of life of any community is reflected through its culture. By '*Naga-Culture*' it mean the way of life of the Nagas, the inherited behaviours and thoughts of their fore-fathers passed on to the new generation, through oral traditions and day to day practices and conservative life styles in the form of customs, traditions, norms, values beliefs and conventions; evolution and growth; contact, diffusions, integration, imitation and acculturation.

The concept and belief in the existence of supernatural beings, their power and the practice of population through the forms of rituals and worship, distinguishes men from other biological animals. Whatever men encounter hardship, danger, storm, flood, lightning, epidemic, famine, dangerous animals, death of the family members, etc., they seek some invisible power for assistance, motivation, strength and help. Encountering such fear and curiosity in life awake in men, the tendency of religious concept is in the existence of a super power in nature. The traditional Naga religion is animistic, though conceptions of a supreme creator and an afterlife exist. Nature is seen to be alive with invisible forces, minor deities and spirits with which priests and medicine men mediate. In the 19th century, with the advent of British rule, Christianity was introduced and Baptist missionaries became especially active in the region. As a result, the population now is predominantly Christian.

Transition in the Economy in Nagaland

Nagaland, the 16th state of the Indian Union, got its statehood on December 1, 1963 missed out on the direct benefits of the first three Five Year Plans. The State also suffered the consequences of continued insurgency, frequently having to commit its scarce resources on establishment costs. Because of these, despite the tremendous strides made in the last 50 years, Naga economy is still confronted by many developmental challenges. Foremost among these are the inaccessibility, hilly and landlocked nature of the State and lack of infra-structure. There is also continued insurgency, high labour costs, lack of industrial culture etc. During 1999, the Eleventh Finance Commission ranked Nagaland (with an index of 76.14) as the 7th most remote State in the country but there was only a difference of about seven points with Arunachal Pradesh which was ranked the most remote with an index of 69.71. One of the areas where this remoteness has affected the people of the State in a real way is in the poor Credit-Deposit ratio.

Area	16,579 sq kms
State Capital	Kohima (1,444.12 m above sea level)
	E/NE—Myanmar/Arunachal Pradesh
	W&N—Assam
	N—Arunachal Pradesh
	S—Manipur
Population	19,80,602 (0.16 per cent of total Indian population, 2011 census)
Density	119 per sq km
Sex ratio	931:1000 (Female: Male, 2011 census)
Literacy	80.11 per cent (Male: 83.29 per cent Female: 76.69 per cent, 2011 census)
No. of Districts	11
No of villages	1286
Official language English	
Average rainfall	2500 mm
Forest covers	13,345 sq kms (80.49%)
Airport and Railway head Dimapur	

Source : Directorate of Economics and Statistics, Govt. of Nagaland.

The Nagas remained outside the influence of modern civilization for a very long time. They lived a simple life completely isolated even from their immediate neighbours mainly due to the practice of head-hunting. Their needs were few and they could manage to be self sufficient of their basic requirements like food, shelter and clothing in their own way within their limited resources. This was the condition even towards the end of the nineteenth century and early part of the twentieth century in villages. In fact, salt and agricultural implements, the two indispensable things were got by exchanging agricultural products with the plains people of Assam, articles of exchange were generally ginger, cotton, chilies, ham and arum. Before the introduction of British administration over the Nagas hills, the Nagas carried their agricultural products to plain and exchanged them for their requirements which comprised of salt, dried fish, agricultural implements, yarn, ornaments, cattle, etc., they also exchanged goods for goods within their village or the neighbouring villages and tribes. For the exchange of goods they set a reasonable rate of quantity for particular commodity according to its value and utility.

A concise glance at the present Nagaland economic scenario reveals that the sectoral structure of the economy began to evolve since the beginning of the planning era with building up of social overheads and infrastructures for economic development. Nagaland state has made little progress in several fields like agriculture, transport, banking, power and human development like education, health institutions and water supply. However, in general it appears that the state has failed to lead its economy into the right direction regardless of the tremendous efforts and investments made towards economic development. The various indicators of economic development prove that Nagaland could not achieve the expected level of development. Although known as a largely mountainous state, Nagaland's economy is based primarily on agriculture. In the state, the agriculture sector employs about 70 per cent of the State's population and its share to the State Domestic Product is about 33 per cent. There is convincing evidence as to why examining this sector is a good starting point for finding solutions to livelihood security and employment stability. Agriculture also has the greatest dominance of female employment in the poorest regions of the world. Nagaland has 40 per cent of women work force employed in the agriculture sector. The Nagas generally follows two methods of cultivations: *Jhum cultivation or Shifting cultivation* on the hill slopes and *Terrace cultivation*. The main crops include fibers, rice, corn, tobacco, oilseeds, sugarcane, potatoes, threads, millets and pulses. Other contributors to the state's economy are forestry, tourism, real estate, insurance and cottage industries. Agriculture in Nagaland is considered a prime source of revenue for the state. Economy of Nagaland gets a major boost through the agricultural activities of the state. The crops that have a high yield in the state of Nagaland include rice, tobacco, oilseeds, pulses, fibers, potato and sugarcane. The local people of Nagaland earn their living by growing a number of crops in their fields.

One of the major reasons behind the flourishing agricultural economy of Nagaland is the developed state of irrigation in the place. The water channels that are controlled by bamboo sticks provide unhindered irrigation facilities to the crop fields of Nagaland. Apart from major crops the farmers of Nagaland also produce plantation crops like coffee, tea and cardamom. Potato and sugarcane are the two prime cash crops that generate revenue for the Nagaland economy. Then there are many vegetables that are grown by the peasants of Nagaland like that of carrots, chillies, onion, melon, spinach leaf, cucumber, brinjal, tomatoes and mustard. Sugarcane, maize, yams, potato, millet and arums are considered as the principal crops of Nagaland state. The farmers of Nagaland grow their crops on the basis of the rain conditions in the place. Having an agri-climatic condition Nagaland is known to have high yield. Since agriculture contributes significantly towards the economy of Nagaland hence the government of the state is taking major initiatives to develop this particular field. From seed farms to irrigation projects the government is leaving no stones unturned to encourage the Nagaland agriculture. Although the crops grow in a large variety, Nagaland is still focused on importing food provisions from states outside its borders. The soil found in the eastern districts of Nagaland can no longer be used for agriculture as the extensive practice of tilling and jhum has made an impact on the soil's fertility. Terracing techniques are performed only by a couple of local tribes from the Phek and Kohima districts. Other tribes, including most of the Aos, Zeliangs and Lothas have also corroded the soil by practicing tilling in many valleys of several Nagaland districts such as Mokokchung, Peren and Wokha.

As agriculture is the mainstay of the State's Economy, it continues to be the main source of livelihood and employment for majority of the population, particularly in the rural areas where almost 82 per cent of the population live. In order to achieve the growth rate of 10 percent envisaged in the 11th Five Year Plan, agriculture sector was targeted to grow at four per cent during the current five year plan period. But the agricultural sector is still dominated by the primitive traditional system of shifting cultivation with very short cycle. Consequently the yield from land is precariously low, thus peasants continue to live at a subsistence level. This system is not only uneconomical but also associated with serious ecological problems like soil erosion, deforestation, loss of flora and fauna, etc. Efforts are required to increase the growth rate, wherein lies opportunities for employment to maintain the tempo of growth in agriculture sector. Added to the development of agricultural sector for economic development as a whole, the sector can significantly contribute to livelihood security, employment and reduction of poverty. Due to regular monsoon, agricultural growth has been highest in Nagaland at 10 percent during 2006-2007. This is much higher than the National average of 2 per cent, which implies a tremendous potential for livelihood and employment opportunities in agricultural and horticultural based food processing industry.

The secondary sector in the state is also underdeveloped, where only a few simple light small and cottage consumer goods industries exist. A few large and medium scale industries that have been set up in the state are as follows: (a) Sugar Mill, which was commissioned in during 1973-74 with an installed crushing capacity of 100 MT sugarcane per day at Dimapur, (b) Paper Mill at Tulli, commissioned in 1983 with a crushing capacity of 100 MT, a joint venture of the State Government and Hindustan Paper Corporation, (c) Ply Wood Factory at Tizit in 1978, (d) Distillery unit of sugar mill, and (e) Mini Cement Plant at Wazeho in Phek district. It is very upsetting to state that most of these industries have ceased to operate. Thus, huge amount of capital has been blocked, which may be due to lack of infrastructures and lack of efficient managerial skill, ongoing political unrest situation in the state.

In case of the cottage industries, crafts such as woodwork, weaving and pottery are considered basic sources of revenue. The development of tourism is limited in Nagaland because of the insurgency that has affected the state's peace for the last 50 years. The forests, which cover about 17 per cent of Nagaland, are its most important source of income. There are varied mineral reserves, including oil deposits, but commercial use of these resources is yet to be done. Until the early 1970s, only cottage industries (e.g., weaving, woodwork, basketry, and pottery) existed in the state. Lack of raw materials, financial resources, and power, as well as poor transport and communications in the state has hindered industrial growth. Dimapur, the state's leading industrial centre, now has a sugar mill and distillery, a brick factory, and a television assembly plant. Other industries in the state include a khandsari (molasses) mill, rice mills, fruit-canning plants, a paper and pulp factory, a plywood factory, and cabinet and furniture factories. Chromium, nickel, cobalt, iron ore, and limestone are found in Nagaland, but only low-grade coal deposits are mined at present. Boreholes drilled in the western district of Wokha have yielded oil, and seepages in the Dikhu valley, near Assam, suggest the presence of exploitable oil reserves. Power generation in Nagaland depends mainly on diesel plants, though hydroelectric potentiality is very high.

Although Nagaland depends mostly on roads for transportation, but development of road and transportation is found to be unsatisfactory. A national highway runs from Dimapur to Kohima and then on to Imphal in Manipur. Another main road links Mokokchung with Amguri in Assam. A short stretch of the Northeast Frontier Railway passing through Dimapur from Assam is the only rail link with the rest of India. Air service is available from Dimapur to Guwahati in Assam and to Calcutta in West Bengal. Among tertiary sector, Nagaland has made significant progress in the development of banking services, as the need for capital requires the existence of financial institution through which savings can be collected and canalised into productive channels.

Recent Initiatives Taken to Revitalise the Economy of the State Based on Local Resources

Progress has been made since the publication of State Human Development Report 2004, which distinctly identified the need to address infrastructure development and agriculture technology towards strengthening the agriculture sector for generation of livelihood and employment opportunities. In line with the spirit and aspiration of the agriculture policy vision *"Food for all by 2020"*, during 2008-2009, the food grain production is anticipated to go beyond its target. It is important to generate mass awareness in the state about the potentiality of horticulture and other agro based sectors with emphasis on commercial farming. Horticulture is considered to be the most suitable farming enterprise in the State. The total area available under horticultural crops is 6299 hectares and a further area of around 4000 hectares is being brought under horticulture farming. Although considerable progress has been made in the horticulture sector, various segments of marketing network such as processing, transport and other post-production activities is yet to be developed. Activities in these sectors can potentially generate employment and entrepreneurship opportunities.

The market infrastructure in the state is quite underdeveloped. Presently most of the product is marketed in the local markets leading to a huge volume of surplus and wastage. The Government of India accords top priority to preservation and processing of fruits and vegetables and has introduced several schemes of assistance for fruit and vegetable processing. Of late, organic horticultural products have been given significant attention, as it commands a premium which would translate into better income for farmers. There is an ongoing effort to access necessary certification. The State Department of Horticulture has entered into a memorandum of understanding (MoU) with the International Competence Centre for Organic Agriculture, October, 2008, to draw up a comprehensive project for development of organic horticultural crops in the State. Under this initiative an initial area of 250 hectares under Dimapur and Peren districts was earmarked for development under organic farming in the year 2008-2009. Recognising the importance for institutional support for development of horticulture in the Northeast, the Government of India approved the establishment of a Central Institute of Horticulture at Medziphema, Nagaland in January 2006, with a financial outlay of 20 crore spread over a period of five years. Horticulture in Nagaland is a non-traditional activity, which has been given a major thrust under the Government of India scheme of Integrated Development of horticulture in the North East since 2001. Under this scheme, the Department is working on area expansion for various horticulture crops all over the 11 districts of the State and which would benefit 5515 beneficiaries spread over about 400 villages. In line with the centrally sponsored scheme, the State has been crop zoned on the basis of climatic conditions. Cultivation of focused crops like banana, pineapple, passion fruit, oranges, large cardamom, ginger, turmeric, Naga chili, medicinal and aromatic plants, coconut and cashew nut has been taken up on a commercial scale. Thus, the horticulture sector in Nagaland continues to offer a vast and promising potential for livelihood improvement and employment generation.

Industrialisation is an integral part of any development. However, the remoteness of the State along with poor infrastructure like road linkages and acute shortage of power, special land laws that restrict transfer of land to outside investor continue to be major challenges. Despite the prevailing constraints, efforts for improvement are being made in some areas in the State. The Paper Mill in Tuli is the most significant, having been reopened after a gap of 15 years. The Nagaland Pulp and Paper Company Ltd. (NPPC), Tuli, with an enhanced capacity from 100 metric tonnes per day (MTPD) to 200 MTPD (white writing paper) is expected to be commissioned, infusing an amount of about' 600.00 crores, with a requirement of about three lakh tonnes of bamboo annually. With the commissioning of the mill, it is expected that both direct and indirect employment along with wealth generation will take place. Though the state has high potential for the development of agriculture and other manufacturing sector but adequate efforts have not been made to develop these as a commercial venture. Factors inhibiting development in the state are mainly absence of proper land tenure system in hill areas, poor cultivation practices which ultimately results in low yield, lack of marketing facilities, scarcity of trained manpower and extension support, inter-state border dispute, high labour costs, lack of industrial culture, financial constraints, etc. The long insurgency problem in the states of Nagaland has considerable impact on diversification of its economy.

Conclusion

Thus to conclude that the Nagas, inhabitants of Nagaland, are said to belong to the indo-mongoloid stock, a race whose presence was first noted ten centuries before Christ, at the time of the compilation of the Vedas. The Nagas form many tribes, as well as numerous sub-tribes, each having a specific geographic distribution. Each tribe is distinct in character from the other in terms of customs, language and dress. The linguistic situation of Nagaland is marked by numerous complicated dialectical variations. Before the advent of the British, the Nagas belonging to different communities used to communicate with one another in Nagamese or broken Assamese. The Nagas are traditionally animistic. Nature is seen to be alive with invisible forces, minor deities, and spirits. In the 19th century, with the advent of British rule, Christianity was introduced, and Baptist missionaries became especially active in the region. Now the most of the Nagas are Christian. The state economy of Nagaland is still traditional one. Primary sector dominates the state economy with traditional practices and low yield rate. Industrially the state is quite backward due to many reasons like poor infrastructure and social unrest, etc., and the service sector now is in growing stage. Nagaland is not resource less but adequate measures are not taken to use the domestically available resources in commercial ventures.

References

1. A.N.M Irsad Ali and Indranosee Das, *'Tribal Situation in North-East India.*
2. Bela Malik, *'The problem of shifting cultivation in the Garo hills of NE India,* 1860-1970.
3. A.K. Agarwal, *'Economic problems and planning in North-Eastern India'.*
4. K. Alam (Edited), *'Agricultural Development in North-East India-Constraint and Prospects'* Deep and Deep Publication.
5. NUTA (Nagaland University, edited publication), *'Economic development in Nagaland, prospects and constraints'.*
6. Bose, Saradindu (Ed) (1990), *Shifting Cultivation in India, Anthropological Survey of India*, Calcutta.
7. Thomas, C.J.A. and Das, G., (edited) *"Dimensions of Development in Nagaland"*, Regency Publication, New Delhi.
8. Thong, J.S., *"Glimpses of Nagas legacy and culture"*, published by 'Society for Naga Students' welfare', Kerala.
9. Smith, W.C., *"The Ao Naga Tribe of Assam"* Mittal Publication, New Delhi, 2009.
10. Chaube, S.K., *"Hill Politics in Northeast India"*, Third Edition, Orient Blackswan.
11. *"Livelihood and Employment Opportunities in Nagaland-Sectoral Issues (a Thematic Report 2009)"*—Department of Planning and Coordination, Government of Nagaland.

12. Chasie, Charles, *"Nagaland"*, Chapter 7.
13. Baral, K.C., (guest editor) *"Indian Folklife—A Quarterly News Letter, Serial No. 22 July 2006, Globalization and Tribes of Northeast India."*
14. Deka, P K and Longkumar, SR (2009): *"Socio-Economic Development of Rura India—A Case Study"* Edition 2009, Adhayan Publisher, New Delhi.

17

Autonomous District Councils in Mizoram: Needs and Government Initiatives

R. Prasad and *Sukanta Sarkar*

Introduction

Tribal society is the stable social system with a division of labour organised around extended family relations, in which people lived before the rupture into social classes. It is a description which covers a vast array of societies, from the earliest humans who first stood upright and who have long since disappeared from the Earth. The citizens of the early Greek polis before about 600 B.C. and indigenous people in many remote parts of the world today live in settled villages and engage in a certain amount of trade. Tribal society has survived up to the present day in many parts of the world where intercourse with the outside world has been prevented by mountain ranges or other natural barriers. It has frequently been obliterated by the intervention of outsiders with their guns, their diseases, their greed and their cheap commodities, but on every continent, at a certain stage in its development, tribal society has given birth to class society. Mizoram is a land of rolling hills, valleys, rivers and lakes. As many as 21 major hills ranges or peaks of different heights run through the length and breadth of the state, with plains scattered here and there. The average height of the hills to the west of the state is about 1,000 metres (3,300 feet).

Historical Perspectives

The origin of the Mizo people, like those of many other tribes in the northeastern India is shrouded in mystery. Mizo history in the 18th and 19th century is marked by many instances of tribal raids and head hunting led by the village chieftains. The Lushai Hills Autonomous District Council was formed in 1952 and it led to the abolition of chieftainship. The autonomy however only partially met the aspirations of the Mizo people so representatives of the District Council and the Mizo Union pleaded with the States Reorganisation Commission (SRC) in 1954 for integrating the Mizo-dominated areas of Tripura and Manipur with the District Council in Assam. The Mizo National Famine Front dropped the word '*famine*' and a new political organisation Mizo National Front (MNF) was born on 22 October 1961 under the leadership of Laldenga with the specified goal of achieving sovereign independence of Greater Mizoram. It resorted to armed insurrection with the 28 February 1966 uprising against the Government, attacking the government installations at Aizawl, Lunglei, Chawngte, Chhimluang and other places. In Aizawl, on 5 and 6 March 1966, the Government of India bombed the city of Aizawl with Toofani and Hunter Jet fighters. This was the first time India used its air force to quell a movement of any kind among its citizens. The Mizo National Front was outlawed in 1967 and the demand for statehood increased. The Mizo District Council delegation met Prime Minister Indira Gandhi in May 1971 and demanded full fledged statehood for Mizoram. The Indian government offered to convert the Mizo Hills into a Union Territory (U.T.) in July 1971. The Mizo leaders accepted on the condition that Statehood occurred sooner rather than later.

There are three Autonomous District Councils (ADCs) for ethnic tribes in Mizoram, namely Chakma Autonomous District Council (CADC) for ethnic Chakmas in South-western Mizoram bordering Bangladesh, Lai Autonomous District Council (LADC) for Lai people in Southern part of the state, and Mara Autonomous District Council (MADC) for Mara people in the Southern-eastern corner.

Chakma Autonomous District Council

Chakma Autonomous District Council is one of the three autonomous district councils of Mizoram. Prior to 1972 it was a part under the Pwi-Lakher Regional Council. It was created on 29th April,

1972 under the Sixth Schedule to the constitution of India by trifurcating the Pwi-Lakher Regional Council into Mara Autonomous

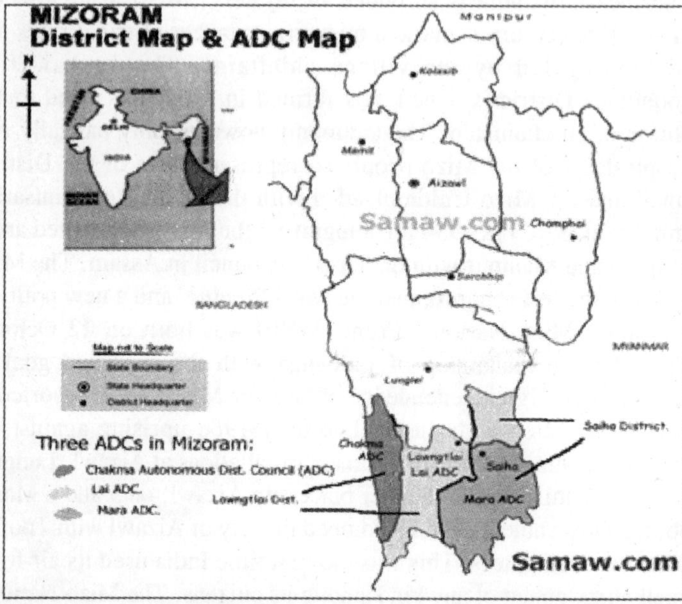

District Council (MADC), Lai Autonomous District Council (LADC) and Chakma Autonomous District Council. While MADC remained under a single district of Saiha, CADC and LADC were accommodated under Lawngtlai district with the district headquarters at Lawngtlai. The then Chakma leaders of the Mizo District Council and Pwi-Lakher Regional Council actively engaged themselves with the Government of Assam and the Government at the Centre for the creation of an autonomous council for the Chakmas of Mizoram with the inclusion of all Chakma inhabited areas which presently remains outside CADC. Unfortunately only the portion under Pwi-Lakher Regional council got considered. Out of that also many Chakma inhabited villages along the eastern bank of river Toijong were not considered under CADC. Thus two-third of the Chakmas of Mizoram had to remain outside the Council. CADC falls between 21 p 58' (N) and 22p 45' (N) and between 92 p 30' (E) and 92 p 45' (E). The tropic of cancer passes over it and its climate is hot and humid. The gentle foothills of the mighty Himalayas adorn its landscape. The two main rivers, i.e., Toijong and Thega weave along the eastern and the western sides respectively forming its natural boundaries. In the north it is bounded by Lunglei District, Myanmar in the South, LADC in the east and Bangladesh in the west. CADC so far witnessed eight General Elections. The first was held on 26th December, 1972. Initially there were only eight MDC constituencies. Today as many as 17 constituencies are contested. The council started functioning with only some departments, namely General Administration, Education, Forest, Land Revenue and Settlement, Legislative, Judiciary and etc. With the enhancement of power in 1994 the council was entrusted with as many as 19 subjects/departments. DRDA and ICDS were also included but with a rider, subject to approval from the Central Government, they being centrally sponsored programmes. Again, in the year 2011, a gazette notification of the Government of Mizoram reviewed the powers of the three Autonomous District Councils by entrusting all the functions so entrusted with proportionate plan-allocation, which were so far executed by the offices of the State Government in the Council areas.

System of Governance in the Council has been structured on the basic frames of Modern Democratic system of Government with Legislative, Executive and Judicial organs. The Chakma Autonomous District Council has an Executive Committee consisting of Seven Members headed by a Chief Executive Member. Major decision and policy formulation are executed by the Executive Committee. Although, the Council has a Judicial wing but it is yet to be elevated to an independent institution in the pattern of the country's judicial system. The Judicial Court in the Chakma Autonomous District Council was constituted in the year 1972 under the provisions of '*Pawi-Lakher Autonomous Region (Administrative of Justice) Rules, 1954*'. The Judiciary in the Chakma Autonomous District Council is a three tier institution viz. *(a) the Village Council Courts, the lowest court, (b) the Subordinate district Council Courts, the intermediate court and (c) the District Council Court, the appellate court*. On the basis of the powers conferred under the Sixth Schedule to the Constitution of India, various Departments have been created on the basis of the subjects entrusted with the Council from time to time through various government orders. So far, 29 departments have been created to administer the council. Judicial Court in the Chakma Autonomous District Council (CADC) was constituted in the year 1972 under the provisions of Pawi-Lakher Autonomous Region (Administrative of Justice) Rules, 1954. The Chakma Autonomous District Council Administration of Justice Rules and Chakma Customary Laws were drafted by Shri Birendra Lal Dewan, the first Court President and Recorder of the Chakma Autonomous District Council Court. These bills were placed in the Chakma Autonomous District Council Legislative Session House and were unanimously passed. Thereafter, these were sent to the Law and Judicial Department, Government of Mizoram, for Gazette Notification.

The Chakmas are one of the Buddhist communities in the Indian sub-continent. They have their own age old culture, language and scripts. They practice shifting cultivation called JUM. They grow paddy, maize, cotton, sesame etc. in their JUM along with vegetables and spices. They also know the art of low land cultivation. They primarily live in the Chittagong Hills Tracts of Bangladesh, Chin and Arakan provinces of Myanmar (Burma), in the North-Eastern Indian states of Mizoram, in the northern and southern districts of Tripura, in the Tirap, Changlang, Subansuri and Lohit districts of Arunachal Pradesh, in the Langsilet area of Karbi-Anglang and north Cachar Hills districts and Cachar districts of Assam and a few families in West Bengal. The present population of the Chakmas is about 5-6 lakhs in Bangladesh, 80,000 - 100,000 in Mizoram, 60-70 thousands in Arunachal Pradesh, 40-50 thousands in Tripura and about 30 thousands in Assam.

The Chakma women wear an ankle length cloth around the waist which is called a Pinon. Chakma women are excellent weavers and creative designers, who weave their own traditional dresses, using the Chakma traditional handloom called BEIN. The equipments that make up the chakma traditional handlooms are collectively known as Sozpodor. Earlier the Chakmas would grow cotton in their jhums alongside rice, maize, fruits, spices and vegetables. A part of the cotton would be paid as taxes to the Chakma King who would then pay the cotton in tribute to the Mughal Emperor and later to the British Empire. British historians record that this cotton was of the finest quality. The Chakma women use the remaining cotton to weave their dresses. This cotton would be softened, made into yarn and dyed using traditional methods that use roots and herbs before being woven into beautifully designed clothes the Chakmas wear. They are extremely hospitable people and very often will go out of their way to delight their guests. The Buddha Purnima is the most important religious festival of the Buddhists and commemorates the birth, enlightenment and Parinibbana of the Buddha. On this auspicious occasion the Chakmas gather at the temples and offer prayers and offerings to the monks and listen to Dhamma talks. At night they perform play(s) on the life of the Buddha.

Lai Autonomous District Council

Lai Autonomous District Council (LADC) is one of the three Autonomous District Councils in Mizoram state in North-east India. It is an Autonomous District Council for ethnic Lai people earlier known as *Pawi*, living in South-eastern Mizoram bordering Myanmar and Bangladesh. The L.A.D.C. has its headquarters at *Lawngtlai town*, which is the District Capital of Lawngtlai District. In 2011, Lawngtlai had population of 117,444 of which male and female were 60,379 and 57,065 respectively. There was change of 59.53 percent in the population compared to population as per 2001. In the previous census of India 2001, Lawngtlai District recorded increase of 34.87 percent to its population compared to 1991. The other two Autonomous District Councils in Mizoram are Mara Autonomous District Council (MADC) to the south and Chakma Autonomous District Council to the west. Thus the three ADCs filled one third of Mizoram in the Southern part of the state. The Lai Autonomous District Council occupies a strategic position in Mizoram, located in the Southern most corner of the state. It shares its political border with the erstwhile Burma (Myanmar) and MADC, the west by CADC, in the north Lunglei Administrative District and in the south by Myanmar. The Lai Autonomous District Council covers an area of 1870.75 sq. km. with a population of 73,620 as on April 2008 and its density is 39 persons per sq. km. The whole/entire population belonged to Schedule Tribes.

The Lai Autonomous District Council was constituted on 29 April, 1972 under the Sixth Schedule to the Constitution of India. The council is a replication of the State Legislative Assembly. It exercises power over specifically allocated subjects. At present it looks after 18 subjects departments. The Lai Autonomous District Council has also the power to determine language and in the manner in which education should be imparted in the Primary Schools within its jurisdiction. The council has a separate set of laws governing the area. It has the power to make laws as provided under the sixth Schedule to the Constitution of India. The people of Lai Autonomous District Council area enjoyed special safeguard granted by Article 371-9 of the Constitution of India. The headquarters of the council is situated at *Lawngtlai* which is also the headquarters of Lawngtlai Administrative District. It is well connected by the NH-54 and is 296 km away from the state capital Aizawl. The power and functions of the Council is mainly three, viz., Legislative, Executive, and Judiciary. It has a chairman to conduct the business of the Council in session and presided over its meeting. The executive functions of the Council are vested in the Executive Committee headed by the Chief Executive Member. The Executive Committee can dispose of all matters falling within its purview. Each Member of the executive is allocated specifies subject for which a member of the committee is collectively responsible for all executive orders issued in the name of Council.

The main occupation of the people of Lai Autonomous District Council is Agriculture (the backbone of its economy) having Rice as its staple food, other crops like ginger, sesame, banana, chili, tilt, pine-apple, orange, mango, etc., are also cultivated. The Council also possesses rich natural resources of self-generating bamboo forest as well as thick tropical forest. The highest mountain in the state of Mizoram known as *'The Blue Mountain'* or *'Phawngpui'* with its Phawngpui National Park and Ngengpui Wildlife Sanctuary are located within the Lai Autonomous District Council area. The peculiarity feature of these two places came to be known as *'Vavu'* the state *'Bird'* of Mizoram found only within the Phawngpui National Park with varieties of flora and fauna. Ngengpui Wildlife Sanctuary, the only Sanctuary in the State possessing elephant is also located within the Lai Autonomous District Council jurisdiction.

From a historical point of view, Lai is a dominant tribe of the so-called *Chin-Kuki-Lushai*, the community is scattered in different parts of the world, mainly concentrating in Mizoram, Chin Hills of Burma, South Bangladesh, Manipur, etc. Historians and Anthropologists are of the opinion that the Lai Community belongs to Tibeto-Burman of the Mongoloid stock. In tracing out the origin of Lai, most of the

Indian and British Researcher's could establish the fact that the Lai people moved towards the North West along the Chindwin River, and then settled down in the Chin Hills. The possible date of their settlement in this place, as suggested by F.K. Lehman is 750 A.D. Haka. The present capital of the Chin Hills (Laitlang) State was said to have founded by the young prince of Lai, Hluansang by name. Subsequently many important places such as *Thlantlang, Lungzarh, Khuafo, Sunthla, Thlanrawn* etc., were founded in which the clans, Chinzah, Zathang, Hlawnchhing, Khenglawt, Hlawncheu, Zahau, Fanai, etc., were found living there. After some generations, in an effort to stretch them out, they moved towards the North and West crossing the River Boinu (Kaladan) and settled in Manipur, Bangladesh and Mizoram. The first group who left the Chin Hills in 1770 under the leadership of Vanhnuaitlira, the prince of Sunthla moved towards the south west and settled down at Rengtlang, Chittagong Hill Tract and Bangladesh. After coming down to the present Mizoram, they occupied the whole eastern belt of Mizoram. The entire eastern belt of the Mizo district, as far as the Tuichang River on the West and Champhai on the North, and the entire areas South of Lunglei are Pawi (Lai) territories. Lai are the people of rich culture, customs and traditions distinct from that of their neighbours. Their cultural heritage include language, folk songs or folklore, moral and social ethics, legends, myth, festivals, dances etc. The Lai people do qualify to seek a Regional or District Council in which they could protect their own customs and culture and to develop their own language and ways of living. Lawngtlai is the district headquarters of Lawngtlai district in the state of Mizoram in India. It is also the headquarters of Lai Autonomous District Council.

Mara Autonomous District Council

It is situated in the southern tip of Mizoram state bordering Myanmar. Its autonomy was established as part of Lai District on 29 May 1971 and separated the next year as Lakher Autonomous District Council and renamed to it current name in 1988. It covers 1445 square kilometers. Mara Autonomous District Council looks after many departments in her area including fisheries, schools (up to Middle school) and education, judiciary, land and revenue, forestry, Public Health Engineering (PHE), etc. The government has jurisdiction over land administration, administration of justice, and limited legislative powers, and a few other local powers.

The Maras occupy the southern portion of Mizoram, the hill tracts situated in the areas of Indo-Myanmar border. The whole region inhabited by the Maras is commonly called *"Marara"* in the local language meaning the *"land of the Maras"* or *"Maraland"*. In the early British period, it was popularly known to the Britishers as *"Lakherland"* as the Maras were then designated as *"Lakher"*. In 1922, the whole region occupied by them was divided up into different parts among the three districts viz *the Lushai hills, the Chin Hills and the Arkan Hill Tracts*. From 1924, the Maras's villages which had fallen to the Lushai hills had been administered as part of the district under the Chief Commissioner of Assam. In 1953 the Mara area of the erstwhile Lushai Hills was loosely amalgamated with the Lai area to create an autonomous region under the name *"Pawi-Lakher Region"* under the Sixth schedule of the Indian Constitution. It is flanked on the north and east by the Lai Autonomous District of Mizoram and on the east and the south by the Chin State of Myanmar. Geographically, the Mara Autonomous District is isolated from the rest of India both its distance and forbidding nature of hills terrain. Several rivers run through the land. The more prominent rivers are the *Beino*, otherwise known as *Kolodyne, the Tisi, the Pala, the Lakie, the Sarau, the Titlao and the Salyu*. The first named river is the bigest, and is also known as *Kolodyne or Chhimtuipui* which means *"the big rivers of the south"*. This river has its source in the Lai lake of the Chin State of Myanmar and after a course due south it makes abrupt turn in the Indo-Myanmar bordering areas and then after running south it joins the Bay of Bengal. Lying below the striking point of the Tropic of Cancer, the Mara District is bestowed with a pleasant climate enjoying cool in summer and temparate winter. The Mara District is very rich in forest resources. The entire area is covered with thick forest which is a continuation of Mizoram hill system. About 289 square kilometres of the area is under forest of which reserve forest occupies above 82 square kilometres the protected Reserve Forest covers 20.5 square kilometres, and Riverine Reserved Forest 72.5 square kilometres. The Maras belong to Mongoloid, the eastern third mankind. They belong to central Chin sub-groups of the Kuki group of the Assam-Burma branch of the Tibeto-Burman family. Some writers have classed them as a number of the Kuki section. Maraland have various Tourist hot spots, like:

1. ***Siaha (Saiha):*** Siaha is the capital town of the Maraland Autonomous District Council. It is the third most developed and also the third most populous town in Mizoram State apart from the state Capital—*Aizawl and Lunglei*. It is also the capital of the third largest tribe—the Maras in Mizoram. It is one of the eight district headquarters in Mizoram and the seat of one of the first three Christian Mission fields in Mizoram. It is situated in the northern part of Maraland and is at the southern part of Mizoram which is at 375 Km from the Aizawl, where the nearest modern Aiport is connecting Mizoram to most of the Indian cities. Siaha is a scenic beauty of one of the Hill stations in India

2. ***Tipa 'V':*** This scenic beauty town is the sub-headquarters of the Autonomous district council. Almost all the tribes of the Maras make up this beautiful town. The National Highway which starts from J and K ends in this town. In Lusei it is commonly known as Tuipang.

3. ***Saikao: The spiritual town:*** The Missionaries to Maraland chose to centered their mission headquarter in this town due to its geographical location and the language of the people in this town. The missionaries' House which was built some 60 years ago is still intact and is one of the most tourist visited places. It is built purely on wood imported from thick forest in Myanmar. This town is the headquarters of Congregational Church of India. It is the second biggest church denomination within Maraland. Lorrain Ville is a very scenic and beautiful street where London missionaries have been living from 1920s. The cemetary of the departed missionaries is one of the most visited sites within this town apart from Lorrain Ville.

4. ***BLUE Mountain:*** A very popular tourist spots like the BLUE Mountain, the highest mountain in Mizoram is just 70 km away from Siaha, and also the Kolodyne fishing and picnic spots. The highest Mountain in Maraland is also just 75 km from Siaha.

5. ***Pala Tipo (Lake):*** The Lake is surrounded by thick a forest unspoilt by the so called modern man, his machines and technologies. The lake is around two square kilometres, elephants and many more wild animals are found around this lake. The government of Mizoram

is planning to decorate more and to beautify with the stae of the modern amusements and many entertainments around this lake apart from the existing tourist lodge run and maintained by the autonomous government of Maraland.

6. ***Phura Town:*** Phura town is just lying side by side with the great paddy fields of Maraland. The only town situated in plain area. It absorbed all kinds of people. It is the melting point of different tribes and people.

7. ***Lodaw Wildlife Sanctuary:*** This Wildlife Sanctuary comes under the administration of the State government. Here different kinds of animal lives naturally. It is not far from the capital town—Siaha.

8. ***Zero Point:*** Zero Point is the entrance town of Maraland, from this town the main road to the Capital—Siaha town and the sub-headquarter town parted to different directions, thus this town acquired the name Zero Point. This town is famous for variety of vegetables and fruits.

9. ***Mt. Mawma:*** The highest peak in Maraland is the fifth highest mountain in Mizoram. It stood 6370ft above sea-level. It lies just next to the second highest mountain in Maraland, which is Mt. Tliatlu. It is situated in the eastern part of the district and below this mountain is river Koldyne which separates India and Myanmar. One can have bird's eye views of neighbouring country. One can see the Dams in Bangladesh during winter. Many wild flowers adorn this mountain which blooms successively throughout the four seasons.

10. ***Mt. Kahrie:*** This Mountain is just above the ancestral home of the Chapi language speaking people, Chapi town. The importance of the mountain does not lie on its height, but rather on the beautiful true love story that surrounds this mountain. Hundreds of Lovers have taken shelter on the tip of the mountain which offers unless heartbreaking view of the surrounding unspoiled land of Myanmar and oversees Kolodyne River the biggest river in Mizoram.

Mizo Society

The fabric of social life in the Mizo society has undergone tremendous change over the last few years. Previously the village and the clan formed units of Mizo society. The Mizo code of ethics or dharma focused on "*Tlawmngaihna*", an untranslatable term meaning that it was the obligation of all members of society to be hospitable, kind, unselfish, and helpful to others. The majority (87 per cent) of Mizos are Christian. Hindus form a small minority (3.6 per cent) and there are also around 8.3 per cent Buddhists according to the 2001 census, mostly made up from Chakma settlers of Arakan origin. The major Christian denomination is the Presbyterian Church.

The fabric of social life in the Mizo society has undergone tremendous changes over years. Before the British moved into the hills, for all practical purposes the village and the clan formed units of Mizo society. The Mizo code of ethics or Dharma moved around *"Tlawmngaihna"*, an untranslatable term meaning on the part of everyone to be hospitable, kind, unselfish and helpful to others. Tlawmngaihna to Mizo stands for the compelling moral force which finds expression in self-sacrifice for the service of the others. The old belief, Pathian is still in use in term God till today. The Mizos have been enchanted to their new-found faith of Christianity with so much dedication and submission that their entire social life and thought-process been transformed and guided by the Christian Church Organisation and their sense of values has also undergone drastic change. The Mizos are close-knit society with no class distinction and no discrimination on grounds of sex. Ninety per cent of them are cultivators and the village exists like a big family. Birth of a child, marriage in the village and death of a person in the village or a community feast arranged by a member of the village are important occasions in which the whole village is involved. Mizos are fast giving up their old customs and adopting the new mode of life which is greatly influenced by the western culture. Many of their present customs are mixtures of their old tradition and western pattern of life. Music is a passion for the Mizos and the young boys and girls take to the western music avidly and with commendable skill. The fascinating hills and lakes of Mizo-land literally pulsate and resound with the rhythms of the sonorous songs of the youths and the twang of guitars everywhere.

Conclusion

Atonomous district council is the real fact of Mizoram. Lai, Chakma ana Mara autonomos district councils are playing vital roles for the development of the southern part of the state. It also helps for soving the insurgency. Each district council is unique for its culture and religious believes. While MADC remained under a single district of Saiha, CADC and LADC were accommodated under Lawngtlai district with the district headquarters at Lawngtlai. The Lai Autonomous District Council occupies a strategic position in Mizoram, located in the Southern most corner of the state. The Maras occupy the southern portion of Mizoram, the hill tracts situated in the areas of Indo-Myanmar border. The majority (87 per cent) of Mizos are Christian. Hindus form a small minority (3.6 per cent) and there are also around 8.3 per cent Buddhists according to the 2001 census.

References

1. *Chakma Autonomous District Council (2012).* Retrieved from http://www.cadc.gov.in/governance/the-judiciary
2. *Chakma Autonomous District Council (2012).* Reprieved from http://en.wikipedia.org/wiki/Chakma_Autonomous_District_Council
3. *Chakma people (2012).* Retrieved from http://en.wikipedia.org/wiki/Chakma_people
4. Dr. K. Zohra (2003). *Mara history, Maraland location and Physical locations,* Retrieved from http://www.maraland.net/maraland/mara-history.html
5. *Mizoram (2012).* http://en. Udalguri district.org/wiki/Mizoram
6. *Mizoram (2012).* See http://mizoram.nic.in/
7. *Tribal society (2012).* Retrieved from http://www.marxists.org/glossary/terms/t/r.htm
8. *Varios information from* Wikipedia, i.e., *Udalguri district, Maraland, Mizoram, Lai People, Lai Autonomous District Council, and Mizoram.*

18

Gorkhaland Territorial Administration: Conflict and Progress

P.K. Pandey

Introduction

Lives of every people are not equal. Tribal's generally live in hilly areas and face variety of challenges. Many tribes and castes on the mainland of India live by hunting, fishing or gathering. Tribal areas are the remotest as well as the most secluded and generally inaccessible hilly tracts. The life in these areas is full of adventure and susceptible to natural calamities. The process of slow and continuous contact between the tribal communities who practiced a comparatively simple form of production with peasants and artisans with greater specialisation must have gone on for centuries. One of the common characteristics of the tribal social system is self-management. Every tribal community is a self-managed and self-sustained group. They produce their own necessities for living, settle inter personal disputes and resolve other problems by themselves. Before independence of the country every tribe of India lives according to its own social system.

The Autonomous District Council has become an important phenomenon in North-East India. Besides Assam, the tribes of Tripura also demanded an Autonomous District Council and it was established in 1985. The demand reflects the political aspiration of the tribes and at the same time disappointment with the state leadership.

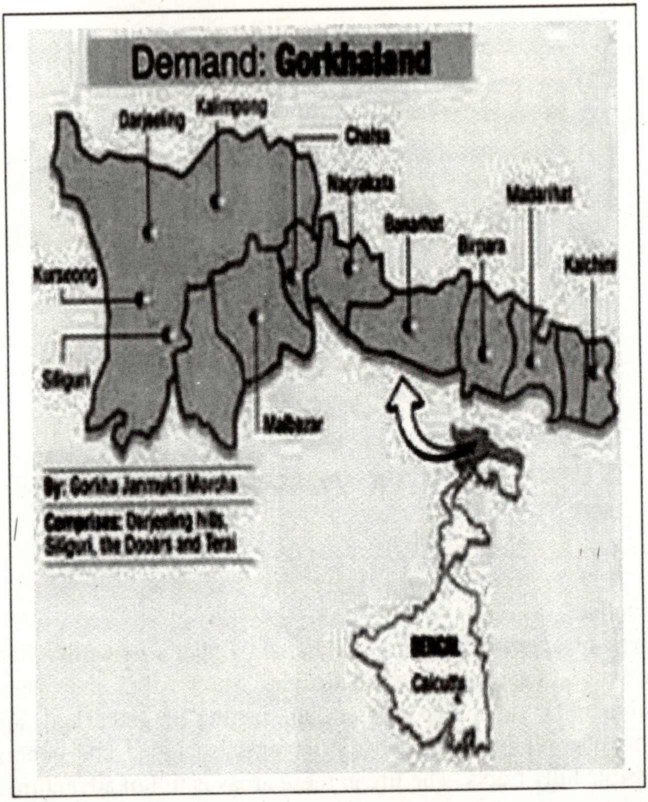

The Autonomous District Council is perceived to be a better alternative to other political arrangements for the plants tribe communities for their development.

Historical Perspectives

In 1789 Nepal concurred a track of lands in Sikkim but Sikkim recaptured this land through British and this land is Darjeeling now Gorkhaland. In early stage about a hundred *'Lepcha'* families were living in Darjeeling and they were the real aborigines, later joined by *'Mecha'* and *'Bhutia'*. But Gorkhas were migrated from Nepal in large numbers in search of works in the Tea gardens. Lepcha, Mecha and Bhutia were become minority. The Gorkhaland movement grew from the demand of Nepalis living in Darjiling District of West Bengal for a separate state for themselves. Historically, Darjiling belonged to the kingdom of Sikkim, which had lost it several times since the eighteenth century. The ethnic identity *"Gorkha"* comes from the kingdom with that name that united Nepal in the late eighteenth century and was the focal point of Nepalese in the British army. Immigration from Nepal expanded with British rule in India and some 34 percent of the population of Darjiling in 1876 was of Gorkha ethnicity. By the start of the twentieth century, Nepalese immigrants made a modest socioeconomic advance through government service and small anglicized elite developed among them. In 1917 the Hillmen's Association came into being and petitioned for the administrative separation of Darjiling in 1917 and again in 1928 and 1942. In 1928 the Akhil Bharatiya Gorkha League (All India Gorkha League) was formed. Before the 1780s, the area of Darjeeling formed a part of the dominions of the Chogyal of Sikkim who had been engaged in unsuccessful warfare against the Gorkhas of Nepal. From 1780 the Gorkhas made several attempts to capture the entire region of Darjeeling. By the beginning of the 19th century they had overrun Sikkim as far eastward as the Teesta River and had conquered and annexed the Terai. In the meantime the British were engaged in preventing the Gorkhas from over running the whole of the northern frontier. The Anglo-Gorkha War broke out in 1814 which resulted in the defeat of the Gorkhas and subsequently led to the signing of the *treaty of Sugauli* in 1815. According to the treaty, Nepal had to cede all those territories which the Gorkhas had annexed from the Chogyal of Sikkim to the British East India Company (the area between Mechi River and Teesta River). Later the East India Company by virtue of the *Treaty of Titalia* reinstated to the Chogyal of Sikkim and restored all the tracts of land between the Mechi and the Teesta to the Chogyal of Sikkim and guaranteed his sovereignty. Later, in 1835, the hill of Darjeeling including and enclave of 138 squad miles was given to the East India Company by Sikkim .In November 1864 Bhutan by virtue of the *treaty of Sinchula* ceded Bhutan Dooars with passes leading to the hills and Kalimpong to the E.I.C. The present Darjeeling district can be said to have assumed its present shape and size in 1866 with an area of 1234 square miles.

It gained additional support after World War II with the influx of ex-soldiers from the Gurkha regiments who had been exposed to nationalist movements in Southeast Asia during service there. During the 1940s, the CPI organised Gorkha tea workers. In presentations to the States Reorganisation Commission in 1954, the CPI favoured regional autonomy for Darjiling within West Bengal, with recognition of Nepali as a Scheduled Language. The All India Gorkha League preferred making the area a union territory under the national government. The state of West Bengal nominally has been supportive of the use of the Nepali language. The West Bengal Official Language Act of 1961 made Nepali the official language of the hill subdivisions of *Darjiling, Kalimpong, and Kurseong,* where Nepalese are a majority. The state legislative assembly passed a resolution in 1977 that led Parliament to amend the national constitution to include Nepali as a Scheduled Language. However, the Gorkhaland National Liberation Front has accused the state government of failure to actually implement use of the language.

Gorkhaland was the name of the proposed state in India that the Nepali/Gorkhali-speaking Gorkha ethnic group in Darjeeling and the Dooars in North West Bengal has expressed a desire to create. The term *Gorkhaland* was coined by Subhash Ghisingh, leader of Gorkha National Liberation Front, who led a violent agitation for its formation in the 1980s. This movement culminated with the formation of Darjeeling Gorkha Hill Council in 1988. The DGHC did not fulfill its goal of forming a new state, which led to the downfall of Subhash Ghisingh and the rise of another party Gorkha Janmukti Morcha headed by Bimal Gurung in 2007, which launched a second agitation for a Gorkhaland state. In the 1980s, Subhash Ghisingh raised the demand for the creation of a state called *Gorkhaland* within India to be carved out of the hills of Darjeeling and areas of Dooars and Siliguri terai contiguous to Darjeeling. The demand took a violent turn, which led to the death of over 1,200 people. This movement culminated with the formation of *Darjeeling Gorkha Hill Council (DGHC)* in 1988. The DGHC administered the Darjeeling hills for 23 years with some degree of autonomy. The fourth DGHC elections were due in 2004. However, the government decided not to hold elections and instead made Subhash Ghisingh the sole caretaker of the DGHC till a new Sixth Schedule tribal council was established. Resentment among the former councillors of DGHC grew rapidly. Among them, Bimal Gurung, once the trusted aide of Ghising, decided to break away from the GNLF. The Gorkhaland movement vis-à-vis the signed *treaty of Gorkhaland Territorial Administration (GTA)* estranged Darjeeling, Kalimpong and Karshiung now from West Bengal. It was evidence that the Gorkhaland movement had been instigated and influenced by inside and outside reactionary forces, the movement launched by rising middle-class Gorkhas and in long run they will be frustrated for non fulfillment of their economic demand. The GTA territories located in near corridors to Nepal and Bangladesh and any political turmoil leads to separation might be a big problem of India. Sikkim is also concerned in formation of GTA as its original habitants - *Lepcha, Mecha and Bhutia* were become minority and they are afraid that the separate Gorkhaland state may expand in Sikkim. GTA is a *'Landmine'* implanded, *"democracy does not consist of majority rule but of majority rule with consideration for minorities"*.

In 1995 it was unclear whether the region would remain content with autonomy rather than statehood. In August 1995, Sherpa complained to the state government that Ghising's government had misused hill council funds, and West Bengal chief minister Jyoti Basu promised to investigate. Both Gorkha parties showed willingness to use general shutdowns to forward their ends. The fact that so many people were willing to follow Sherpa instead of the hitherto unchallenged Ghising may indicate that they will be satisfied with regional autonomy. There is a supposition in intellectual circles that the statehood movement in the Darjeeling hills has its origin in a revolt against the political and socio-cultural hegemony of West Bengal over a people far removed from Bengalis in terms of character and culture.

Gorkha People

Gorkhas are Nepali/Gorkhali-speaking citizens of India. The term *"Indian Gorkha"* tries to make a distinction between the citizens of Nepal living in India and the Indian citizens of Gorkha ethnic group. The Gorkhas of India are citizens of India as per the Gazette Notification on the issue of citizenship of Gorkhas of India. However, there are many Nepalese citizens of Nepal living in India as per the Indo-Nepal Treaty of Peace and Friendship (1950) that permits *"on a reciprocal basis, the nationals of one country in the territories of the other the same privileges in the matter of residence, ownership of property, participation in trade and commerce, movement and other privileges of a similar nature."* The quest of the Indian Gorkhas for a distinct Indian identity has given rise to the demand for a state of Gorkhaland within the Constitution of India under Article 3(a). The proposed state of Gorkhaland comprises the district of Darjeeling and the adjoining areas of the Dooars in North Bengal. It is estimated that there are about 10,000,000 Gorkhas in India but a true count will be possible after the India Census 2011. In the Darjeeling district of West Bengal there is an estimated 900,000 Gorkhas. The Jalpaiguri district of West Bengal has about 400,000 Gorkhas. There is an estimated 500,000 Gorkha population in Sikkim—the only state in which majorities of the population are Gorkhas. In Northeast India (states of Assam, Meghalaya, Nagaland, Manipur, Tripura, Mizoram and Arunachal Pradesh), there are several million Gorkhas. The Gorkhas of India are a mixture of Indo-Aryan castes and Mongoloid-featured clans.

The Gorkhas, an ethnic group originally from Nepal, migrated to India during and after British rule. Many were recruited for service in the colonial army. In today's Darjeeling, however, the term Gorkha tends to be applied to all Nepali-speaking people. It is a political rather than an ethnic label to embrace a multi-ethnic group consisting of indigenous tribes of the area and Nepali immigrants with Indian citizenship.

Autonomous District Council

Gorkhaland Territorial Administration (GTA) is a semi-autonomous administrative body for the Darjeeling hills in West Bengal, India. The GTA will replace the Darjeeling Gorkha Hill Council, which was formed in 1988 and administered the Darjeeling hills for 23 years. GTA presently has three hill subdivisions Darjeeling, Kalimpong, and Kurseong and some areas of Siliguri subdivision under its authority. The movement for a separate state under Gorkha National Liberation Front (GNLF) and its suoremo Subash Ghishing gained serious momentum during the 1980s, before signing an agreement on August 22, 1988 with the central and West Bengal governments for creation of the Darjeeling Gorkha Hill Council (DGHC)—an autonomous governing body for the hills. **The Salient Features of the Darjeeling Gorkha Hill Council:**

1. *The name of the Council will be* Darjeeling Gorkha Hill Council.

2. The Council will cover the three hill sub-divisions of Darjeeling district, namely, Darjeeling, Kalimpong and Kurseong, plus the Mouzas of Lohagarh Tea Garden, Lohagarh Forest, Rangmohan, Barachenga, Panighatta, Choto Adalpur, Paharu, Sukna Forest, Sukna Part-I, Pantapati Forest-I, Mahanadi Forest, Champasari Forest and Salbari Chatt Part II within Siliguri subdivision.

3. The State Government agrees to lease to the Council after it is formed, or acquire for it the use of such land as may be required and necessary for administrative and developmental purposes, anywhere in the State and in particular in or around 'Darjeeling More' in Siliguri subdivision.

4. The Council shall exercise general powers of supervision over Panchayat Samities, Gram Panchayats and Municipalities falling within the area of the Council's jurisdiction.

5. The General Council will have a total of 42 Members out of which 28 will be elected and the rest nominated by the State Government.

6. There will be an Executive Council and the Chairman and Vice-Chairman of the General Council will be ex-officio members of the Executive Council with the Chairman of the General Council functioning as the Chief Executive Councillor. The Chief Executive Councillor will nominate five members to the Executive Council from out of the elected members of the Council and the State Government will nominate two members of the Council and the State Government will nominate two members to the Executive Council from out of the non-official nominated members of the General Council.

7. The Chairman of the General Council-cum-Chief Executive Councillor will have the ex-officio status and privileges of a Minister in the Council of Ministers in the State.

8. The Bill for setting up the Hill Council will be introduced and passed in a special session of the State Legislature which has been summoned. The election to the Hill Council will be held by the 15th December 1988.

The Salient Features of the Gorkhaland Territorial Administration:

1. The Bill for setting up the Hill Council will be introduced and passed in a special session of the State Legislature which has been summoned. The election to the Hill Council will be held by the 15th December 1988.

2. While under the provisions of the Constitution transfer of legislative powers to the new Body is not possible, the power to frame rules/regulations under the State Acts to control, regulate and administer the departments/offices and subjects transferred to the new Body will be conferred upon the new Body ;

3. The administrative, executive and financial powers in respect of the subjects transferred will be vested in such a way that the new Body may function in an autonomous and effective way ;

4. The subjects alongwith all Departments/Offices to be transferred to the new Body is appended as Annexure – 'A'

5. The area of the Gorkhaland Territorial Administration shall comprise the areas of the entire sub-divisions of Darjeeling, Kalimpong with extended areas of Kurseong. In regard to transfer of additional areas of Siliguri Terai and Dooars to the new Body, a High-Powered Committee will be formed comprising four representatives of GJM, three representatives of the State Government (one from the Home Department; the District Magistrate, Darjeeling; the District Magistrate, Jalpaiguri); the Director of Census Operations representing Government of India, apart from the Chairman of the Committee to be appointed by the State Government. The Chairperson of the Board of Administrators, DGHC will be the convener of this Committee. The Committee will look into the question of identification of additional areas in Siliguri Terai and Dooars that may be transferred to the new Body, having regard to their compactness, contiguity, homogeneity, ground level situation and other relevant factors.

6. The work of this High-Powered Committee will run parallel to the electoral process which will be based on the existing area delimitation. However, the empowering statute will have a provision for transfer of the additional areas from Siliguri Terai

and Dooars that may be agreed upon, based on the recommendation of this Committee.

7. In regard to transfer of all forests including reserved forest, it was agreed that the State Government will make a reference to the Central Government on the issue of reserved forest as the power delegated to the State Government under the Central statute cannot be delegated to any other authority straightaway. However, all offices catering to the unreserved forests under the jurisdiction of GTA would also be transferred to GTA.

Gorkhaland is the name of the proposed state in India demanded by the majority people of Darjeeling hills and the people of Gorkha ethnic origin in Dooars in northern West Bengal. The movement for Gorkhaland has gained momentum in the line of ethno-linguistic-cultural sentiment of the people who desire to identify themselves as Gorkha. After three years of agitation for a state of Gorkhaland led by GJM, the GJM reached an agreement with the state government to form a semi-autonomous body to administer the Darjeeling hills. A bill for the creation of GTA was passed in the West Bengal Legislative Assembly on 2 September, 2011. The GTA will have administrative, executive and financial powers but no legislative powers. A 10-member joint verification committee headed by a retired High Court judge would examine the demand to bring the Gorkha-inhabited pockets of the Dooars and the Terai under the GTA. The memorandum of agreement for the formation of a Gorkhaland Territorial Administration (GTA) which is a semi-autonomous administrative body for the Darjeeling hills was signed on 18 July, 2011. Earlier, during the West Bengal assembly election (2011) campaign, Mamata Banerjee had promised that the issue of Gorkhaland would be resolved. While Mamata implied that this would be the end of the Gorkhaland movement, Bimal Gurung reiterated that this was just another step towards statehood. Both spoke publicly at the same venue in Pintail Village near Siliguri, where the tripartite agreement was signed. A bill for the creation of GTA was passed in the West Bengal Legislative Assembly on 2 September, 2011. The West Bengal government issued a gazette notification for the GTA Act on 14 March, 2012, signalling preparations for elections for the GTA. In the elections of the GTA held on 29 July, 2012, GJM candidates won from 17 constituencies and the rest 28 seats unopposed.

The tripartite agreement on the Gorkhaland Territorial Administration (GTA) was signed by West Bengal government, the Centre and the Gorkha Janmukti Morcha. The accord will pave the way for a separate state *"Gorkhaland"* which will fulfil the Gorkhas' century old quest for self-rule. The agreement was signed on 18 July, 2011 at Pintail village, the epicentre of the Gorkha campaign for their ethnic identity in the Terai in presence of Indian home minister P. Chidambaram, West Bengal chief minister Mamata Banerjee and Gorkha Janmukti Morcha (GJM) chief Bimal Gurung. Darjeeling District is the northernmost district of the state of West Bengal in eastern India in the foothills of the Himalayas. The district is famous for its beautiful hill stations and Darjeeling tea. Darjeeling is the district headquarters. Kalimpong, Kurseong and Siliguri, three other major towns in the district, are the subdivisional headquarters of the district. Geographically, the district can be divided into two broad divisions, the hills and the plains. The foothill of Darjeeling Himalayas which comes under the Siliguri sub-division is known as the Terai. The Terai is bounded on the north by the mountains, on the south by Kishanganj district of Bihar state, on the east by Jalpaiguri district and on the west by Nepal. The economy of Darjeeling hill area depends on tea production, horticulture, agriculture, forestry and tourism. The major portions of the forests are today found at elevations of 2000 meters and above. The area located in between 1000–2000 meters is cleared either for tea plantation or cultivation. About 30 per cent of the forest covers found in the lower hills are deciduous. Evergreen forest constitutes only about six per cent of the total forest coverage. The district was previously divided into five assembly constituencies. According to the 2011 census Darjeeling district has a population of 1,842,034.

The original inhabitants of the Darjeeling Hills were the Lepchas or Rongpa. They are decidedly Mongolian in physical features. The Limbus is another ancient inhabitant of this district. The greater bulk of the people in the hills today are the Gorkhas. They are industrious and enterprising as a race and speak Nepali and various other dialects. Among the population are the *Sherpas*. They are well known for their contributions to mountaineering. Also much in evidence in the hills are the *Bhutias*. There is also a sizable population of Tibetans who arrived from Tibet since the 1950s. In the plains, one will find several communities like the Gorkhas, the adivasi people originally from Chottanagpur and Santhal Parganas and a greater bulk of Bengali people. Wildlife in the district is protected by the wildlife wing of the West Bengal Forest Department. The Darjeeling Himalayan Railway is a 60 cm (24 in) narrow-gauge railway that was declared a World Heritage Site by UNESCO in 1999 for being *"an outstanding example of the influence of an innovative transportation system on the social and economic development of a multi-cultural region, which was to serve as a model for similar developments in many parts of the world"*, becoming only the second railway in the world to have this honour.

Darjeeling Sadar subdivision consists of the Darjeeling municipality and three community development blocks: *Darjeeling Pulbazar, Rangli Ranglot and Jorebunglow*. The three blocks contain one census town Pattabong Tea Garden and 50 gram panchayats. The subdivision has its headquarters at Darjeeling. Kalimpong subdivision consists of the Kalimpong municipality and three community development blocks: Kalimpong–I, Kalimpong–II and Gorubathan. The three blocks contain 42 gram panchayats. The subdivision has its headquarters at Kalimpong. Kurseong subdivision consists of the Kurseong municipality, Mirik municipality and two community development blocks: Mirik and Kurseong. The two blocks contain 20 gram panchayats. The sub-division has its headquarters at Kurseong. Siliguri subdivision consists of the Siliguri municipal corporation and four community development blocks: *Matigara, Naxalbari, Phansidewa and Kharibari*. The four blocks contain 22 gram panchayats and two census towns: *Bairatisal and Uttar Bagdogra*. The subdivision has its headquarters at *Siliguri*.

Darjeeling is the headquarters of Darjeeling district which has a partially autonomous status within the state of West Bengal. The development of the town dates back to the mid-19th century, when the colonial British administration set up a sanatorium and a military depot. Subsequently, extensive tea plantation was done in the region and tea growers developed hybrids of black tea and created new fermenting techniques. Darjeeling has several British-style public schools which attract students from India and neighbouring countries. The varied culture of the town reflects its diverse demographic milieu consisting of Nepalese, Tibetan, Bengali and other ethno-linguistic groups. Darjeeling with its neighbouring town of Kalimpong was a centre of the Gorkhaland movement in the 1980s.

The Dooars are the floodplains and foothills of the eastern Himalayas in North-East India around Bhutan. *Duar* means door in Assamese, Nepali, Maithili, Bhojpuri, Magahi and Bengali languages and the region forms the gateway to Bhutan from India. There were 18 passages or gateways through which the Bhutanese people can communicate with the people living in the plains. The native people of this region generally have Mongoloid features. They are composed of numerous tribes, including the Bodo in Assam, and the Rabha, the Mech, the Toto, the Koch, the Tamang/Murmi, the Limbu, the Lepcha and the Rajbongshi in Bengal. The Dooars are famous for the tea gardens which were planted by the British. For working in the gardens, they imported labour from Nepal and the Chota Nagpur and Santhal Parganas. The *Oraons, Mundas, Kharia, Mahali, Lohara and Chik Baraik* are the tribal's from these areas.

The All Assam Gorkha Students' Union (AAGSU) declared unconditional support to the Gorkhaland movement. It said that if need, in the future, AAGSU along with other Gorkhaland supporters of the North Eastern states will take on democratic movement from this region of the country. AAGSU submitted a memorandum by fax and email to Union Home Minister P. Chidambaram seeking justice for the Gorkhas by creation of Gorkhaland. The copies of the memorandum have been sent to Leader of Opposition, Sushma Swaraj, Darjeeling MP Jaswant Singh, West Bengal former CM Buddha Dev Bhattacharjee, National Human Rights Commission Chiar, K.G. Balakrishnan, President Gorkha Jan Mukti Morcha (GJM), Bimal Gurung and Smt. Dil Kumari Bhandhari, President, Bharatiya Gorkha Parisangh (BGP). The detailed memorandum threatens central government of vigorous democratic movement from Assam in support of Gorkhaland. It demands immediate creation of Gorkhaland state, adequate compensation to the martyrs and those critically injured lives and security of Gorkhas in bordering states to be ensured and high level judicial enquiry on violation of human rights. Darjeeling is not only about Gorkhas of Darjeeling, Siliguri and Dooars but it is about 12.5 millions Gorkhas of this nation.

Greater autonomy for the hills has been an emotive issue and dates back to 1907 when the first effort was made. The issue is not about territory, but about identity and preservation of culture as also a way of life. Most Gorkhas are residents of hill states, which historically suffer from poor infrastructure and lack of education facilities at grass root level. There is also a need for subsidised higher education for Gorkha youth who lack this basic facility. The creation of a State hopefully quickens the pace of these and removes infrastructure bottlenecks which bedevil development.

Progress

Ahead of the 2009 general elections in India, the Bharatiya Janata Party announced its policy of having smaller states and to create two more states, *Telangana and Gorkhaland*, if they won the general election. GJM supported the candidature of Jaswant Singh of BJP, who won the Darjeeling Lok Sàbha seat with 51.5 per cent votes in his favour. In the July 2009 budget session of Parliament, three Parliamentarians—*Rajiv Pratap Rudy, Sushma Swaraj and Jaswant Singh*—strongly pleaded for creating a state of Gorkhaland. The demand for Gorkhaland took a new turn with the assassination of Madan Tamang, leader of Akhil Bharatiya Gorkha League. He was stabbed to death allegedly by Gorkha Janmukti Morcha supporters on May 21, 2010, in Darjeeling, which led to a spontaneous shutdown in the three Darjeeling hill sub-divisions of Darjeeling, Kalimpong and Kurseong. After rejecting the offer of parleys with the West Bengal government, the Gorkha Janamukti Morcha said it was ready for talks with the Centre and that Gorkhaland should not be considered a separatist demand. In most parts of Darjeeling, the Nepalis there either didn't know who Jaswant Singh was or didn't care about him. An overwhelming majority voted for him all in the belief that the party with the lotus symbol will help create Gorkhaland if it comes to power at the Centre. Jaswant's campaign was pitched to convey the sense to a gullible mountain population that this is the man for the long cherished dream of Gorkhaland, a separate homeland away from West Bengal.

The Akhil Bharatiya Adivasi Vikas Parishad (ABAVP) which has an uneasy alliance with Gorkhaland Janmukti Morcha (GJM) has warned the latter that if it tries to spread the Gorkhaland agitation in the Dooars and Terai region, its consequences would be *"lethal"*. The tribal body is now desperate to prove its strength in the plains following its defeat in the Kalchini by-elections. Gorkhas and tribal's are coming close to each other, thus posing a threat to the non-tribal population. In the West Bengal state assembly election, 2011 held on 18 April, 2011, GJM candidates won three Darjeeling hill assembly seats, proving that the demand for Gorkhaland was still strong in Darjeeling. GJM candidates Trilok Dewan won from Darjeeling constituency, Harka Bahadur Chhetri from Kalimpong constituency, and Rohit Sharma from Kurseong constituency. Wilson Champramari, an independent candidate supported by GJM, also won from Kalchini constituency in the Dooars. Recent developments over Telengana issue are about to reignite the separate statehood demand in queen of hills Darjeeling in West Bengal. After keeping Darjeeling hills boiling for last couple of years, the movement for separate state '*Gorkhaland*' took a low key following formation of a separate autonomous body for Darjeeling by state Government under support from Center in July 2011.

Since the Gorkhaland Territorial Administration (GTA) came to power, the state is yet to transfer financial and administrative powers to the newly elected hill administration. There are plans to set up as many as 59 departments and GJM wants control over 26 of them in which the state government has a say. It also wants the state to address the budgetary gap for GTA which arose due to a technical glitch in the agreement. Teething problems over financial and administrative powers to be transferred to the Gorkhaland Territorial Administration by the state continue to plague the newly elected hill administration. The Gorkha Janmukti Morcha wants *"absolute control"* over the nearly 26 departments of the 59 expected to be set up where the state government has a say. It also wants the state to address the budgetary gap for GTA which arose due to a technical glitch in the agreement. The GJM also wants control over the forests that fall under the concurrent list. The GTA is all set to take over the Tauzi department which includes looking after the tea gardens, the department of agriculture, animal husbandry, information and cultural affairs, school education, land and land reforms, PHE, urban development and municipal affairs. Some of these departments, GJM feels could be able to generate revenue for the GTA. The other demand by GJM also demanded that tribal status be granted today was also regarding the demand for granting Tribal Status to the Gorkhas, excluding the scheduled castes. As far as the latter is concerned, the GJM has already made an application to the backward class's welfare department of the state government. The state and the Centre have pledged to provide all financial assistance to the GTA for all-out development of the region.

With the advent of a new era in the Hills, effort is on in full swing to preserve the lost history of the region. The Gorkhaland Territorial

Administration (GTA) took a step forward and laid the foundation stone for a Gorkha War Museum near Batasia Loop, six km from Darjeeling town. The project is pegged at Rs 1.50 crore and plan to begin work from tomorrow itself so that the museum can be set up within a year. Earlier, it was planned that the museum would be set up next to the war memorial at Batasia Loop. But due to space constraint the museum could not be built there. The 2000 square feet land that will house the two-storey museum belongs to the land and land reforms department. While various artifacts associated with Gorkha soldiers, belonging to the Indian and British Army will be on display on the first floor, the second and third floor will house a research centre and personnel souvenirs respectively. There will also be a lecture and cinema hall. Most of the artifacts, souvenirs and war collection will be provided to the museum by Hemant Pradhan, a local private collector. Pradhan, over the past forty years has managed to collect over 200 medals associated with the Indian and British Army. His collection includes army souvenirs from 1890 till that of Kargil war, army uniforms and photographs dating back to World War I and II. The idea is to make people and tourists coming to the Hills aware of the rich history of the region.

Conclusion

The Gorkhaland movement grew from the demand of Nepalis living in Darjiling District of West Bengal for a separate state for themselves. The Gorkhaland National Liberation Front led the movement which disrupted the district with massive violence between 1986 and 1988. The issue was resolved, at least temporarily in 1988 with the establishment of the Darjiling Gorkha Hill Council within West Bengal. Not to be left behind in the separate state demand race, the Gorkha Janmukti Morcha (GJM) has threatened to resurrect the Gorkhaland agitation if the Union government initiates the process of creating the separate state of Telangana. The proposed creation of Gorkhaland Territorial Administration (GTA) is an important institutional innovation of multilevel federal structure in India. As a sub-state structure of autonomy it intends to create space for self rule for the people of the region.

References

1. Amitava Banerjee (2012). *Gorkha Janmukti Morcha threatens to resurrect Gorkhaland agitation*, Retrieved from.

2. Archana Rai (2011). *AAGSU threatens movement for Gorkhaland*, Retrieved from http://isikkim.com/aagsu-threatens-movement-23-for-%E2%80%98gorkhaland%E2%80%99-4/
3. Deepak Roy (2011). *Gorkhaland – a state within a state*, Retrieved from http://www.weeklyblitz.net/1608/gorkhaland-a-state-within-a-state
4. *Darjeeling (2012)*. Retrieved from http://en.wikipedia.org/wiki/Darjeeling
5. *Darjeeling District (2012)*. Retrieved from http://en.wikipedia.org/wiki/Darjeeling_district.
6. *Darjeeling Sadar subdivision (2012)*. Retrieved from http://en. wikipedia.org/wiki/Darjeeling_Sadar_subdivision.
7. *Dooars (2012)*.Retrieved from http://en.wikipedia.org/wiki/Dooars
8. Dr.Gaur Ghosh and Abhijit Datta (2012). *Gorkhaland, the hot bed of crisis in the North-East*, Retrieved from.
9. *Gorkhaland (2012)*. Retrieved from http://www.gorkhacreed.com/groups/gorkhaland/forum/topic/download-full-points-gorkhaland-territorial-administration-gta-memorandum-of-agreement/
10. *Gorkhaland (2011)*. Retrieved from http://www.gorkhacreed.com/tag/gorkhaland-movement/
11. *Gorkhaland Territorial Administration (2012)*. Retrieved from http://en.wikipedia.org/wiki/Gorkhaland_Territorial_Administration
12. *Gorkhaland (2012)*. Retrieved from http://en.wikipedia.org/wiki/Gorkhaland
13. *Gorkhaland movement-Revolt or assertion?*, Retrieved from http://www.thestatesman.net/index.php?option=com_contentand view= article andid=362087andcatid=57
14. *Indian Gorkhas (2012)*.Retrieved fromhttp://en.wikipedia.org/wiki/Indian_Gorkha
15. *India-Gorkhaland Uttarakhand (2012)*. Retrieved from http://www.mongabay.com/history/india/india-gorkhaland_uttarakhand.html
16. *Is Gorkhaland movement contained for formation of GTA?,* Retrieved from http://www.dailypioneer.com/state-editions/dehradun/85733-is-gorkhaland-movement-contained-by-formation-of-gta.html
17. *Kalimpong subdivision (2012)*. Retrieved from http://en.wikipedia.org/wiki/Kalimpong_subdivision
18. *Kurseong subdivision (2012)*. Retrieved from http://en.wikipedia.org/wiki/Kurseong_subdivision
19. Kusumbar Bhuyan (2008). *Sixth schedule in North-East India: A Case Study of Karbi Anglong District*, First edition, Guwahati: DVS Publishers.
20. M.S. Jairth (1991). *Tribal economy and society*, First edition, New Delhi: Mittal Publications.
21. *Museum for Gorkha war heros (September 14, 2012)*, Retrieved from

http://articles.timesofindia.indiatimes.com/2012-09-14/kolkata/33843589_1_gorkha-soldiers-gta-gorkhaland-territorial-administration

22. N.K. Bose (2004). *Tribal life in the India*, First reprint, New Delhi: National Book Trust.
23. *Siliguri subdivision (2012)*. Retrieved from http://en.wikipedia.org/wiki/Siliguri_subdivision
24. The Economic Times (October 8, 2012), *Telengana developments is likely to reignite Gorkhaland movement in Darjeeling,* Retrieved from http://articles.economictimes.indiatimes.com/2012-10-08/news/34322996_1_gorkhaland-gorkha-janamukti-morcha-gjm
25. *The Hindustan Times (2011)*.More autonomy for Gorkhaland, Retrieved from http://www.hindustantimes.com/India-news/WestBengal/More-autonomy-for-Gorkhaland/Article1-722522.aspx
26. *The Times of India (Aug 20, 2009)*. Big setback for Gorkhaland dream, Retrieved from http://articles.timesofindia.indiatimes.com/2009-08-20/india/28193000_1_gorkhaland-gjm-gorkha-janmukti-morcha
27. *The Times of India (December 12, 2009)*. Stay away from Dooars, tribal's warns GJM, Retrieved from http://articles.timesofindia.indiatimes.com/2009-12-12/kolkata/28102235_1_gorkhaland-dooars-and-terai-tripartite-talks
28. *The Times of India (September 12, 2012)*. Morcha wants more money, absolute control, Retrieved from http://articles.timesofindia. indiatimes. com/2012-09-12/kolkata/33788659_1_gta-gorkhaland-territorial-administration-concurrent-list
29. *The Economic Times (2012)*. Darjeeling to have the Gorkhaland Territorial Administration (GTA) election on July 29, Retrieved from http://articles.economictimes.indiatimes.com/2012-06-27/news/32441533_1_darjeeling-hills-gta-election-gjm
30. *The history of Gorkhaland demand (2012)*. Retrieved from http://www.redgage.com/blogs/nischaldj/the-history-of-gorkhaland-demands.html
31. *The Times of India (June 14, 2008)*. GJM ready for talks with govt on Ghorkhaland, Retrieved from http://articles.timesofindia.indiatimes.com/2008-06-14/india/27770835_1_gorkhaland-gorkha-janamukti-morcha-gjm-general-secretary.

19

TTAADC in Tripura and Tribal Welfare: An Overview

Satyajit Das

Introduction

On 15th august 1947, India got Independence after a long freedom struggle against British crown. On 26th January 1950, India got its own constitution. The leaders and framers of Indian constitution had a deep thought about the poor condition of the tribal areas and tribal people. Basically they gave special stress in the condition of tribal people of North East India. To protect the tribal people from rapid and sudden change of the society the leaders wanted to make those people attach with the modernisation and democratic process without any change in their own life pattern. For that the 5th and 6th schedule of Indian constitution initiated few provisions for the smooth conduct of administration in those tribal areas. In the initial stage, the provisions of 5th schedule were applicable to all areas except Assam, Meghalaya, Tripura and Mizoram. The provision of 6th schedule, at the very out set, were applicable to only tribal areas of Assam. But afterwards it has been expanded to Meghalaya and Mizoram. At last by the amendment of constitution, Tripura has come under 6th schedule.

Historical Background of TTAADC

Autonomous district council is one of the types of self government and a part of democracy. In connection to that the constitution of India provides for the special assistance and opportunities to the people of those areas as the people come under special category guaranteed by the Constitution. Before the accession to the Indian Union, Tripura was a princely state. Even in that time it has been assumed by the then king *Maharaja Bir Bikram Kishore Manikya Bahadur* that for the development and protect and safeguard the interest of tribal people of Tripura, there might have reserved areas for them. It has been seen that the land of tribal people are segregated by the non-tribal people. To protect this trend, the then Maharaja of Tripura declared 70,000 and 400 acre land of kalyanpur under Khowai subdivision reserved for the tribal people of Tripura. The Maharaja prohibits non tribal people from buying and selling the land. In this kind of situation the government will buy this as Khas land. But this was not enough for the upgrading of the tribal people of Tripura.

In 1943, huge areas of low land, about 1950 sq mile have been declared as reserved land for tribal people. It was assumed that no one can sell the land without the prior permission of the government. It was also applicable to the tribal people also. In the year of 1952 the then prime minister of India pandit Jawahar lal Nehru convened a conference to discuss problems affecting the scheduled Caste and Scheduled Tribe people of the country. In that conference, Sree Dasarath Deb the then Member of Parliament described the miserable conditions of the tribal people of Tripura and proposed that a definite area should be declared as reserved for the Tribal people of Tripura where the non-tribal people should not be allowed to live permanently and buy and sell any land.

TTAADC and Tribal Welfare

TTAADC is an indicator of local self government. The introduction of the TTAADC is a great step taken by the central government for the tribal people of Tripura. Since its establishment it is working for the development of the tribal people of Tripura. The TTAADC was formed with a view to provide internal autonomy in the areas inhabited by tribal people. At the same time it is formed to protect the social, economic and cultural interests of the tribal population and to promote the all-round socio-economic development of the territory covered by the TTAADC. Basically the council came under the purview of the sixth Schedule with effect from 1st April 1985 by 49th amendment of the Indian constitution. The total areas of the TTAADC are about 7,132.56 sq.km. which covers about 68 per cent of the total area of the state. There are 30 members in the TTAADC out of which two members are nominated by the Governor while 28 members are directly

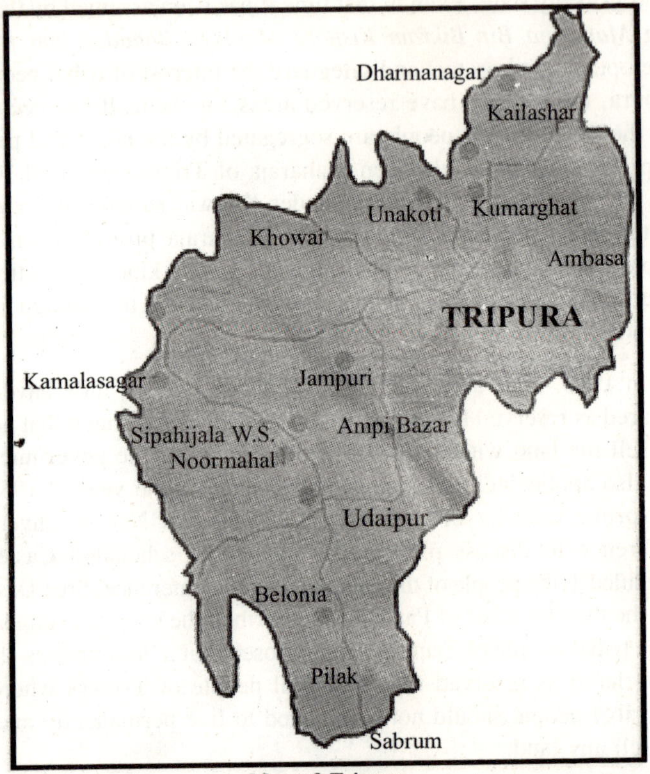

Map of Tripura.

elected through Adult suffrage but it is to be noted here that three seats are unreserved out of 30 seats and in the unreserved seats even non-tribal people can contest in the election too.

The constitution of India by 49th amendment, in its sixth schedule provides a big opportunity for the tribal people of Tripura. As a result of that the tribal people of Tripura made their own council for their development. The main aim of forming the council was to protect and safeguard the right and freedom of the tribal people of Tripura. The TTAADC has been working to implement various state plan, Central plan and centrally sponsored schemes to make sure overall economic and social development of the people of these areas. There are 19 departments of TTAADC work in maximising the development upshot. In the year 2006, the election of 527 nos. village committees were organised. As a result of that community involvement in decision making process has become easier to a large number of people of these areas. It also been noticed that the representation of the community has been done in a democratic way and people also took part in this process quite freely. Government also takes initiative to empower the people of these areas through the Council. In order to make quality education is mandatory for one and all; the TTAADC has given special stress to improve quality in education at primary level by establishing Residential Schools for the children of remote areas where schools do not function properly. Through these schools the ST boys and girls are being brought to the school for their proper education. They all do that from the hostels provided by the government. The Council is working continuously for this quality education. The Council is organising Tripura Adhibasi Sahitya O Sanskriti Mela. It's a symbol of harmony among the different communities of the Tribal as well as with the other people of Tripura. The 13th Finance Commission made special allocation of Rs 20 crore of strengthening of TTAADC administration and Rs 10 crore for development of Kok-Borok language. The land under TTAADC is mostly hilly and roads are not well equipped for the proper communication from one place to another. The central government as well as state government is taking steps for the development of the hilly areas and construction of the roads. Infact initiatives are being taken for the development of horticulture, piggery and fishery cultivation. The TTAADC is also taking steps for economic development of the people of those areas. For that the Council giving emphasise on rubber plantation, capacity building of elected representatives and construction of road connectivity in the villages.

Conclusion

Tripura tribal areas autonomous district council is a milestone in the path of development process of tribal people in Tripura. About 30 per cent of the total population of Tripura is scheduled tribe. They are still back ward in 21st century than that of other communities. These tribal communities even today depend on their primitive type or traditional pattern of agriculture. From time immemorial, they live their life in a measurable way such as on hunting, traditional way of agriculture, collecting fruits from the forest, exchange system has not been in practice and they were not acquainted with the division of labor. Their societal structure is based on traditions, customs. They are not acquainted with the good side of science and technology. After the independence of India the local as well as national leaders of country gave a special emphasis on the development of tribal people of Tripura. After a long journey, the constitution of India made a historical decision regarding tribal welfare. Eventually TTAADC has been formed. Since its birth, it is working for the improvement of tribal areas and tribal people. Although the TTAADC is formed with a view to develop the socio-economic condition of the people of those areas but due to lack of sufficient fund the council can not able to reach its goal.

References

1. Dr. Jagadish Gan Chaudhuri, *'A Constitutional History of Tripura'*, Parul Prakashani, Agartala, 2004.
2. Website:www.ttaadc.nic.in
3. Dr. Chandrika Basu Majumder, *'Democratic Decentralisation and Tripura Tribal Areas Autonomous District Council: A Review'*, presented in the Annual Conference of IASSI and Seminar on Democratic Decentralisation, New Delhi, 2011.
4. Memorandum to 13th Finance commission.
5. Dr. Chandrika Basu Majumder in 'Tripura Tribal Areas Autonomous District Council: Problems and Prospects' published in book, *Decentralised Planning and Development New Directions*, edited by Amalesh Banerjee, Kanishka publishers, 2004.

Index